W9-ABG-879

TENNYSON IN AMERICA

TENNYSON IN AMERICA

HIS REPUTATION AND INFLUENCE FROM 1827 TO 1858

by

John Olin Eidson

1943
The University of Georgia Press
Athens

TO

MY FATHER AND MOTHER

AND MY AUNTS,

MISSES EVA AND JESSIE RUSHTON

PREFACE

THIS STUDY BEGINS WITH THE PUBLICATION OF *POEMS BY Two Brothers,* Tennyson's earliest work, in 1827, and closes with the publication of the first of the *Idylls of the King* in 1859. It traces Tennyson's rise to fame. From 1859 till the coming of the reaction against him soon after his death, Tennyson was firmly ensconced as the chief Victorian poet.

The largest part of my work has been done in four places: the Library of Congress, the New York Public Library, the Harvard College Library, and the Boston Public Library. To all departments of these libraries I am greatly indebted for the use of their facilities. Also, the libraries of Duke University, the University of North Carolina, and the University of Georgia have rendered much assistance. Two libraries in which I have spent less time but in which I found several of the most significant items contained in this work are the Pierpont Morgan Library of New York City and the Boston Athenaeum.

The Union Catalogue of the Library of Congress, the Union Library Catalogue of the Philadelphia Metropolitan Area, the Cleveland Regional Union Catalog, and the Bibliographical Center for Research (Denver, Colorado) have helped me ably in my search for American editions and impressions of Tennyson. And I am grateful to the Houghton Mifflin Company, successors to Ticknor and Fields, Tennyson's authorized American publishers, for furnishing me with detailed records of Ticknor and Fields's editions.

It is impossible for me to name here all of the libraries and individuals who have contributed to my work, but some of the contributions cannot be left unacknowledged. The Henry E. Huntington Library of San Marino, California, the Wrenn Library of the University of Texas, and the Victoria University Library of Toronto, Canada, have given me valuable material from their large Tennyson collections. Dr. Henry Wadsworth Longfellow Dana kindly allowed me free use of his valuable Longfellow papers in the Craigie House, Cambridge, Massachusetts. Mr. Edward Waldo Forbes permitted me to use Emerson's unpublished journals and the unpublished letters to Emerson owned by the Ralph Waldo Emerson Memorial Association of Cambridge. Mr. Thomas Franklin Currier of Harvard University and Mr. Charles E. Goodspeed of Goodspeed's Book Store, Inc., Boston, have helped me in my gathering and recording of information concerning American editions and their sales. Mr. J. Francis Driscoll of Brookline, Massachusetts, placed at my disposal his enormous collection of American sheet music. Mr. Clarence S. Brigham, Director of the American Antiquarian Society, Worcester, Massachusetts, supervised for me the checking of hundreds of American literary annuals and gift-books owned by the Society but not included in any index or catalogue of annuals. Mr. Duncan Burnet of the University of Georgia Library secured for me through inter-library loan numerous periodicals from all sections of the country. Mr. M. M. Hoover allowed me the use of his Park Benjamin Collection in the Columbia University Library; and Professor Oscar Cargill kindly directed me in the use of his unpublished index of American magazines in the New York University Library.

To Professors Paull F. Baum and Clarence Gohdes of Duke University and Professors Edwin M. Everett and Edd Winfield Parks, my colleagues at the University of Georgia,

I am grateful for valuable suggestions; and to Professor Jay B. Hubbell of Duke University I am especially indebted for his continual interest and scholarly criticism.

Several research workers have given me valuable assistance by checking periodicals and scanning newspapers in search of needed items. Miss Annie A. Nunns, Assistant Superintendent of the Wisconsin Historical Society, Madison, supervised for me the checking of rare periodicals in the Society's unusually large American collection. Miss Mary H. Seem scanned numerous periodicals in the Enoch Pratt Free Library, Baltimore, Maryland. Also, Misses Anita Fennell and Willene Flanigan, student assistants at the University of Georgia, and Miss Helen Marie Chew, of Washington, D. C., have carefully gathered material from the periodicals.

Finally, I am indebted to the following publishers and copyright holders for permission to quote from their books: Mrs. George M. Gould, Atlantic City, New Jersey (Laura Stedman and George M. Gould, *Life and Letters of Edmund Clarence Stedman*); Miss Mildred Howells, Boston, Massachusetts (William Dean Howells, *My Literary Passions*); Mrs. Mary Thacher Higginson's estate, Cambridge, Massachusetts (*Letters and Journals of Thomas Wentworth Higginson*); D. Appleton-Century Company (Hildegarde Hawthorne, *The Poet of Craigie House*); A. S. Barnes and Company (R. H. Stoddard, *Recollections Personal and Literary*); Thomas Y. Crowell Company (*The Complete Works of Edgar Allan Poe*); Alfred A. Knopf, Inc. (Frederick Goddard Tuckerman, *Sonnets*); Cassell and Company, Limited (T. Wemyss Reid, *The Life, Letters, and Friendships of Richard Monckton Milnes*); The Macmillan Company (*Alfred, Lord Tennyson, A Memoir by His Son* and *Tennyson and His Friends*); L. C. Page and Company (*The Works of Alfred Tennyson,* ed. William J. Rolfe); The University of Wisconsin Press (J. F. A. Pyre, *The Formation of Tennyson's Style*); Yale University Press (Thomas R. Lounsbury, *The Life and Times of Tennyson*); and Houghton Mifflin Company (*Journals of Ralph Waldo Emerson; The Heart of Hawthorne's Journals;* Caroline Ticknor, *Hawthorne and His Publisher;* Thomas Wentworth Higginson, *Studies in History and Letters;* John T. Morse, Jr., *Life and Letters of Oliver Wendell Holmes;* Samuel Longfellow, *Life of Henry Wadsworth Longfellow; The Complete Writings of James Russell Lowell;* Edward Everett Hale, *James Russell Lowell and His Friends;* Horace E. Scudder, *James Russell Lowell;* Marie Hansen-Taylor and Horace E. Scudder, *Life and Letters of Bayard Taylor;* and *Letters of Charles Eliot Norton*).

J. O. E.

FOREWORD

THE STUDY OF ALFRED TENNYSON'S REPUTATION IN AMERICA is the study of a poet who embodies, as does no other, the qualities which we think of as especially characteristic of the mid-nineteenth century. By their reaction to Tennyson, American poets and critics of the period may be rather clearly divided into those who liked best the poetry of the eighteenth century and those who preferred the poetry of their own time. Again and again in the eighteen-forties and fifties, Americans referred to Tennyson as the spokesman of a "new poetry." This fact, in itself, makes the study of Tennyson's American reputation a significant chapter in the history of Anglo-American literary relations.

Another important fact, which has been consistently ignored by scholars of English and American literature and which the study of Tennyson's American reputation illustrates, is the influence which American criticism has had upon the careers of leading English literary figures. This influence can be traced distinctly in the work of Carlyle, Elizabeth Barrett, Macaulay, Tennyson, and others. Concerning the popularity of Macaulay in America, the London *Morning Chronicle* wrote on August 27, 1853: "We owe much to America. Not content with charming us with the works of her native genius, she teaches us also to appreciate our own. She steps in between the timidity of a British author and the fastidiousness of the British public, and using her 'good offices' brings both parties to a friendly understanding." This British debt to America is shown nowhere more distinctly than in the career of Tennyson.

The general assumption that an English author's reputation in America was a duplicate of that in his own country is strikingly disproved by the course of Tennyson's American fame. America accepted Tennyson much earlier than did his own country. In the eighteen-thirties Americans who knew his poems were unanimously praising them while the leading British journals were subjecting Tennyson to one of the bitterest attacks in the history of literary criticism. It was through the "good offices" of Americans that Tennyson was persuaded, in spite of the British censure, to venture into print again in 1842. Both the *Poems* of 1842 and Tennyson's next work, *The Princess,* received greater praise in America than in England. In their acclamation of *The Princess,* American periodicals directly reprimanded the British for failure to understand so excellent a work. With the coming of *In Memoriam,* American critics again exhibited their independence of British criticism. Many disliked the poem, and they said so, in the face of England's first wholehearted approval of Tennyson. The peculiar reception given the peculiar poem, "Maud," in America is another example of originality in criticism. The reputation of Tennyson in this country through 1858 offers evidence of an almost unbelievable independence in American literary criticism at the time.

CONTENTS

TENNYSON IN AMERICA

Chapter I

BEFORE THE *POEMS* OF 1842

IT IS EVIDENT THAT THE BRITISH PUBLIC JUDGED TENNYSON'S early poetry more by the satiric and entertaining reviews of it than by the poems themselves. Many read the reviews; few read the poems. There is some justification for the conjecture that the American public, given the choice, would not have done likewise; but that theory will have to remain conjectural. Few Americans had an opportunity to read Tennyson before the first American edition of his poems in 1842.

Probably no copy of Alfred Tennyson's first book, *Poems by Two Brothers* (dated 1827, published December, 1826), written in collaboration with his brother Charles, reached America before Tennyson's fame became firmly established in the eighteen-fifties.[1] It is entirely possible that no printed reference to the book appeared in an American publication before 1842.[2] Written anonymously by two boys, both under twenty, and published by a firm of provincial booksellers in Louth, Lincolnshire, the book attracted little attention in its own country. The only one of three notices long enough to be called a review is a twenty-eight line paragraph in the *Gentleman's Magazine* for June, 1827. Booksellers' newspaper advertisements show that copies of the *Gentleman's Magazine* were reaching America as early as 1827, but this paragraph could not be expected to cause any comment.

Because Edgar Allan Poe quoted in the preface to his *Tamerlane and Other Poems* the same sentence from Martial which the Tennysons quoted upon the title page of their book, some biographers of Poe have suggested the possibility that Poe saw *Poems by Two Brothers* before publishing his first tiny booklet.[3] It seems certain, however, that such was not the case; evidence to support the possibility is slight.[4]

More plausible is the suggestion that Fanny Kemble may have brought with her a copy of *Poems by Two Brothers* when she came to America in September, 1832. Her brother John had given her a copy, and she had become already one of the most ardent of Tennysonians. During her stay in America, she played a significant part in making Tennyson known. Often she read and praised to those about her the *Poems* of 1833, which a friend had sent to her from London, but there is no direct evidence that she brought her highly prized copy of *Poems by Two Brothers* to America.[5]

Tennyson's second published work was the poem *Timbuctoo,* which won the Chancellor's Medal at Cambridge University in 1829. It was published, along with other Cambridge University prize poems, in *Prolusiones Academicae* of the same year, and a very few copies of the poem were published separately.[6] The Boston Athenaeum acquired its copy of *Prolusiones* in 1847.[7] Probably no copy of *Timbuctoo* reached America any earlier. The brief but remarkably eulogistic review which it received in the London weekly *Athenaeum* seems to have attracted no notice in this country.[8]

Tennyson's next literary ventures were his two small volumes: *Poems, Chiefly Lyrical* (1830) and *Poems* (dated 1833, published December, 1832). It was upon these two volumes that Tennyson's fame, both in England and America, rested until 1842. The editions were small, and since Tennyson took steps to withdraw them from circulation when they were ridiculed by the critics, they had become scarce by the late thirties.

Certainly only a few copies of these poems came to America,[9] but, also certainly, there was a demand for them among the few literati who had seen them. Professor William J. Rolfe's statement that it is doubtful whether a dozen copies had crossed the Atlantic by 1842 is reasonable, and his further statement, as late as 1898, that neither of the volumes "is to be found in any of our great libraries," though not strictly accurate, is indicative.[10] James Freeman Clarke wrote in his Louisville, Kentucky, magazine, the *Western Messenger,* in December, 1836, that having borrowed a copy of *Poems, Chiefly Lyrical,* "we copied it half off into our common place book; as no other copy could be found in any book store." James Aldrich, editor with Park Benjamin of the *New World,* having tried often to find a copy, wrote in 1840 in desperation to his friend, F. W. Tappan, "If you chance to see in London a book with this title 'Poems, Chiefly Lyrical' by Alfred Tennyson, I pray you buy it for me *at any price.*" [11] The 1833 volume also was sought after. Unable to find a copy for sale, James Russell Lowell borrowed Emerson's in 1838 or 1839 [12] and set himself the task of copying the entire volume page by page. Making no selection, he began at the beginning and copied the poems, as they came, to page 38, where he broke off in the middle of a stanza of "The Miller's Daughter." [13] Although the manuscript shows little sign of use, probably it was passed about among Lowell's associates. It seems that reading the poems from manuscript was not uncommon among early American Tennyson admirers.

II

The American recognition of Tennyson had its source in the Harvard College group of writers. Nearly every step of advancement in his fame before 1842 can be traced to a member of the so-called Transcendental School or to another who received his or her inspiration in Cambridge. Although he could never make up his mind about Tennyson and never praised him superlatively, Ralph Waldo Emerson in these early years did more than any other single person to make Tennyson known in America. Emerson owned a copy of *Poems, Chiefly Lyrical* as early as December, 1831,[14] and when in 1833 he visited England, he brought back with him a copy of the 1833 *Poems*.[15] Lowell and other Harvard men first read Tennyson's poems in these books, and with that reading their enthusiasm for Tennyson began.[16] What seems to be the earliest American review of Tennyson was written for the transcendental *Western Messenger* by James Freeman Clarke, graduate of Harvard and personal friend of Emerson.[17] Transcendentalist John Sullivan Dwight wrote for the *Christian Examiner* the earliest full and comprehensive review of both of Tennyson's volumes, and he borrowed the two books, and probably the inspiration for the review, from Emerson.[18] Henry Wadsworth Longfellow, Margaret Fuller, Thomas Wentworth Higginson, and Sophia Peabody, who around 1839 made a drawing of the "Lady of Shalott," one of the earliest illustrations of Tennyson,[19] were others of the group who early admired Tennyson.

Edward Everett Hale, writing years later, reminisced interestingly if vaguely concerning the beginning of Tennyson's fame at Harvard:

> I cannot remember—I wish I could—whether it were Longfellow or Emerson who introduced Tennyson in college. That first little, thin volume of Tennyson's poems, with "airy, fairy Lillian [*sic*]" and the rest, was printed in London in 1830. It was not at once reprinted in America. It was Emerson's copy which somebody borrowed in Cambridge and which we passed reverently from hand to hand. Everybody who had any sense knew that a great poet had been born as well as we know it now. And it is always pleasant to me to remember that those first poems of his were handed about in manuscript as a new

ode of Horace might have been handed round among the young gentlemen of Rome.[20]

In striking contrast to Hale's description is that of another Harvard writer, Cornelius C. Felton, who, fifty years earlier, wrote of the same time and the same group:

Strange to say, his [Tennyson's] poems found their way across the Atlantic, and gained favor in the eyes of a peculiar class of sentimentalists. Young ladies were known to copy them entire, and learn them by heart. Stanzas of most melodious unmeaningness passed from mouth to mouth, and were praised to the very echo. The man who possessed a copy was the envy of more than twenty persons, counting women and children; until at length Mr. Tennyson came into possession of a very considerable amount of reputation. His admirers sent to England for copies; but singularly enough not one was to be had.[21]

Clearly, Felton had a motive other than merely describing Tennyson's rise. The phrase, "a peculiar class of sentimentalists," gives a clue. It was doubtless aimed at the transcendentalists, whom Felton did not like. John Sullivan Dwight in 1848 wrote rather proudly of the "martyrs" who had praised Tennyson so enthusiastically in the early days as to be "found guilty of rank literary heresy and transcendental infatuation." [22] Attacks in several quarters seem to have had their origin in Tennyson's American admirers rather than in his poems. Perhaps this is America's version of the Northian lesson concerning becoming "the Pet of a Coterie." [23]

Emerson and Longfellow showed in their letters and journals their interest in Tennyson during the 1830's. In 1834, Emerson copied into his journal two lines of "A Dirge" from *Poems, Chiefly Lyrical,*[24] and in 1836 in explaining how one learns through reading, he wrote, "I go to Shakspear, Goethe, Swift, even to Tennyson, submit myself to them, become merely an organ of hearing, and yield to the law of their being." [25] A well-known statement of Emerson's is that "Tennyson is a beautiful half of a poet." [26] The poems had beauty, but needed more serious matter. They lacked rude truth: "I think Tennyson got his inspiration in gardens and that in this country where there are no gardens, his musky verses could not be written." [27] He found in Tennyson, however, a few "moral sentences" that affected him deeply, and his impression of the *Poems* of 1833 was favorable:

> I have read the second volume of poems by Tennyson, with like delight to that I found in the first and with like criticism. Drenched he is in Shakspear, born, baptized and bred in Shakspear, yet has his own humor, and original rhythm, music and images. How ring his humorsome lines in the ear,—
>
> "In the afternoon they came unto a land
> In which it seemed always afternoon."

Of all the poems in the volume, Emerson liked best "The Death of the Old Year." [28]

Longfellow also was favorably impressed by the volume. He wrote in 1837 or 1838 to Frances Appleton:

> Did you ever read Tennison's [*sic*] Poems? He too is quaint, and at times so wondrously beautiful in his expressions, that even the nicest ear can ask no richer melody:—and the most lively imagination no lovelier picture nor more true. For instance, what words could better describe the falling of those silver streams in the Lauterbrunnen Valley, than these two lines from page 109.
>
> "A land of streams; some like a downward smoke,
> Slow-dropping veils of thinnest lawn, did go."
>
> Or the description of Rosalind on p. 121.
>
> "To whom the slope and stream of life,
> The life before, the life behind,
> In the ear, from far and near,
> Shineth musically clear." [29]

If Miss Appleton had not already read Tennyson, she did soon afterward, for she and Fanny Kemble, who were good friends, were quoting Tennyson to one another in their letters as early as February, 1840.[30] Probably Fanny Kemble imparted some of her own enthusiasm for Tennyson to Miss Appleton; Fanny imparted it to many in America, even, with doubtful success, to Pierce Butler.[31]

Margaret Fuller after 1839 was as enthusiastic about Tennyson as anyone in Cambridge. An important force in the introduction of foreign literary figures into this country, she wrote in 1846: "It has been a great object of my life to introduce here the works of those great geniuses . . . which might give the young, who are soon to constitute the state, a higher standard in thought and action. . . ." [32] She had been deeply impressed by a copy of Tennyson borrowed from Emerson in 1839,[33] and in 1841, reviewing Tennyson in the *Dial,* she praised him extravagantly.[34] When Margaret Fuller visited England in 1846, Emerson tried to arrange for her to see Tennyson and Browning because she had "a sort of right to them" since she had "made their merits widely known among our young people." [35]

Thomas Wentworth Higginson's reminiscences concerning his college days at Harvard testify to the appeal which Tennyson's early poems had for even the younger students there. In 1840 Higginson, seventeen, and Levy Lincoln Thaxter, two classes below him, borrowed from Maria White, Tennyson's "first thin volumes," which seemed to them to "double the value of words"; [36] and a year later Higginson closed his Commencement oration on "Poetry in an Unpoetical Age" with a dramatic peroration coupling the names of Spenser and Tennyson as the greatest of poets. When Professor Edward T. Channing, correcting the speech, wanted to delete the passage, Higginson stoutly defended it, declaring that he considered both Tennyson and Spenser "as among the gods." The passage stood and, according to Higginson, met with much applause from faculty and students alike.[37]

III

Writing in *Graham's Magazine* in 1842, Rufus W. Griswold suggested that "of the works of contemporary English poets of the second class," perhaps none had been "more commented upon or less read in America than those of Alfred Tennyson." [38] The little reading is easily explained by the scarcity of the books, and if Tennyson was much commented upon, that fact may be traceable to Americans' reading the English reviews and to the idea that Tennyson was heading a new school of poetry. The school was often attacked as an infamous one, and many American poets were designated as imitators—plagiarists. All of this would make good gossip.

The general assumption, so often made, that Tennyson was almost unknown in America before 1842 fails to take into account the reading of the English magazines in this country.[39] True, American diaries, letters, and periodicals say little of the English reviews of Tennyson, but certainly the reviews by Christopher North and John Wilson Croker made interesting reading, and the magazines which contained the reviews were circulating widely. Enterprising publishers, pirating the leading English journals and reprinting them in American editions, were doing a thriving business,[40] despite competition with numbers of booksellers who were importing the original editions.[41]

With the possible exception of the *Edinburgh Review, Blackwood's Edinburgh Magazine* seems to have been the most popular of the foreign literary journals, and it was in *Blackwood's* that Christopher North spoke of Tennyson in the "Noctes Ambrosianae" and wrote his famous review of *Poems, Chiefly Lyrical.* Emerson read *Blackwood's* continually in the 1830's; Poe corresponded with Christopher North and may have contributed to *Blackwood's;* [42] and Cornelius Mathews, an editor of the *Arcturus,* was accused in 1842 of having blamed the competition with *Blackwood's* for the failure of his magazine.[43]

When the American magazines and newspapers reviewed individual numbers of the English periodicals, they usually confined themselves to bare summaries of the articles. Infrequently, however, the reviewers expressed their own opinions. Such an exception is the *Albion's* notice of the *Quarterly Review* for April, 1833. John Wilson Croker's review of Tennyson's 1833 *Poems* [44] thoroughly convinced the *Albion's* reviewer of their absurdity:

> The muse of this gentleman belongs to the milky-way of poetry, according to our reviewer, and certainly from the extracts submitted, the versification is as meager and affected as possible. There are unquestionably a few beauties scattered through the numerous verses, but the accumulation of images without rhyme or reason, the pedantry of expression without reference to sense, the laboured accentuation to mark particular phrases, and the painful absurdity of his comparisons, put them without the pale of approbation, and force the regret that an ability, which under proper tuition and restraint, might have produced sweet fruit and pleasant flowers, should have yielded only the glaring poppy and the worthless weed.[45]

In another notice of an English magazine, this time of *Blackwood's* for May, 1836, Horace Greeley's *New Yorker* (July 9, 1836) sympathized with "poor Tennyson," whom Christopher North delighted to lash and who had "experienced some pretty severe handling from the Professor."

The eclectic magazines, composed of articles and reviews copied from foreign periodicals, were an important means of making Tennyson known in America. Eliakim Littell's attractive and popular *Museum of Foreign Literature and Science* republished Christopher North's review of *Poems, Chiefly Lyrical* in August, 1832; and the Boston *Select Journal of Foreign Periodical Literature,* one of the best edited of all the American eclectic periodicals, republished John Wilson Croker's review of the 1833 *Poems* in July, 1833, both republications coming within three months after their originals. Croker's article was copied word for word without comment, but North's was subjected to a significant revision. In the midst of his review, the editor of the *Museum* inserted a footnote: "We have omitted several pages of well-deserved animadversion on the mystical affectation, and 'not unfrequent silliness' of Mr. Tennyson, and subjoin the commendatory part of the article as more likely to interest our readers." The omission, approximately a third of the review, included the harshest of the ridicule and none of the praise. The passages concerning the patriotic songs, "The Poet's Mind," "The 'How' and the 'Why,' " and the examples of Alfred's kissing like a cod-fish and out-Wordsworthing Wordsworth were all omitted. The Americanized version of North was less deadly than the original.

The talk in America of a new school of poetry with Tennyson as its leader obviously had its origin in the descriptions of such an infamous school in the English reviews. The titles of "milky way" and "God-help-you-silly-ones" were dropped, but some of the early descriptions of the school vie with the English in acrimony. The *American Monthly Magazine* of New York for October, 1833, offers a good example:

> . . . the English poets have become the most affected, misty, and unnatural beings in creation. They see visions and they dream dreams. . . . They have a set of pretty little silly phrases, that mean about as much as the simpering sentimentalism of a boarding-school miss, who has sighed away her insipid little soul over the musical nothings of Thomas Moore. When they get into a passion, or rather get a passion into *them,* they make it wondrously like a thunder storm in a tea pot; and they pour it out with a sort of mental hissing, which betokens the bubbling up and boiling over of the vapory stuff within. Nothing is told in plain words. All thought is twisted into strange shapes, till nobody would believe it to be thought at all. They have a pious horror, not of common-place ideas, for ideas

are the last things looked after, but of what they deem to be common-place expressions. All the natural forms of speech, all the hearty ways of telling what the heart feels, are shut out from the poets' 'word-book' with as much care as if they were pestilential. They have sounded the depth of *unmeaningness* and gone to the bottom of that almost bottomless pit. Rising in slowly widening circles, a countless throng of poets and poetasters crowd on each others' heels, like the souls of the dead sinners in Dante's hell, with Alfred Tennyson, like Lucifer, below them all.[46]

At first the school was represented as entirely English, and two tendencies of the time—to promote Americanism and to glorify the classicism of the eighteenth century—sharpened the attacks. But soon Tennyson and Elizabeth Barrett began to share the honors with James Russell Lowell and Longfellow, and with Tennyson's gradual rise, references to the group became more and more favorable. In February, 1842, four months before Tennyson's 1842 volume, Evert A. Duyckinck spoke of him in the *Arcturus* as "a most respectable lawgiver and governor of his peculiar province," and of the "good society at his court, if we named no others than Miss Barrett and Lowell." The following month, Edgar Allan Poe, annoyed by the talk of "the good old Pope" and "the good old Goldsmith school," named Tennyson side by side with the greatest of the Romantics, saying concerning the work of "Keats, Shelley, Coleridge, and Tennyson in England; Lowell and Longfellow in America . . . [that] such poetry and such alone has fulfilled the legitimate office of the muse." [47]

A review in 1842 of Lowell's *A Year's Life* [48] bore the title "A New School of Poetry at Hand." According to the review Tennyson was the undisputed leader of the school; however, he was not a "MESSIAH": it would require "a dozen Tennysons to make a Spencer [*sic*]." Lowell, one of the best poets of the school, could be expected to prove a beneficial leaven: he might "soften their errors" and "elevate their style," for he could "emulate the ideality of Tennyson and Keats without the affectation of the one, or the redundancy of the other." Though far from faultless, the school was to be welcomed:

> It will have none of the jaundiced views of Byron, and little of the *petit maître* style of Pope. It will be intellectual, and, we fear, pedantic also. It threatens to be disgraced by conceits . . . so far as we can foresee now, the Tennysons, Longfellows, and poets of that cast of mind, will give the tone to the coming change in the public taste. Indeed they are already bringing about a revolution.

IV

Many contemporary critics spoke of American imitators of Tennyson from 1840 to 1842. Rufus W. Griswold wrote in *Graham's Magazine* that the scarcity of the two early volumes of Tennyson "enabled some persons to steal the author's livery and achieve great reputation." [49] Henry T. Tuckerman "had no idea" until he read the 1842 volume "how many barefaced imitators he [Tennyson] had in this country." [50] And Park Benjamin's *Brother Jonathan,* reviewing the volume, facetiously grieved that "divers of our poetasters who have parodied and plundered by wholesale, an author hitherto comparatively little known in this country, will find their daw's feathers now revealed, in uncomfortable nakedness." [51]

One of the closest followers of the early Tennyson was James Russell Lowell. When in 1840 he submitted a "sheet of sonnets" for publication in the *Dial,* Margaret Fuller called them imitations of Tennyson,[52] and when his first volume of poems, *A Year's Life,* appeared in 1841, reviews were almost unanimous in noting the Tennyson influence. An exception was Charles Stearns Wheeler's review in the *Christian Examiner,* which quoted lines from "Ianthe" to show how distant were the poems "from the cold and accurate appreciation of beauty, which marks some of the portraits of Alfred Tennyson." [53] On the other hand, a typical example is that in the *North American Review,* making its earliest reference to Tennyson. The reviewer, George S. Hillard, disliked Lowell's "daintinesses and prettinesses of expression":

He abounds with those affected turns, with which the poetry of Tennyson (which we suspect our friend has studied more than is good for him) is so besprinkled. He is too liberal in the use of the poetical vocabulary. . . . Speaking of a lady's hair, he says it is "parted flowingly" and "maidenwise," and in the same poem, we have "rosy white," "red moon-rise," and "far liefer." Why not "far rather"? He does not listen to a bird's song, but he "drinks" its "jargoning." Leaves are "rifted fitfully"; eyes have a "sunset-tinted haziness," and a "mysterious shine. . . ." [54]

Hillard objected also to the compounding of words and to the use of "the solemn termination *eth,* as 'dwelleth' for 'dwells.' " The criticism closely resembled the British reviewers' comments upon Tennyson's diction.

The young Lowell loved sheer melody, music purely for the sake of the sound, and this he found in Tennyson. Calling Tennyson the only English poet whom Lowell "seemed to have read with admiration" in 1841, R. H. Stoddard wrote that to say Lowell "was impressed by Tennyson is to say that he was impressed by whatever is most purely poetic in English verse." [55] Tennyson's influence upon Lowell is evident less in verbal similarity than in a similarity of melody, mood, and atmosphere. Lowell has few lines or phrases which can be called clear echoes of Tennyson, but the influence is unmistakable.

The poems which show the influence most strongly may be conveniently divided into two groups. First, there are the pictures of loveliness and desolation in chivalric setting. The mood is melancholy, and the atmosphere, dreamy and mysterious. A forsaken maiden, a moaning night wind over a barren moor, strange shadows, and a waning red moon form the scene, which is described in verses of lulling music. Such material is, of course, a part of the whole Romantic movement. It is in Keats, and that Lowell was deeply impressed by Keats is certain. Some of his admiration for Tennyson may be accounted for by the fact that they had Keats as a common master. Many of Lowell's borrowings from Tennyson are passages in which Tennyson is most Keatsian. But, as the reviewers pointed out, Lowell frequently borrowed Tennyson's mannerisms or eccentricities. And in these early years Lowell was going to great lengths to get Tennyson's poems, reading all that he could get his hands on. A commonplace book which he kept from 1837 to 1839 contains six quotations from Tennyson, fewer from Coleridge, Byron, and Shelley, and none from Keats.[56] Then, too, Lowell's distinctly Tennysonian and not at all Keatsian "girl-name poems," to be considered later, strengthen the Lowell-Tennyson relationship. Many of Lowell's poems of dreariness and melancholy seem directly traceable to Tennyson's "Mariana," "The Ballad of Oriana," "Mariana in the South," "The Lady of Shalott," "Oenone," or "The Lotos-Eaters."

A good example is Lowell's uncollected poem, "A Ballad":

> Gloomily the river floweth,
> Close by her bower door,
> And drearily the nightwind bloweth
> Across the barren moor.
>
> It rustles through the withering leaves
> Upon the poplars tall,
> And mutters widely 'neath the eaves
> Of the unlighted hall.

The waning moon above the hill
Is rising strange and red,
And fills her soul, against her will,
With fancies lone and dread.

The stream all night will flow as drearly,
The wind will shriek forlorn,
She fears—she knows that something fearful
Is coming ere the morn.

The curtains in that lonely place
Wave like a heavy pall,
And her dead mother's pale, pale face
Doth flicker on the wall.

And all the rising moon about,
Her fear did shape the clouds,
And saw dead faces staring out
From coffins and from shrouds.

A screech-owl now, for three nights past,
Housed in some hollow tree,
Sends struggling up against the blast
His long shriek fearfully.

Strange shadows waver to and fro,
In the uncertain light,
And the scared dog hath howled below
All through the weary night.[57]

Compare "Mariana":

About a stone-cast from the wall
A sluice with blacken'd waters slept,
And o'er it many, round and small,
The cluster'd marish-mosses crept.
Hard by a poplar shook alway,
All silver-green with gnarled bark:
For leagues no other tree did dark
The level waste, the rounding gray.

She only said, 'My life is dreary,
He cometh not,' she said;
She said, 'I am aweary, aweary,
I would that I were dead!'

And ever when the moon was low,
And the shrill winds were up 'nd away,
In the white curtain, to and fro,
She saw the gusty shadow sway,
But when the moon was very low,
And wild winds bound within their cell,
The shadow of the poplar fell
Upon her bed, across her brow.
She only said, [etc.]

All day within the dreary house,
The doors upon their hinges creak'd;
The blue fly sung i' the pane; the mouse
Behind the mouldering wainscot shriek'd,
Or from the crevice peer'd about.
Old faces glimmered thro' the doors,
Old footsteps trod the upper floors,
Old voices called her from without.
She only said, [etc.] [58]

"Serenade," in *A Year's Life,*[59] is in the same mood, and a refrain, "Alone, alone, ah woe! alone!" is in the same key as that of "Mariana in the South":

I am all alone,
Love-forgotten and love-forlorn.[60]

Lowell's "Rosaline" is another in the mood of "Mariana":

The death-watch ticked behind the wall,
The blackness rustled like a pall,
The moaning wind did rise and fall
Among the bleak pines, Rosaline! [61]

The name Rosaline is repeated twice in each stanza much in the manner of Tennyson's "Oriana." The chivalric setting in which the grief stricken lover looks upon his dead Rosaline is again like "Oriana." Rosaline is the traditional lady of chivalry with her mystic halo.

"Farewell," uncollected in Lowell's late editions, contains a portrait of the traditional lady which reminds one of the Lady of Shalott. The ethereal lady of "Farewell" is named Marian. Tennyson usually described his ladies in the third person, but Lowell always had the lover do the talking:

> Fair as a single star thou shinest,
> And white as lilies are
> The slender hand wherewith thou twinest
> Thy heavy auburn hair;
> Thou art to me
> A memory
> Of all that is divinest:
> Thou art so fair and tall,
> Thy looks so queenly are,
> Thy very shadow on the wall,
> Thy step upon the stair,
> The thought that thou art nigh,
> The chance look of thine eye
> Are more to me than all, Marian,
> And will be till I die.[62]

Lowell's "The Syrens" has the drowsy, soothing atmosphere of Tennyson's "The Lotos-Eaters," as these lines indicate:

> All around with a slumberous sound,
> The singing waves slide up the strand,
> And there, where the smooth, wet pebbles be,
> The waters gurgle longingly,
> As if they fain would seek the shore,
> To be at rest from the ceaseless roar,

To be at rest for evermore,—
For evermore.[63]

The "Syrens" was probably inspired by Tennyson's little song, "The Sea-Fairies," in the 1833 *Poems.* The sirens and the fairies sing enticingly to the weary mariners in much the same manner; however, Tennyson's singers become gay and sprightly, while Lowell's preserve the atmosphere of "The Lotos-Eaters." [64]

The second group which show marked Tennysonian influence is Lowell's "girl-name poems." Tennyson's 1830 and 1833 volumes contain several portraits of girls written in a light and fanciful vein. "Lilian," "Madeline," "Adeline," "Margaret," "Rosalind," and "Kate" are all of a kind, and "Lilian" is often used to typify the group:

Airy, fairy Lilian,
Flitting, fairy Lilian,
When I ask her if she love me,
Claps her tiny hands above me,
Laughing all she can;
She'll not tell me if she love me,
Cruel little Lilian.

When my passion seeks
Pleasance in love-sighs,
She, looking thro' and thro' me
Thoroughly to undo me,
Smiling, never speaks:
So innocent-arch, so cunning-simple,
From beneath her purfled wimple
Glancing with black-beaded eyes,
Till the lightning laughters dimple
The baby-roses in her cheeks;
Then away she flies.

Prythee weep, May Lilian!
Gaiety without eclipse
Wearieth me, May Lilian;

Thro' my very heart it thrilleth
When from crimson-threaded lips
Silver-treble laughter trilleth:
Prythee weep, May Lilian!

Praying all I can,
If prayers will not hush thee,
Airy Lilian,
Like a rose-leaf I will crush thee,
Fairy Lilian.[65]

Lowell's "Sonnets on Names" in *A Year's Life* resemble Tennyson's portraits in sprightliness.[66] Some verbal similarity also may be noted. "Rose" is an example:

My ever-lightsome, ever laughing Rose,
Who always speakest first and thinkest last,
Thy full voice is as clear as bugle-blast;
Right from the ear down to the heart it goes
And says "I'm beautiful! as who but knows?"
Thy name reminds me of old romping days,
Of kisses stolen in dark passage-ways,
Or in the parlor, if the mother-nose
Gave sign of drowsy watch. I wonder where
Are gone thy tokens, given with a glance
So full of everlasting love till morrow,
Or a day's endless grieving for the dance
Last night denied, backed with a lock of hair,
That spake of broken hearts and deadly sorrow.

Rose's fickle heart suggests Tennyson's "Madeline," and the "ever-lightsome, ever laughing" recalls the thrice repeated refrain, "Ever-varying Madeline." [67] Two others of the "Sonnets on Names" have phrases suggesting "Lilian." Mary is a "gold-haired, laughing little fairy"; and Anne is quiet and pensive;

Yet is she not of those who, all they can,
Strive to be gay, and striving, seem most sad.

Lowell's "Isabel" and two songs, "Lift up the curtain of thine eyes" and "What reck I of the stars when I," are in the same group.[68] "Isabel" in its closing lines resembles also the "Mariana" group. The second of the songs described the lady's brown hair with a phrase, "parted maidenwise," which may be akin to Tennyson's phrase in "Isabel":

> locks not wide-dispread,
> Madonna-wise on either side her head.[69]

Several circumstances contributed to the resemblance between the two serious portraits, Lowell's "Irené" and Tennyson's "Isabel." "Irené" was inspired by Maria White, and "Isabel," by Tennyson's mother. They were women of much the same type. Both poems emphasize a gentleness, a wisdom in counsel, a God-like quality, and perfect womanhood.[70] That the poems should speak of many of the same qualities is to be expected, but it is evident that Lowell's owes something to Tennyson.

A note in the *New World* reversing the charge of the influence gives interesting evidence of the early resemblances between Lowell and Tennyson. The writer had looked over the English reviews of Tennyson's 1842 volume and was disappointed that "none of the London journals charge the author with stealing either his style or thoughts from that first of modern bards, James Russell Lowell." [71]

No other major American poet of the period fell under the spell of Tennyson as did Lowell. Longfellow, however, felt the influence of Tennyson to some extent. In 1840 Poe, always the zealous detector of plagiarism, loudly proclaimed one borrowing from Tennyson: that of the "Midnight Mass for the Dying Year" [72] from "The Death of the Old Year." This, Poe labeled "plagiarism too palpable to be mistaken"; Longfellow had stolen "nearly all that is valuable in the piece of Tennyson": "the conception of personifying the Old Year as a dying old man, with the singularly wild and fantastic *manner* in which that conception is carried out." Both poems capitalized "Old Year"; both had an absence of rime at the end of each stanza; and they were alike in "the general peculiarity of the rhythm." [73] When Longfellow heard of the accusation, he wrote, "I did not even know that he [Tennyson] had written a piece on this subject." [74] Longfellow, however, had owned in 1837 a copy of Tennyson's 1833 volume containing the poem.

In his heated arguments on plagiarism, Poe himself did not escape the charge of copying Tennyson. His "The Haunted Palace," first published in N. C. Brooks's *American Museum of Literature and the Arts,* for April, 1839, was called a copying of Tennyson's "The Deserted House"; and "The Sleeper," written early and having several versions and varying titles, was also called Tennysonian.[75] An anonymous article in the *Foreign Quarterly Review* (London), which worried Poe greatly, quoted passages from "The Haunted Palace" as examples of a "strong Tennysonian tinge." [76] The following lines were called a "metrical imitation":

> In the greenest of our valleys
> By good angels tenanted,
> Once a fair and stately palace
> (Snow-white palace) rear'd its head.
>
> . . . .
>
> And all with pearl and ruby glowing
> Was the fair palace-door,
> Through which came flowing, flowing, flowing,
> And sparkling evermore,
> A troop of echoes—

"The Haunted Palace" metaphorically described an insane mind as "The Deserted House" described a dead body.

James Aldrich, New York editor and minor poet,[77] owed nearly all that is poetic in his work to Tennyson. His son nets and short poems, scattered through New York magazines and newspapers, abound in dreamy imagery, desolate scenes, and also sprightly feminine portraits. "The Dreaming Girl" immediately suggests Tennyson:

> The clusters of her dusky hair
> Are floating on her bosom fair,
> Like early darkness stealing o'er
> The amber tints that daylight gave,
> Or, like the shadow of a cloud
> Upon a fainting summer wave.
>
> . . . .
>
> Up waking from her blissful sleep,
> She stalks with fear too wild to weep;
> Through the trailing honeysuckle,
> All night breathing odorous sighs,
> Which her lattice dimly curtains,
> The morn peeps in with his bright eyes.[78]

Poe noted Aldrich's "Molly Gray" as one of the clearest imitations of Tennyson's "Lilian":

> Pretty, fairy Molly Gray!
> What may thy fit emblems be?
> Stream or star or bird or flower—
> They are all too poor for thee.
>
> No type to match thy beauty
> My wandering fancy brings
> Not fairer than its Chrysalis
> Thy soul with its golden wings! [79]

Such verses were tremendously popular in newspapers and magazines in the early 1840's. For some of them Tennyson was undoubtedly the source, and probably he was in some measure responsible for the great wave of interest in airy feminine descriptions at this time. They form a rare evidence that some Americans other than the select literati were reading Tennyson's poems before 1842. The following two, the first as early as 1834, will exemplify the large group:

Sweeter than the sweetest manna,
Lovely, lively, chaste Susannah
You're the girl that still I muse on,
Pretty little smiling Susan.
Oh! if verses can amuse ye,
Fairest, sweetest, laughing Susy,
I'd write on, but never rebuke ye
Handsome and good natured Suky!
Every rhyme should flatter you,
Sprightly, dimpling, tender Sue. . . .[80]

There is a witchery about you, Kate,
'Tis not the saucy sparkle of your eye,
Nor step with conscious victory elate,
Spurning the suppliant earth in passing by,
Nor smile that seems all comers to defy—
It is not these, but all of them combined,
And voice that varies with each fancy wild,
Playing, like noon-tide shadows, o'er thy mind:
As wilful art thou as a petted child,
Fickle, alluring as an April wind!
None ever yet have touched that heart of fire
Burning far down with all this dross above—
Ah! that were prize where bold heart may aspire,
'Twere worth a world to tame thee into love! [81]

V

The American criticism of Tennyson before 1842 consisted very largely of praise. Only the poems now universally classed as Tennyson's worst were condemned. "O Darling Room," of which Croker had made much fun, was rejected by his most ardent admirers. Lowell in 1838 quoted its first stanza as an example of "floods of verses with all the childishness and none of the redeeming points of Wordsworth's earlier style." [82] Fanny Kemble, reading the 1833 *Poems* sent to her in America, thought Tennyson "to possess in a higher degree than any English poet except, perhaps, Keats, the power of writing pictures." "The Miller's Daughter,"

"The Lady of Shalott," "Mariana," and "Eleanore" she thought "full of exquisite form and color," but "The little room with the two little white sofas" she hated. As Miss Kemble noted, the three stanzas, each one of which rimed *exquisite* with *white* lent themselves "temptingly to the making of good burlesque." [83]

Oliver Wendell Holmes singled out another of the early poems as one of Tennyson's worst. Lecturing upon Tennyson's poetry in 1853, Holmes, according to a newspaper reporter, recalled a lecture which he had made before 1842 and in which he had discussed the poems of Tennyson which were then published. He had thought poorly of the poems, "one especially, a war-song, not republished, which was the dowdiest, crushed old woman's bonnet of a battle-song that ever Bellona figured in." [84] But "The Lady of Shalott" was excellent: he had "heard it read from the manuscript before publication to a company which it held in magnetic silence." [85]

The theory that early American reviews of Tennyson were mere copies of the English, lacking "even the slight merit of originality," [86] is not at all applicable to the period before 1842. *Poems, Chiefly Lyrical* and *Poems,* 1833, received at least five reviews or notices in American magazines, and they were, without exception, loud in praise of Tennyson. If the authors knew of the harsh criticism in the British periodicals, they were not influenced by it. The American notices were, if nothing else, original.

The *Western Messenger* of Louisville, as has been said, seems to have been the first to review the poems. Although founded primarily as an organ of Unitarian religion, it was an important literary periodical. Oliver Wendell Holmes, Theodore Parker, and Ralph Waldo Emerson were among its contributors, and some of Keats's poetry was first published in its pages.[87] *Poems, Chiefly Lyrical* was reviewed by its editor, James Freeman Clarke, in December, 1836. The review was extravagant in praise of the poems:

No music we ever heard was half so sweet in its ripple and cadence—no warm June morning so full of soft influences of woods, winds and waters—nothing in conversation, literature, or oratory so wholly charming as the bits of poetry in this little book. And yet this is wholly and merely the beauty of expression. The thoughts are often very trivial, the sentiment wholly insignificant, but the *form* is so exquisite, that we smack our lips, as though tasting some rare delicacy, which, when it has left our mouths, we think no more of forever.

"The Deserted House," "Claribel," and "The Sleeping Beauty" were quoted in full. In "Claribel," the sound was "so sweet we can well dispense with any meaning." Its music reminded one of Mozart. "The Sleeping Beauty" resembled the pictures of "some glittering Lombard or Venetian Painter." The editor closed with an invitation to his readers to ask for more: if they "appear to enjoy these sweet sounds as much as we have, we can give them some further specimens of the dainty Alfred Tennyson." [88]

In March, 1837, *Every Body's Album,* a Philadelphia periodical devoted to "humorous tales, essays, anecdotes and facetiae," contained a brief notice of Tennyson's two volumes. Edited by Charles Alexander, a founder of the *Saturday Evening Post* and editor from time to time of several short-lived papers, the *Album* had no literary pretensions. During its brief existence from July, 1836, to June, 1837, the *Album* printed some American poems and a few selected poems of Thomas Campbell, Mrs. Hemans, and Tennyson. Only Tennyson's were noticed. The reviewer placed Tennyson in the forefront of living English poets. Of that group "who have sprung into notice, since those brilliant masters of the lyre, who figured in the latter part of the last century, and the earlier part of the present, have retired, none has attracted more favorable regard" than Alfred Tennyson:

> His felicity of diction, wild originality of conception, and melody of numbers, can hardly be surpassed. Most of his poems are short—small but priceless gems—.

The notice quoted "The Death of the Old Year" in full, and promised that, since Tennyson's two volumes were "exceedingly rare in this country," the *Album* would present occasionally to its readers "some of the happiest effusions of this original and highly popular poet." [89]

The most comprehensive American review of Tennyson before 1842 was that by John Sullivan Dwight in the *Christian Examiner* for January, 1838. A Unitarian magazine published in Boston, the *Examiner* was for more than half a century one of the most important of American reviews not only because of its theological work but also because of its distinctive literary criticism. Dwight, a frequent contributor, was a young Boston minister and music critic. A graduate of Harvard and a member of the Transcendental Club, he later became a leader in the Brook Farm movement. In 1838 he was already accomplished in the criticism of music. His review of Tennyson's two volumes—the titles of both were listed as the heading of the article—was wise and understanding, and in spite of evidences of a strong admiration for Christopher North, it was independent. The review showed the musician's love of melody and, less frequently, the minister's demand for moral purpose.

Dwight had read the witty review in the *Quarterly,* which showed "what ludicrous constructions *can* be put" upon the poems. He had read also North's review in *Blackwood's,* which he thought much better, for though it made merry with Tennyson's faults, it paid due reverence to "the genuine poetic spirit, which always finds its way into the warm poet's heart of Christopher North." Because of North's sanction, Dwight had "no misgivings in introducing the poet to the American public." He did not feel called upon to drag to light the least successful poems. Some were "fruit not worth the gathering." Tennyson "seems often to have descended to the mechanical task of trying to make up something, which may look like the living product of some old remembered inspiration." But even these pieces had one excellence which pervaded everything of Tennyson's: "they charm by their melodious sound." Tennyson had "the true instinct of rhythm" and could not "write unmusically." Although he had much to outgrow, he had a "poet's faculty to answer for."

"Claribel" was quoted as an example of melodious music. It had, according to the review, in common with many of Tennyson's poems, a Wordsworthian truth and freshness of diction, which was one sure sign, among others, of the poet's intimacy with nature:

There is a minute reality in his pictures of the outer world; a dainty selection, as by the surest instinct, of the most delicate and significant features of nature. He has looked on her calmly, with an eye of his own, till all that is common place vanishes, and the thing appears as it *is,* with a renovated beauty, so perfect that the heart is never weary of it. So vivid are his allusions to natural sights, that we know that all this is the poetry of experience;—it was lived first, and then written. This poet, we know, must have been an observer. He has the true insight, or onsight, (Anschauen) as the Germans call it. Hence the transparency of his style. Every phrase is genuine; it stands for something felt; it is frank and out-speaking, shunning neither homeliness nor strangeness, unlike the empty phrases which pass current often where poetry will not. Every word stands for a thing; remove a word, and you erase a feature.

"The Miller's Daughter" was quoted to show Tennyson's minute fidelity to nature in all his descriptions. "The May Queen" and "New-Year's Eve," also quoted, were "two exquisite little pieces" in the style of simple feeling.

"The Lady of Shalott" had "exquisite beauty of imagery, yet of most obscure meaning." "The Ballad of Oriana," quoted in full, received the highest praise:

> This is all but perfect. Why shall we not call it one of the best ballads in the English language? There is not a line or a phrase which we would willingly spare. In what bold relief it stands forth! what a holy calm invests him! It is the height of the passive heroic.

But, Dwight thought, perhaps the best of Tennyson's poems were his female portraits: "a gallery of lovely ideals, which all but breathe from the canvas." "Adeline" and "Margaret" were quoted as examples. These, together with such poems as "The Lotos-Eaters," "The Hesperides," and "A Dream of Fair Women," were beautiful. Their one fault was that they "make no appeal to any active sentiment within us." They "shine for nothing—insulated as in a vacuum." Tennyson had sacrificed too much to beauty. He possessed "great excellences, remarkable everywhere," but what he had yet done was "not worthy of himself." We might hope for better things.

In July, 1841, Margaret Fuller's notice of Tennyson's poems appeared in the *Dial,* a quarterly which during its four years of existence from 1840 to 1844 served as the chief organ of the New England transcendentalists. Margaret Fuller and Emerson were its editors, and most of the transcendental group contributed to it. The Tennyson notice testifies to the admiration felt for Tennyson by the members of this group:

> Tennyson is known by heart, is copied as Greek works were at the revival of literature; nothing has been known for ten years back more the darling of the young than these two little volumes. "If you wish to know the flavor of strawberries or cherries, ask children and birds." We understand he is preparing for a new edition, which will, we hope, be extensively circulated in this country.

Evert A. Duyckinck wrote a review of Tennyson's poems for his *Arcturus, A Journal of Books and Opinions* in February, 1842. A New York monthly designed to have "the mixed character of a Review and a Magazine," the *Arcturus* lasted only a year and a half. Its editors were Duyckinck and Cornelius Mathews. Duyckinck was an early admirer of Tennyson, but it was long before he classed Tennyson as anything but a minor poet. In August, 1841, Duyckinck listed him with the "minor names" who "will live with the Donnes, the Carews, and the Marvells," [90] and in December of the same year he spoke of Charles and Alfred Tennyson as of equal rank, admitting that all he knew of either one of them was what he had found in Leigh Hunt's *Tatler*.[91] Duyckinck, however, was one of the few Americans to own a copy of *Poems, Chiefly Lyrical,* and in his collection of books given to the Lenox Library in 1878, there were more copies of Tennyson's works than of any other English poet except Shakespeare.

The review in *Arcturus* welcomed the news of preparations for a new edition of Tennyson: "Right welcome to the taste of the better judges and the popular enjoyment" would the poems be. "New Year's Eve" was set before the readers as "a provocative to the banquet." It exhibited "several characteristics of the true poet; and, chief of all, a sympathy with common and familiar things, not holding verse, as formerly it has been practiced, a grammarian's exercise of words, but a living tabernacle of the spirit, filled with thought and sensibility."

The "highest kingdom of the art poetical" Duyckinck thought Tennyson had not "aimed at," and a peculiar school of poets had gathered around him:

> The turn this plaintive school of poets has for melancholy, is one of their chief characteristics: it is associated with gentleness, grace, and much beauty; but its predominance is not evidence of a high order of poetry. . . . This is an unhappy

tendency of the Tennyson school of poets: yet, there are many moods of the mind, when such a gentle voice of grief comes to relieve the burdened heart of many of its cares, by its words of sympathy.

Except for the few reviews, American literary periodicals had little to do with Tennyson before 1842. One looks in vain for any selected poems of his in such magazines as the *North American Review,* the *Southern Literary Messenger,* or *Graham's Magazine.* It was left almost entirely to New York weekly newspapers to do the selecting that was done.[92] James Aldrich's *New York Literary Gazette* led all others by printing seven of Tennyson's poems during its six months of existence in 1839.[93] The *New World,* edited by Park Benjamin and James Aldrich, printed six in its quarto edition in 1841 and 1842.[94] Aldrich, an ardent Tennysonian, was probably responsible for Tennyson's appearance in both of these papers. Horace Greeley's *New Yorker* selected "The Mermaid" and "The Death of the Old Year," [95] and the *New York Mirror* selected "Kate," "Margaret," and "The Sleeping Beauty." [96]

Forty-one poems by Tennyson, counting each appearance as a separate poem, have been located in American periodicals, either as quotations in original reviews or as separate selections, before the appearance of the *Poems* of 1842. Nine are poems which were not reprinted in 1842. Nineteen are from *Poems, Chiefly Lyrical* and twenty-two from the *Poems* of 1833. Twelve are from the "girl-name poems," and six are from the "Mariana group." "Mariana" appears twice, and "Lilian" once. Most reprinted is "Margaret," which appears four times. "Adeline," "The Ballad of Oriana," "New Year's Eve," "The Sleeping Beauty," and "The Death of the Old Year" each appears three times.

VI

The first move to reprint Tennyson's early poems came in America in 1838. John Sullivan Dwight's review in the *Christian Examiner* in January of that year deplored the fact that enterprising American booksellers had not republished Tennyson, and by April, Emerson had persuaded one to risk the venture. C. C. Little & Company, of Boston, wrote to Longfellow on April 27, 1838, that Emerson had urged them to republish Tennyson's poems and that they intended to do so. They had Emerson's permission to print from "his volume," which Longfellow then had, and they wished to borrow also Longfellow's "own volume." [97] Apparently, the proposed edition was to include *Poems, Chiefly Lyrical* and the *Poems* of 1833 complete. But the plan was never carried out. Why it was rather abruptly abandoned is not known. Possibly Tennyson himself heard of the plan and in some way remonstrated.

In 1840 the desire for a new edition again asserted itself in America, and this time the first step was to ask Tennyson to give his permission or to prepare an edition himself. Charles Stearns Wheeler, tutor in Greek at Harvard, and a friend of Lowell and Emerson, wrote to Tennyson in December making such a request.[98] Little & Brown, successors to C. C. Little & Company, still wished to publish the poems, and Wheeler was eager to edit them. Cheerfully diligent and untiring in clerical duties, Wheeler had helped Emerson edit Carlyle's *Miscellanies* in 1838 and 1839,[99] and when Lowell suggested that he write Tennyson offering similar services,[100] Wheeler was delighted at the prospect.

Of Wheeler's offer, Tennyson wrote to Edward Fitzgerald early in 1841, "You bore me about my book; so does a letter just received from America, threatening, tho' in the civilest terms, that, if I will not publish in England, they will do it for me in that land of freemen." Concerning what he styled a threat Tennyson added, "I may curse knowing what they will bring forth. But I don't care." [101] Tennyson, however, did care very much. Undoubtedly he was inwardly pleased by this compliment to his poems, but the thought of seeing again in print his much ridiculed early verses was galling. He might have held out against the entreaties of his English friends to publish, but against the menace of this new peril from across the Atlantic, his only defense lay in the preparation of a new edition of his own. On February 22, 1841, he answered Wheeler:

I thank you for your polite & kindly communication, as also for the offer of your services in the correction of the press, supposing that my book were published in America. I am rejoiced that I have made myself friends on the other side of the Atlantic, & feel what a high privilege it is for a writer to be born into a language common to two great people; & so believe me not insensible, or if that seem to savour too much of the coldness of mere courtesy, believe me deeply sensible of the honour my American friends have done me even in making a request to which I feel it impossible to accede as they perhaps might wish. I am conscious of many things so exceedingly crude in those two volumes that it would certainly be productive of no slight annoyance to me, to see them republished as they stand at present either here or in America, but I will tell you what I will do, for when I was wavering before, your letter decided me. I have corrected copies of most that was worth correction in those two volumes & I will in the course of a few months republish them in England with several new poems & transmit copies to Little & Brown & also to yourself (if you will accept one) & you can then of course do as you choose with them.[102]

Knowing nothing of Wheeler's correspondence with Tennyson, Evert A. Duyckinck, in his *News-Gong* for December, 1841, urged an American reprint of Tennyson, and a few days later Lowell wrote to him that Tennyson was at work upon a new edition.[103] Concerning the news, Lowell added in the same letter:

I do not wish you to [Lowell first wrote, "You need not," then marked it out] state your authority for this—but you may depend on it, for my authority is the poet himself. I have the great satisfaction of thinking that the publication is in some measure owing to myself, for it was by my means that he was written to about it, and he says that "his American friends" are the chief cause of his reprinting.

Duyckinck was delighted, hoped we could have also the sonnets of the brother Charles,[104] and in his *Arcturus,* became enthusiastic over this example of Americans' recognition of a minor poet:

It is understood that Moxon, the London publisher, is about to issue a new edition of the poems of Alfred Tennyson, undertaken by the author, we believe, at the solicitation of his *American* friends and readers. It is a handsome compliment, this, to the "American Market," and one that is richly deserved. For the enthusiasm for good verse, even including the recent minor poets of England, is far greater here than at home.[105]

Before the new English edition had appeared, preparations were under way for an American edition, to be its exact duplicate. The *Dial* announced, belatedly, in July, 1842, that Tennyson, "moved by being informed of his American popularity," was preparing a new edition and had sent the new poems to Wheeler, who was "republishing them here."

The correct meaning of the word *moved* in the quotation might be one which the *Dial* did not intend. The pressure from America may not have left Tennyson in the best of humor. But be that as it may, the new English edition was completed in May, 1842. By mid-June copies were reaching America; within a few weeks Americans had an edition of their own; and the poems were becoming plentiful.

Chapter II

THE RECEPTION OF THE *POEMS* OF 1842

THE NEW EDITION OF TENNYSON'S POEMS APPEARED IN TWO volumes, the first consisting largely of poems which had been published in 1830 and 1833, and the second made up, with two exceptions, of poems hitherto unprinted. The most noteworthy feature of the first volume, and from the standpoint of American criticism, of the entire edition, was the radical revisions of the reprinted selections. Of the poems of 1830 the majority were discarded, and the others retained with little alteration, but the major pieces of 1833—"The Lady of Shalott," "The Miller's Daughter," "Oenone," "The Dream of Fair Women"—were all retained and all extensively revised. The second volume contained such new favorites as "Morte d'Arthur," "Ulysses," and "Locksley Hall." [1]

Early in June, 1842, before any copies could reach America through the book market, Tennyson sent the two volumes to Charles Stearns Wheeler. Wheeler wrote to Emerson on June 11 that the "two beautiful volumes" had arrived and that William D. Ticknor and Company of Boston was busy reprinting them.[2] Just why Ticknor, and not Little and Brown, was given the volumes is not clear, but Wheeler was trying to make for Tennyson the best bargain possible, and it is reasonable to suppose that Ticknor's financial agreement was more favorable to Tennyson than was Little and Brown's. Certainly, if available information is correct, the contract which Ticknor made was one almost unheard of among publishers of that time. After the negotiations, Tennyson wrote to Wheeler, "I have full faith that you have made as good a bargain for me as was possible under the circumstances. . . . These things will all be remedied with the progress of years though perhaps the grass will wave over our graves 'before the coming of the better day.' " [3] Tennyson was speaking of the coming of an international copyright law, still fifty years away. Ticknor had paid him one hundred and fifty dollars for the copyright of his two volumes.[4]

William Davis Ticknor began his career as a Boston publisher in 1832, and in 1845 he took James T. Fields into partnership. Throughout Tennyson's life, he looked upon Ticknor and Fields and their successors [5] as his authorized American publishers. They were always strictly honest. At a time when nearly every American publisher was pirating the works of English authors, Ticknor and Fields insisted upon making full payments for copyright.[6] Tennyson's long relationship with the company was pleasant in the extreme. The copyright payment for his first American edition, Tennyson never forgot. On his eightieth birthday he recalled memories of William D. Ticknor as "one who gave so honorable an example to his countrymen of justice in the highest sense." [7] Ticknor's payment for the *Poems* of 1842 is possibly the earliest copyright payment by an American publisher to a foreign author.[8]

Ticknor issued his edition of the *Poems* on July 7, 1842,[9] three weeks after copies of the English edition had begun to reach American booksellers.[10] At least four Boston booksellers advertised Ticknor's edition prominently during July, and reviewers and advertisers alike were unanimous in their praise of the binding, printing, and general editorial excellence of the books.[11] Bound in two octavo volumes, the edition was, as nearly as Ticknor could make it, an exact duplicate of the English edition. At least one reviewer could not distinguish between the two without looking at the publisher's label.[12] Wheeler had wanted the American edition to add a preface "telling our good people who Alfred Tennyson is," and he had asked Emerson to write it.[13] But the plan was dropped, possibly because of the desire to make the American edition a duplicate of the English. Both were issued without preface or introduction.

Particularly significant is the fact that the first American edition consisted of from fifteen hundred to two thousand copies; whereas, the English publisher was willing to risk only eight hundred. The second English edition (June, 1843) added a thousand more, still little above the American figure.[14] Not until the third English edition appeared in 1845 did the London publisher outdistance Ticknor, and within a few months after the English third edition, Ticknor issued his second.[15] Remembering that the English edition was circulating in America three weeks ahead of the American and that it continued to circulate to some extent after the American appeared,[16] one is forced to the conclusion that the sales in America were but slightly, if at all, behind those in England.

II

First to greet Tennyson's new poems in America were the Boston newspapers. Their reaction was mildly favorable. On the day the poems appeared, the *Transcript* spoke of the "exquisite lyrics and ballads" whose very titles were "melody itself," but within a few days its enthusiasm had cooled: if Tennyson "had written less, he would assuredly have written better"; he should have used the pruning knife more freely.[17] The *Post* (July 12, 1842) was strongly hostile. Confessing that he had read much about Tennyson in English magazines, the reviewer kept his eye on Christopher North. Tennyson was "capable of far greater things," but many of his verses were "mere trash." Tennyson appeared "to be almost one of those great little writers who find most of their originality in truisms, puerility, and affectation." The *Times* (July 14, 1842) in a long rambling review could not make up its mind, and only the *Courier* (July 12, 1842) gave unadulterated praise: Tennyson's remarkable imagination, purest pathos, melodious versification, and originality afforded "the most striking evidence of genius" and combined to make Tennyson "one of the most deeply imaginative and affecting bards of the day."

The *Poems* reached New York by July 12, and there, where the newspapers had paid Tennyson's poems far more attention before 1842, the reception was more favorable.[18] The *New World* was incensed by the Boston *Post's* review. Feeling only pity and contempt for the reviewer's obtuseness and "his utter want of appreciation of the exquisitely beautiful," it assured him that Tennyson's poems "were not made for him, less he for them." [19] In its own review of the *Poems,* the *New World* gave one of the earliest expressions of the idea, later so prevalent, that Tennyson was the oracle of the age:

> Tennyson's poems are everywhere pervaded with a peculiarly tender grace: they are highly imaginative, and eminently suggestive; shadowing forth, with dreamy indistinction, the great Idea of the age. We regard Tennyson as occupying higher ground than any poet of his time—he is a true prophet, somewhat in advance of his age, giving utterance to the unapprehended aspirations of millions.[20]

The New York *Daily Tribune* (July 12, 1842) praised Tennyson's "true poetic vein," and *Brother Jonathan* (July 16, 1842) admired his quaintness, simplicity, and truth of sentiment, calling them traits which would make his fame live far longer than that of many a poet now thought greater. Nearly every New York newspaper which included any literary matter contained during 1842 at least a selection from Tennyson's *Poems* with a brief prefatory comment.[21] Every known comment was favorable. Many lacked thought; none lacked praise.

One of the strongest feelings produced by the new poems in America was that of grief over the many revisions of the early poems. The same feeling was expressed by periodicals in England, and often, strangely enough, by those which earlier could find no good word for the first poems.[22] The American feeling, however, was borrowed from no one. When Sophia Peabody found the lines from "The Lady of Shalott," which she had illustrated in a sketch, altered out of existence, she was sincerely shocked. Her sister, Elizabeth Peabody, who thought every single one of Tennyson's alterations a mistake, wanted her to send the drawing to Tennyson as the best lesson to give him concerning his mutilations.[23]

Fanny Kemble could have no patience with the revisions. In her sixteen-page review of the *Poems* for the *Democratic Review* of New York, she devoted fifteen pages to the poems of 1830 and 1833.[24] For page after page she argued bitterly over the changes, quoting lengthy revised passages side by side with their originals to show that the most beautiful had been ruined and that the mediocre had been turned into "unmitigated twaddle." Tennyson was moving both forward and backward: the new poems—which Fanny never got around to—showed growing genius, but the changes in the early poems showed none at all.[25]

The transcendental group received the new poems with praise equal to that which they had accorded to the earlier. At Brook Farm "the weeds were scratched out of the ground" to the music of Tennyson's songs,[26] and for the *Dial* Margaret Fuller wrote one of the most commendatory reviews which the volumes received.[27] She missed several of her "favorites for years past" which Tennyson had omitted, but in his new poems she thought his genius was deeper and more matured:

The light he sheds on the world is mellowed and tempered. If the charm he threw around us before was somewhat too sensuous, it is not so now; he is deeply thoughtful; the dignified and graceful man had displaced the Antinous beauty of the youth. His melody is less rich, less intoxicating, but deepens, a sweetness from the soul, sweetness as of the hived honey of fine experiences, replaces the sweetness which captivated the ear only, in many of his earlier verses. His range of subjects was great before, and is now such that he would seem too merely the amateur, but for the success in each, which says that the same fluent and apprehensive nature, which threw itself with such ease into the forms of outward beauty, has now been intent rather on the secrets of the shaping spirit.

"Locksley Hall," "The Two Voices," "Dora," and "Godiva," Margaret Fuller liked exceedingly.[28] She even liked "The Skipping-Rope." England had not "shown a due sense of the merits of this poet" and had left to Americans "the honor of rendering homage more readily to an accurate and elegant intellect, a musical reception of nature, a high tendency in thought, and a talent of singular fineness, flexibility, and scope."

Emerson's estimate of Tennyson remained little changed after 1842. If he had harsher words for the new volumes than he had ever spoken of the earlier ones, on rare occasions he gave them higher praise. Emerson's opinion was still as unsettled as ever. Tennyson's poetry had a "monotony of elegance." It wanted "a little north west wind, or a north east storm"; it was "a lady's bower," a "musky greenhouse." [29] And with this artificiality, was combined more skill in craftsmanship than real genius. Although "A perfect music-box for all manner of delicate tones and rhythms," Tennyson lacked matter. His reader remembered beautiful lines and not the scope of the poem.[30] But, on the other side of the ledger, Emerson consistently praised "Ulysses" as poetry of the highest order and wondered whether there was taste in all England to do justice to it. Others of the poems, too, were "liberating": "Locksley Hall" and "The Talking Oak" gave him "a momentary sense of freedom and power." [31]

For the *Dial,* Emerson wrote a second review of the *Poems,*[32] several months later than Margaret Fuller's, and a comparison of the two reviews shows strikingly the difference between Emerson's mild commendation of the poems and his followers' unrestrained enthusiasm. Emerson was the prime mover of Tennyson's American fame, but his highest praise of Tennyson never rivaled that accorded by John Sullivan Dwight, James Freeman Clarke, or Margaret Fuller. Emerson's review in the *Dial* exemplifies his general estimate:

> Tennyson's compositions are not so much poems as studies in poetry, or sketches after the styles of sundry old masters. He is not the husband who builds the homestead after his own necessity, from foundation stone to chimney-top and turret, but a tasteful bachelor who collects quaint stair cases and groined ceilings. We have no right to such superfineness. We must not make our bread of pure sugar. . . . But let us not quarrel with our benefactors. Perhaps Tennyson is too quaint and elegant. What then? It is long since we have as good a lyrist; it will be long before we have his superior.[33]

No one, either in England or America, surpassed Edgar Allan Poe in superlative praise of Tennyson in the years just after 1842. Poe knew of Tennyson before that date and spoke of him casually as if everyone else did, but apparently never reviewed the poems in his magazines.[34] If the loud praise of Tennyson by the transcendentalists, whom Poe hated, caused Poe to withhold his commendation then, certainly nothing restrained him after 1842. Soon after the new poems appeared, he professed for them "a reverence unbounded." "Morte d'Arthur," "Locksley Hall," "The Sleeping Beauty," "The Lady of Shalott," "The Lotos-Eaters," "Oenone," and many others were "not surpassed, in all that gives to Poetry its distinctive value, by the compositions of any one living or dead." For those critics who cavilled at Tennyson's quaintness, or what they chose to term affectation, Poe had no sympathy. Tennyson's quaintness sprang from a keen perception of beauty, which is never "without some *strangeness* in its proportions." No true poet would deny "that he feels impressed, sometimes even to tears, by many of those very affectations which he is impelled by the prejudice of his education, or the cant of his reason to condemn." [35] Later Poe felt that "the injustice done in America to the magnificent genius of Tennyson" was "one of the worst sins for which the country has to answer." [36]

It is difficult to see the American injustice in view of the fact that the English critics had not yet begun to equal in praise the pace set by the Americans, but if injustice there was, Poe went a long way toward correcting it. He wrote in December, 1844:

> I am not sure that Tennyson is not the greatest of poets. The uncertainty attending the public conception of the term "poet" alone prevents me from demonstrating that he *is*. Other bards produce effects which are, now and then, otherwise produced than by what we call poems; but Tennyson an effect which only a poem does. His alone are idiosyncratic poems. By the enjoyment or non-enjoyment of the "Morte D'Arthur," or of the "Aenone" [Poe usually spelled it thus], I would test any one's ideal sense.[37]

And but one year later, Poe wrote a brief notice of Ticknor's second edition of the *Poems:*

> This is a very neat, and altogether tasteful *new* edition of a poet, who (in our own humble, but sincere opinion) is *the greatest* that ever lived. We are perfectly willing to undergo all the censure which so heretical an opinion may draw down upon us.[38]

Poe is often referred to as "the first American author to welcome Tennyson." [39] That, he was not, but no one before or after exceeded his praise. Poe stands after Emerson as the second milestone in the progress of Tennyson's reputation in America. Like Emerson, Poe did much to spread abroad the knowledge and love of Tennyson; and, unlike Emerson, Poe never wavered in his support. Bayard Taylor, later one of the most devoted of Tennyson's admirers, got his first inspiration from Poe. Having read Poe's praise of the 1842 volume, he sought for a copy, was dazzled by its brilliance, and read till his eyes ached.[40] Thomas Holley Chivers, deluged by Poe with praise of Tennyson in conversation and correspondence, was slowly brought to the point of joining in Tennyson's praise.

Chivers' first reaction to the *Poems* of 1842 had been extremely unfavorable, and when during a visit to Poe in New York in 1845 he heard Poe refer to Tennyson as "one of the greatest Poets that ever lived," his immediate reply was, "My God! Poe! how can you say that? . . . Why his Poems are as effeminate as a phlegmatic fat baby." [41] Evidently the two argued vehemently on the subject, for after Chivers returned home he wrote in apology:

> The remarks which I made to you in regard to Tennyson's Poems, were not intended to be critical, as I was too much fatigued always when I saw you to talk as I could were you with me *now*. "The Gardener's Daughter"; "Recollections of the Arabian Nights"; and "Locksley Hall," are the best. He is a lofty imitator of Shelley, without a tithe of his force. He possesses fine ideality, but there is too much conventional grotesqueness of abandon, with too little artistical skill in him to be compared with Shelley. If you think he is even a musical imitator of Shelley, just get his *Poems* and disabuse your mind at once. He has fine ideality, but not the artistical force of Horne. One of his greatest and unpardonable faults consists in his not appealing, in any *understandable* language, to any of the most universal feelings of the heart of Man. He does not

sing Truth—that Angel-mission for the fulfilment of which the Poet was sent down by God out of Heaven.[42]

Chivers' telling Poe to get the *Poems* as if Poe had hardly seen them is amusing. The "disabusing" swung rapidly in the other direction. The next month Chivers was writing, as if prompted, "There is . . . a more elaborate perfection in the Poems of Tennyson than in any Poet that ever lived."[43]

The two most unfavorable reviews accorded the *Poems* of 1842 by American literary periodicals were written by critics of widely diverse experience and environment: Cornelius C. Felton, Professor of Greek in Harvard College, and Henry Charles Lea, a nineteen-year-old Philadelphia school boy. They had had one experience in common: both had read John Wilson Croker's review of the 1833 *Poems* in the London *Quarterly*. Felton's review appeared in November, 1842, in the *Christian Examiner,* the periodical which had warmly welcomed Tennyson four years earlier. A staunch representative of the old school of criticism, Felton bitterly opposed the coming of new poetic influences, and that opposition is sufficient explanation of his hostility to Tennyson.[44] Nevertheless, there are matters which make the review remarkable: Felton's closest associates were enthusiastic about Tennyson,[45] and the American editor and ardent sponsor of the *Poems* was Charles Stearns Wheeler, tutor in Felton's department at Harvard.

In his review Felton harshly satirized Tennyson both as a poet and as a person:

He is a dainty poet. We cannot help fancying him to be altogether finical in his personal habits. He is a sweet gentleman, and delights to gaze upon his image in a glass; his hair is probably long, and carefully curled; he writes in white kid gloves, on scented paper; perhaps he sleeps in yellow curl-papers. We are certain he lisps.

His verses, filled with "sugary sentimentalities," outran "the simplicity of Mother Goose." He would never write in "a direct, unambiguous, and plain fashion, as the older and better poets did." But, Felton assured Tennyson, he had genius, and better poetry than he had yet written was "unquestionably within the range of his powers."

The second of the hostile reviews, appearing in the *Southern Literary Messenger* two years later, was even more in the Croker tradition than was Felton's.[46] Lea was widely read for his age, knew some Latin, worshiped Byron, but nothing that he had read about Tennyson later than the reviews by North and Croker had made any impression upon him. Lea's review is a shallow imitation both in manner and in matter. Ideas and expressions are lifted from Croker. Lea even quoted the lines "To Christopher North," which were not reprinted in 1842 and which he obviously got from Croker's article. Lea's review is a clear instance of American criticism's slavishly following the English in regard to Tennyson, but it cannot be used to indicate a trend. Probably there is not another such example in an American literary periodical of any significance, and possibly not another anywhere.

Lea thought the poems of Tennyson were made up of pilfered thoughts almost smothered beneath piles of meaningless words. "Oriana" was an amusing attempt at pathos; "The Miller's Daughter" was a "wretchedly paraphrastic translation of Anacreon"; "A Dream of Fair Women" was a "silly abortion"; and "The May Queen," one of the "least silly poems," was spoiled by the "snake-like line" which closed each stanza. Tennyson should write no more:

> He would confer a benefit, not only on the world but on himself, if he would only convert his pen into a pruning hook, and his inkstand into a watering-pot; for, though his vanity would no longer be gratified by seeing his own name in print, except as the cultivator of enormous pumpkins and gigantic straw-

berries, yet he might gratify a spirit of large benevolence by raising two blades of grass where one grew before, and his rest would be no longer broken by remorse at sending "such reams of blank among the sons of men."

Lea closed the review with the regret that the poems were meeting with a "ready and extensive sale" in this country and an apology to the reader "for having detained him so long over so poor and fruitless a subject."

American periodicals were never very careful to keep their opinions consistent. A year earlier than Lea's review the *Southern Literary Messenger* had reviewed the *Poems* with high praise: Tennyson possessed "decided ideal tendencies and pure sensibilities" with an uncommon taste in the choice and arrangement of words, and therefore the *Messenger* took pleasure in commending the poems to such of its readers "as would commune with one, who, whatever faults may belong to him, is not only a genuine poet, but one of more individuality than any who has appeared for a considerable period." [47] Such inconsistencies were common. By June, 1845, the *Knickerbocker* had completely reversed its opinion of the 1842 *Poems* twice.[48]

As would be expected, the general trend of opinion was toward a greater appreciation of Tennyson. Coming in 1842 and bearing the name of a well known scholar, Felton's review met with few retorts. Two years later Lea's review aroused more disapproval.[49] And soon no low evaluation could appear in a place of prominence, no matter how well known the critic might be, without drawing attack from many quarters. When Rufus W. Griswold in his *Poets and Poetry of England in the Nineteenth Century* gravely assured his readers that Tennyson's poems had "enough intrinsic merit, probably, to secure him a permanent place in the third or fourth rank of contemporary English poets," [50] he aroused a long lasting storm of disapproval. Later editions of Griswold's work—as late as 1853—retained the biographical notice of Tennyson unaltered; so for years to come the estimate was periodically refuted.[51]

One of the most influential American reviews of Tennyson had its origin in a refutation of Griswold: that of Edwin P. Whipple for the *American Whig Review*.[52] Calling Griswold's phrase, "third or fourth rank," an "amusing slip of the pen," Whipple defended Tennyson at points where he had been most attacked:

> . . . nothing can be more incorrect than to call any poem of Tennyson's unmeaning. Such a charge simply implies a lack in the critic's mind, not in the poet's. The latter always *means* something, in everything he writes; and the form in which it is embodied is chosen with the most careful deliberation. It seems to us that the purely intellectual element in Tennyson's poetry, has been overlooked, owing perhaps to the fragility of some of his figures and the dreariness of outline apparent in others. Many think him to be a mere rhapsodist, fertile in nothing but a kind of melodious empiricism. No opinion is more contradicted by the fact. Examine his poetry minutely, and the wonderful artistical finish becomes evident. There are few authors who will bear the probe of analysis better.

Nearly all of the American periodicals of literary significance noticed Tennyson's *Poems* of 1842, and a majority of the notices were highly favorable. The *New Englander* gave the poems a long review, listed page after page of faults and excellences, thought "naturalness" and "manliness" among his principal charms, and concluded that Tennyson was a poet after its "own heart." [53] Henry T. Tuckerman wrote for the *Columbian Lady's and Gentleman's Magazine* of New York a review praising Tennyson's refined sentiment, felicitous language, and love for Truth.[54] In a comprehensive article for the *Knickerbocker,* Charles A. Bristed argued not only that Tennyson was the first poet of his age but also that placed "in any age, among any men, he would still be a great poet." [55] And the *Orion* in far away Penfield, Georgia, noticed the poems and approved.[56]

In this wide recognition by the literary periodicals, there was but one glaring exception: the *North American Review*. Henry Charles Lea had offered his scurrilous article to the *Review*, but the *Review* had rejected it, not because of any disagreement with Lea's opinion, but because "it is not worth while to gibbet a man who is destined to fall into rapid oblivion." [57] The *North American Review* took pleasure in introducing to the American public Carlyle, Browning, Elizabeth Barrett. But with Tennyson, it waited for the fall. It ignored not only the *Poems* of 1842, but also *The Princess* and *In Memoriam*. Not until October, 1855, did it capitulate, with a review of *Maud*. That review was complimentary. But by that time Tennyson's fame had become so firmly established that the added recognition could hardly be felt.

III

The American reception of the *Poems* of 1842 was undoubtedly influenced to some extent by the British reaction to the volumes as expressed in periodicals and individual literary works. The British periodicals were being widely circulated in America both in their original editions and in American reprints. The Tennyson reviews were being read in them, and the American eclectic magazines were reprinting some of the Tennyson reviews to offer another means of making them available to Americans.[58] Since it is easier to copy criticism than to originate it, American reviewers naturally did some copying; however, the influence of the British reviews of Tennyson upon the American has been greatly exaggerated.

The high praise of Tennyson in American reviews was not copied from the British, for it was not there to be copied. The British reviews of the *Poems* of 1842 were favorable only in comparison with the caustic reviews of the earlier volumes. Although many of the reviewers were Tennyson's personal friends, they were cautious and hesitant, awaiting public approval before committing themselves. As Fanny Kemble said in 1844, the English critics were following rather than leading the public opinion of the *Poems*.[59] Such was not the case in America. American reviewers had praised the early poems long before they had become available in a sufficient quantity for the public to form any opinion, and after 1842 the reviewers, with a few exceptions, redoubled their praise. Even a casual comparison of the most laudatory British reviews [60] with the reviews by Poe, Whipple, or Margaret Fuller will show how far ahead the Americans were in commendation.

It is true, of course, that the differences between the American and the British reviews of Tennyson are not traceable entirely to differences in the evaluation of the poems. Much of the dissimilarity is inherent in the contrast between American and British periodical criticism. Slow to condemn and quick to commend, American magazines of the period had a reputation for overpraise.[61] On the other hand, the established British magazines had built up a tradition for vitriolic attacks. John Sterling's review of the *Poems* of 1842 was, for the London *Quarterly*, quite complimentary; in *Graham's Magazine*, the *New Englander*, or the *Knickerbocker* it would have been, by comparison, barely favorable.

The American and the British reviewers looked at the *Poems* of 1842 from different points of view. Americans considered the poems for what they were, but the British looked upon them as stepping stones to something greater. Tennyson, thought the British, had completed the ground work and now should find a great subject worthy of his powers.[62] Such criticism was what George William Curtis was referring to in 1844 when he complained that critics, unable to realize that a "diamond is no less wonderful than the world," were demanding that Tennyson write an epic.[63] The British took Tennyson more seriously than did the Americans. They were already talking of his duties to his age, and the reviewers felt it incumbent upon them to instruct him in the fulfilment of his promise. Feeling no such obligation, the Americans tended merely to enjoy and praise the poems, emphasizing frequently the light, airy feminine portraits, which most of the British reviewers thought pretty, but too trivial for much consideration. American reviews were shorter, less detailed, and less studied than the British. In the former, Tennyson would have found many passages to give him immediate pleasure; in the latter he found many to give him instruction, which he liked not.

It has already been seen that some American reviewers of 1842 were belatedly copying North and Croker. The comment that Tennyson was at times affected and effeminate, which ran through American reviews, was doubtless borrowed in large part from British criticism, especially the earlier. Many American reviewers, however, sincerely felt that affectation was the chief fault of Tennyson and his school. Other poets who were considered his followers were accused of the fault even more than was Tennyson. Probably what the American reviewers owed to the earlier British critics outweighed the influence of all the British reviews of 1842. The influence of the later British reviews seems to have been slight.

Apparently of greater influence upon America's attitude toward Tennyson were several English books which were widely read in America. Chief among these was R. H. Horne's *A New Spirit of the Age,* a book of literary criticism published in London in 1844 and republished in New York the same year.[64] In a twenty-page chapter devoted to Tennyson, Horne assigned to him a high place and declared that he was destined for an even higher. Horne praised especially Tennyson's originality, his delicacy and refinement, and his sweetness of melody. Henry Charles Lea scornfully referred to the chapter as an attempt to prove that Tennyson was a greater poet than Byron.[65] Most Americans, however, seem to have been highly pleased with Horne's criticism. The magazines reviewed *A New Spirit of the Age* favorably, and *Graham's* singled out the chapter on Tennyson for special praise: "It is, altogether, the most sympathizing and most analytical review of Tennyson which has appeared, and with some abatements for exaggeration, the most searching and correct." [66]

Doubtless many Americans got their first view of Tennyson the man and his environment from William Howitt's *Homes and Haunts of the Most Eminent British Poets.*[67] Few of Tennyson's American admirers saw him earlier than Emerson's brief visit in 1848,[68] and except for Emerson and Henry Reed, the Philadelphia publisher,[69] few Americans had gained any knowledge of Tennyson through intimate correspondence with his English friends. It is natural, then, that American lovers of Tennyson should have read with much interest Howitt's chapter on Tennyson. Howitt described Tennyson's ancestry and early life, his homes, the settings of his poems, and his personal habits. Along with such facts, Howitt reviewed the poems and showed for Tennyson a strong admiration, some of which he possibly had borrowed from an American, Charles Stearns Wheeler, who had read and praised the poems to him in Heidelberg in 1842.[70]

English criticism of quite a different sort reached Americans in 1846 in Bulwer-Lytton's long poem, *The New Timon, A Romance of London.*[71] Through the influence of his friends, Tennyson had been granted a pension by Sir Robert Peel in 1845, and Bulwer-Lytton thought that an older and more widely recognized writer would have been more deserving of the award. An abrupt digression in *The*

New Timon (II, 48–85) crudely attacked Tennyson's pension and Tennysonian poetry in general. Tennyson was described as "outbabying Wordsworth, and outglittering Keates [*sic*]," and as "School-Miss Alfred" venting "her chaste delight" on "darling little rooms so warm and bright." A footnote quoted lines from "O Darling Room" in order to show "to what depth of silliness the human intellect can descend." This poet, *The New Timon* emphasized, was the "puling Muse" which Peel did "with pudding plump." The digression was brief, but it soon became the best known passage in the poem. So universal was the indignation at the passage that within a few months of the poem's appearance a new edition was published from which the opprobrious lines had disappeared. They were, however, far from forgotten. For years the early editions had a special value because of the lines on Tennyson, and the second American edition, issued after the revision, still retained the notorious lines.[72]

It is not likely that *The New Timon* detracted from Tennyson's rising fame in America. In fact, the ill-natured attack and the strong indignation which it aroused may well have helped Tennyson's rise. Writing in the *Christian Examiner,* Cyrus A. Bartol thought the poem "a wholesome protest against the feeble sentimentality and slender ornaments of the whole Tennyson school," [73] but his was not the general attitude. Lowell in the *North American Review* called the lines on Tennyson "presumptuous and in bad taste." [74] And a reviewer in the *Southern Literary Messenger* bitterly denounced the anonymous author for his "peculiar spite": before "pouring out his scorn for Mr. Tennyson, he should have reflected on one thing; that while the author of 'The New Timon' is only a man of *ability,* Mr. Tennyson is a man of *genius.*" [75]

The New Timon was one of the last of the contemptuous treatments of Tennyson. No longer tolerated by the public, such attacks were giving way to genial good-natured burlesquing of Tennyson's eccentricities. In this field America was almost entirely dependent upon England. Almost one hundred per cent of the parodies of Tennyson appearing in American periodicals before 1865 were copied from the British, and those that were not, hardly deserve the name of parody. Many years were yet to pass before America produced clever parodies of Tennyson or anybody else.

British parodies of Tennyson began to reach America even before the *Poems* of 1842. In January of that year, *Brother Jonathan* reprinted from *George Cruikshank's Omnibus* a parody of "Mariana," [76] and in the following year the *Knickerbocker* printed Bon Gaultier's "To Isaac Tomkins' Child," a parody of "Lilian." [77] Two Scotchmen, William Edmondstone Aytoun and Theodore Martin, had formed in 1842 a partnership under the pseudonym "Bon Gaultier," and during the next three years they printed in British periodicals some of the most popular parodies of Tennyson. The only one of their poems which attracted much attention in America was "The Laureate," a parody of "The Merman." [78] When in 1845 the collected parodies by Bon Gaultier were published in London as *The Book of Ballads,* the book went almost unnoticed in America. There seems to have been no American edition till 1852,[79] and then the reviews were more unfavorable than favorable. Many Americans were shocked by the parodies of Tennyson. "The Laureate" they still liked, and the

> Lightsome, brightsome, cousin mine!
> Easy, breezy Caroline! [80]

But *Sartain's Magazine* thought that "Locksley Hall" was "travestied in too shocking a manner to allow of a single line in quotation," [81] and the *Southern Literary Messenger* thought this whole group was flat, stupid, and malicious.[82] Only the genial imitations found favor with Americans.

Apparently Americans wrote no real parodies of Tennyson's 1842 poems. The only things that approached burlesque were the careful and obvious imitations.[83] The following imitation of "Oriana" is characteristic:

> On yesternight awhile the pallid moon,
> Orihula,
> Was passing thro' her fleecy clouds, at noon,
> Orihula,
> I saw thee with thy grave clothes on,
> Sitting beneath the cypress' shade, alone,
> On the gray moss of a broken stone,
> Orihula.[84]

The poem continued in like manner for five more stanzas. It was published with no mention of Tennyson or of any intention to parody, and the reader can never be quite certain whether the burlesque is intended or unintended.

An imitation of "Lilian" by H. W. Parker is also characteristic. The poem copied its prototype closely but made little fun of it:

> Lofty little Emily
> Dimpled, dazzling Emily,
> Throned within my inmost heart,
> There thou shalt be, as thy art,
> My soul-exalting, pure ideal.
> Ever present to my thought,
> Mine eyes shall wake and close
> On thy image, though unsought.
> Unfading, changeless, still it glows,—
> Still it sparkles, dimples, dances,
> In my waking, sleeping fancies.
> As if, no phantom, it were red.
> I cannot clasp nor follow it;
> For, like thyself, 'twill ever flit
> With a far off goddess-grace,

With chaining, yet forbidding, eye;
I bless, I ban that little face,
Floating ever in airy space;
I frown and mutter—then smile and sigh;
I cannot love thee
Yet must adore thee,
Majestic little Emily.[85]

American readers of periodicals in the eighteen-forties and fifties seem to have enjoyed such verses much more than they did parodies, and the parodies they saw little of. In the late eighteen-fifties, American newspapers and magazines printed several parodies of "The Eagle," "The Charge of the Light Brigade," and "Come into the Garden, Maud," but nearly all of them were copied from the British.[86]

The talk of a Tennysonian school of poets, which had begun before 1842, continued thereafter. Lowell, Longfellow, Poe, and many other Americans were designated as Tennyson's followers, but no name was so inseparably linked with Tennyson's as was that of Elizabeth Barrett. Nearly every American reviewer of Elizabeth Barrett's *A Drama of Exile and Other Poems* (1845) referred to a relationship with Tennyson.[87] Poe warned her that she was following Tennyson too closely.[88] Henry Charles Lea discoursed about the "nominalists," a title he had coined for poets who run after shadows and deal with "things earthly but in name"; Tennyson was the "most outré" of the nominalists, but "his twin-sister, Miss Barrett" was close by his side.[89] So often was she called his sister that the *Democratic Review* in January, 1845, felt called upon to explain that she was so only figuratively, and not actually. But after a few years the two began to part company. Such talk as Lea's grew less frequent, and Tennyson was coming to be thought of as standing alone at the head of English poets, an idea greatly quickened in America by his next work: the medley of Princess Ida and her university.

Chapter III

RISING FAME: *THE PRINCESS*

THE RUMORS RIFE IN ENGLAND DURING 1846 AND 1847 CONcerning Tennyson's preparation of a startling and extraordinary work seem not to have reached America till after *The Princess* had been published. On December 25, 1847, the date upon which London newspapers announced the poem as that day published, Duyckinck's New York *Literary World* announced that William D. Ticknor and Company of Boston would republish it "as soon as it is received in this country"; and on February 10, 1848, the Boston *Daily Chronotype* noticed as "yesterday published" *The Princess,* "which is destined to make a sensation in this metropolis, where the 'woman question' is so well up." [1]

Just how great a sensation *The Princess* made upon its arrival in America is difficult to estimate now. Evidently, however, the sale of the book was rapid. Ticknor seems not to have published a second separate edition of *The Princess* till 1855, but the first was reprinted several times in 1848. Longfellow wrote in his journal on February 25, 1848, that on a visit to Ticknor's office he had "found [James T.] Fields correcting the proofs of the second edition of Tennyson's Princess,—the first, one thousand copies, having been sold within a few weeks"; [2] and *Graham's Magazine* stated in May of that year that *The Princess* had already passed "through three editions." [3] Also, Ticknor was including *The Princess* in all of his editions of Tennyson's *Poems* between 1848 and 1855. The fact that a few months after

Ticknor's first edition of *The Princess* he rushed through the press a new edition of *Poems* to include it may be attributed in part to the rapid sale of *The Princess*.[4]

Ticknor's first edition of *The Princess* was a neat little volume which, though differing slightly in size and pagination from the first London edition, was equally as attractive a book as Moxon's. Nearly every reviewer praised the printing and format of the book, and N. P. Willis's *Home Journal* (September 23, 1848), which had earlier proclaimed Ticknor and Company "the Moxon establishment of America," felt that this volume thoroughly justified the parallel.

It must be remembered that the text of this first edition of *The Princess* was quite different from the text as it stands now. The entire poem was in blank verse; even the three songs which it contained were unrimed. Not until the third London edition, which appeared in February, 1850, were the six intercalary rimed songs added, and *The Princess* did not reach its final form till the fifth London edition, October, 1852.[5] No American edition included the songs until Ticknor's *Poems,* published in late 1853,[6] and apparently the final text of the poem was not published in America till 1857.[7]

II

Americans liked *The Princess* from the beginning. Newspaper reviewers praised it immediately. The day following its publication in America, the Boston *Daily Chronotype* pronounced it "perhaps the most exquisite and truthful painting of female character, that was ever thrown upon canvas." Though objecting to the "stereotyped" love story and to certain prosaic lines, the Boston *Daily Atlas* thought that *The Princess* would become a "general favorite," for "it charms the reader and carries him along with it, so that he is loath to leave it unfinished. The more he reads it, the better he likes it." [8] And the praise of the New York *Daily Tribune* knew no bounds. In a manner suggestive of Margaret Fuller, who was then in Europe, the anonymous reviewer declared *The Princess* the "noblest" of Tennyson's works:

If we were to express the feeling of satisfaction with which we have just read every word of this beautiful, charming and profound little book we should be thought extravagant. Nor does it stand in need of any enthusiastic commendation to secure for it a very large circle of readers, for of all living poets hardly any has a wider or more desirable reputation in this country than TENNYSON; the mere announcement of a new Poem from his pen will send thousands on an immediate pilgrimage to their respective bookstores. . . . The poem . . . is full of those delicate, subtle master-strokes of original genius for which Tennyson is remarkable.[9]

In general, Americans took Tennyson at his word and considered the new poem "a medley." If it mixed tragedy and comedy, the real and the fantastic, that was to be expected. Only those readers, who were looking for "a regular poem," thought *Peterson's Magazine,* would be disappointed. It was "a medley like that of the milky way, studded with stars innumerable . . . a string of pearls to the very end." [10] *Graham's Magazine* thought that the poem was "properly called" a medley because it brought "the manners and ideas of the chivalric period into connection with those of the present day." And because of this mingling there was "no less fascination in the general conduct of the story. . . . The whole poem is bathed in beauty, and invites perusal after perusal." [11] Medley or no medley, the narrative itself held the reader's attention throughout: Henry B. Hirst's *Illustrated Monthly Courier* questioned whether it had "ever read a poem in which the chain of interest is so well preserved," [12] and James Russell Lowell felt that "it must argue a poverty in ourselves if we cannot see it as a harmonious whole." [13]

Some reviewers were more concerned with another kind of admixture which *The Princess* represented: the compounding of pure poetry and a utilitarian purpose. They were concerned with it to defend it. One reviewer expounded at length the thesis that *The Princess* was a "work of art," that it was beautiful and entertaining, but that it was not "first-rate poetry." A versified moral treatise might be eminently poetic, but it was not, therefore, a poem. Since, however, such a sentiment was not "the doctrine of the day," the reviewer was not disposed to "quarrel with Mr. Tennyson because he steps from the Delphic tripod into the pulpit of the popular lecturer." It seemed "ungrateful," the reviewer feared, for him to criticize at all this excellent work which had given him such a "pleasant hour." His excuse was that the London *Examiner* in an otherwise commendable approval of Tennyson had made one slip: the statement that "there is hardly an element of first-rate poetry, which is not contained in the Princess." Against such a lack of discrimination in high places, he had to "speak out in a kind of desperation." [14]

John Sullivan Dwight felt that the most gratifying quality of *The Princess* was that it showed Tennyson giving his poetry a purpose. The "faintly smiling Adelines" and the "airy, fairy Lilians" were now becoming "flesh and blood existences in true functions of life." Mingled with his earlier admiration of Tennyson, Dwight had had one fear which made him shudder:

> There lurked a danger in the very tendencies which formed the beauty and the genuineness of his creations; the danger of excess, in the direction of mere beauty, of an existence too exclusively ideal and select, and of becoming spell-bound, as all must, who serve the ideal without grappling with the real.

Tennyson's "poetic visions of society" were not made "any the less poetry by becoming social science." Objecting to *The Princess* on the grounds that it combined pure poetry and a purposeful contribution was like objecting to the use of "the scientific construction of the scale of tones and laws of harmony," which made the creations of Handel, Mozart, and Beethoven possible.[15]

It was of this problem that another of Tennyson's admirers, Christopher P. Cranch, seems to have been thinking as he wrote his poem, "The Bird and the Bell," in 1848 and 1849.[16] That he reached much the same decision as Dwight's in regard to *The Princess* is shown in his poem, written years later, "On Re-reading Tennyson's Princess." [17]

To Edgar Allan Poe, Tennyson in 1848 was still the greatest poet that ever lived. Tennyson's predominant excellence was still the purity of his art:

> I call him, and *think* him the noblest of poets—*not* because the impressions he produces are at *all* times, the most profound—*not* because the poetical excitement which he induces is at all times the most intense—but because it *is,* at all times, the most ethereal—in other words, the most elevating and most pure. No poet is so little of the earth, earthy.[18]

Following this passage in "The Poetic Principle," Poe quoted the song, "Tears, Idle Tears," from *The Princess* to prove his point. John R. Thompson remembered after Poe's death the delight with which Poe recited the little song again and again. The lines,

> . . . when unto dying eyes
> The casement slowly grows a glimmering square,

Poe pronounced unsurpassed by any image in writing.[19]

Of all the qualities of *The Princess,* its exquisite music and lyrical blank verse received highest praise. Tennyson's use of blank verse for lyrical purposes in such songs as "Tears, Idle Tears" and "O Swallow, Swallow" was an innovation. Possibly influenced by Theocritus, Tennyson had used blank verse for lyrical purposes in two shorter poems but never with the confidence he showed in *The Princess.*[20] Longfellow's first impression of *The Princess* was not satisfying, but the music enchanted him:

Fanny read it in the evening. Strange enough! a university of women! A gentle satire, in the easiest and most flowing blank verse, with two delicious unrhymed songs, and many exquisite passages. I went to bed, after it, with delightful music ringing in my ears; yet half disappointed in the poem, though not knowing why. There is a discordant note somewhere.[21]

The music of *The Princess* rang also in the ears of Bayard Taylor. So much did he feel its intoxication that it frightened him. He wrote to his fiancée:

I had the misfortune to be deeply intoxicated yesterday—with Tennyson's new poem, "The Princess," which I shall bring to thee when I return home. I dare not keep it with me. For the future, for a long time at least, I dare not read Tennyson. His poetry would be the death of mine, and, indeed, a *pervadence* of his spirit would ruin me for the great purposes of life. His intense perception of beauty haunts me for days, and I cannot drive it from me.[22]

Even Thomas Powell, author of the only definitely unfavorable American review of *The Princess* which has come to hand, bore witness to its musical quality: "It is impossible for a true poet to write a long poem without revealing some snatches of his genius, and, although generally speaking, this poem is a mournful instance of mistaken powers, it abounds in fine passages." [23] In the few paragraphs devoted to *The Princess* in his *The Living Authors of England* (1849), Powell called the poem Tennyson's "greatest failure," without, however, supporting his position. His review was little more than a summary of the story.

Along with the general praise of Tennyson's language came criticism, always, however, outweighed by the commendation. Dwight Sprague's *American Literary Magazine* thought the blank verse "sometimes obscure and often abrupt; somewhat as an English Tacitus might be." Disjointed clauses and misplaced nominatives perplexed the reader; "yet with these blemishes there are many beautiful and melodious lines, showing the skillful artist." [24] John R. Thompson wrote in the *Southern Literary Messenger* that Tennyson sinned "against the dignity of the muse by frequently resorting to a free and easy style—almost colloquial and in striking contrast with his more elevated strains." Thompson repeated too the old criticism that Tennyson was affected; but, he said, "this Medley abounds with fresh poetical conceptions that cannot but delight every reader of refined sympathy or delicate fancy." [25]

That it did delight American readers is beyond question, and one reason was the genial satire mixed with the serious element which never made it quite clear whether Tennyson was defending the Woman's Rights movement or making fun of it. Readers were thus enabled to give to it the meaning which best suited their fancy. A Yale College student thoroughly enjoyed *The Princess* because it ridiculed "with admirable truth and skill this horde of literary ladies, who always wear *book*-muslin." Like a "skillful angler," Tennyson had "hooked them to his lines, and drawing them out of their natural elements" had "displayed them to us floundering uneasily in the basket of Science and Literature." [26] Another reviewer found the same lesson: the heart of a modern belle would always overrule her head, as by right it should.[27] And still another, a staunch opponent of Woman's Rights, devoted half of his review to a tirade against the movement. The greatest beauty of the poem was its "excellent moral":

All the sciences and all the *ologies* will not satisfy a woman's heart. For which we are thankful. The studious little witches in this manufactory of the new race of women, though "gorged with knowledge," stuffed with sciences and loaded with languages, were not contented with their wisdom. . . . Disappointed old maids and women who are only beardless, petticoated men, may talk long and loudly of the equal rights and the independence of their sex. But in the heart of a true woman such theories have no place. "Love will still be lord of all."

The close to the moral, the reviewer thought, was an appropriate one, the Princess happily married and "her wild follies" serving as "food for merry laughter." [28]

On the other hand, Horace Greeley, a strong advocate of equal rights for women, used it as one of the best arguments for a "wider horizon" for women.[29] *Godey's Lady's Book* in January, 1850, began a series of discussions of woman's intellectual and moral influence with excerpts from, and high praise of, *The Princess.* And crusaders for feminine independence quoted passages from *The Princess* again and again.[30] In announcing a Woman's Rights convention in 1853, the *Home Journal* reminded the ladies where they could "find a whole armory of weapons, ready made, finely wrought and beautifully polished": Tennyson's *Princess* contained "a score of passages on *their* side of the question." [31]

The reviewer in *Peterson's Magazine* explained succinctly how both factions were able to find argument to their liking: it was the purpose of Tennyson to repudiate "the modern idea that the sphere of woman is inferior to that of man, or that she ever does good by stepping out of it." [32] The Yale student had another explanation: readers were to go to the poem for entertainment and not to worry about its purpose. He closed his "Frolic with Tennyson," which exhibited a style and judgment that would do credit to a more experienced critic, by recounting his pleasant hours with *The Princess* and extending to his fellow students an invitation:

Would you enjoy such a quiet dream, such a free and careless reverie, you have but to follow my example. Lock your door against intruders; build up a cheerful fire; throw yourself back in your rocking chair, elevate your slippered feet to a level with your head; clasp a cigar between your teeth; and read—Tennyson's "PRINCESS." [33]

So delighted were Americans with Tennyson's new poem that their praise at times reached unreasoned extravagance. The reviewer in the Philadelphia *Illustrated Monthly Courier,* probably its co-editor, Henry B. Hirst, a close imitator and strong admirer of Tennyson, soared oratorically as he depicted Tennyson's rise:

Little by little, degree by degree, slow at first, but afterward with a steady, manly stride, and lastly, with the triumphal march of a conqueror, he seized upon the mind of England, and took possession of the soil of Shakespeare. Here and there, to be sure, lurked a caviller, a follower of the classic but lifeless, statue-like school of Pope—one of the Keats-killers. . . . But these fellows were few, very few, and although they had their day, like other dogs, that day was one of infinitesmal duration. . . . Tennyson arose like a sun that can know no setting. . . . [Then] one fine day "The Princess" appeared . . . [and] there was marching and counter-marching [criticism], with all the strategy of actual warfare, but it was all in vain; "The Princess" remained and remains a poem that will walk down the vista of posterity the Princess of all time.[34]

Nowhere in American criticism has been found anything resembling the caustic British reviews which greeted *The Princess* during the first few months after its publication.[35] The British reviewers were deeply disappointed.[36] They were expecting a great work, which *The Princess,* they said, was not. Tennyson was not fulfilling his "mission." [37] They refused to accept the poem for what it was, "a medley." [38] Again they instructed Tennyson as they had done earlier, and they could only trust that possibly he might still benefit by the instruction. Again they would look forward to his next work with the hope, now glimmering, that he might yet produce a great work.[39] These reviewers had advanced little beyond those of ten years earlier. With few exceptions,[40] it was not until two years after its publication and after it had gained a hold on the reading public that *The Princess* was received with favor by the English periodicals.

The three reviews—by Charles Astor Bristed, James Russell Lowell, and James Hadley—which might be singled out as the most significant ones that *The Princess* received in this country, all used as their theme the correction of the harsh and stupid criticisms which British periodicals had given it. Bristed made his review into a dialogue between himself and two fictitious characters, "Fred Peters" and "The General." Peters had read the British reviews; once he had seen notices in three separate London journals all the same day. The General had mingled with the "literati in England," had noted their disappointment with *The Princess,* and thought their feeling thoroughly justified. Into the mouths of these, Bristed put the stock criticisms, and, one by one, he refuted them. The plot of *The Princess* was absurd, they said; its subject was "too slight"; its language was unrefined; Tennyson was justly called "namby-pamby." For all of these Bristed had answers. The scenes called absurd he explained. As for the plot and subject, the poem was only intended as a "medley." The language was appropriate to the action. And as for some people's calling Tennyson "namby-pamby," that simply showed that "some people are dummies." There the matter rested, and the gentlemen, still in disagreement, closed their conversation with wafers and wine.[41]

James Russell Lowell had read the harsh criticisms before he had read the poem, and with the fulmination of the critics ringing in his ears, he had opened the little book with a tremulous hand, but then all fears vanished:

We read the book through with a pleasure which heightened to unqualified delight, and ended in admiration. The poem is unique in conception and execution. It is one of those few instances in literature where a book is so true to the idiosyncrasy of its author that we cannot conceive of the possibility of its being written by any other person, no matter how gifted.

Tennyson's conception was always clear, "his meaning exactly adequate, and his finish perfect." With Tennyson "perfection of form" seemed to be "a natural instinct, not an attainment." The growth of the poem was as natural as its plan was original. Its organization was perfect: "We know of no other man who could have mingled the purely poetical with the humorous in such entire sympathy as nowhere to suggest even a suspicion of incongruity." Tennyson's humor was like "a delicate flower which we can perceive and enjoy, but which escapes definition." "In short," said Lowell, "it is Tennyson's." The poem had "repose and equilibrium," with "nowhere the least exaggeration." The reader was never "distracted by the noise of the machinery." No single beauty marred the reader's perception of the poem's completeness. Its concentration of imagery marked "the sincere artist" and was "worthy of all praise." *The Princess* was Tennyson's best:

On the whole, we consider this to be the freest and fullest expression of Tennyson which we have had. The reader will find in it all the qualities for which he is admirable so blended and interfused as to produce a greater breadth of effect than he had elsewhere achieved. The familiarity of some passages, while it is in strict keeping with the character he assumes at the outset, indicates also the singer at last sure of his audience, and reposing on the readiness of their sympathies.[42]

Coming a year later than the other two, the twenty-three-page review by Professor James Hadley of Yale College methodically analyzed the criticism which had gone before and gave one of the most logical defenses that *The*

Princess ever received, earlier or later. Systematically opening his paragraphs with quoted or paraphrased criticisms from British journals, Professor Hadley followed the criticisms with his defenses of Tennyson's practice. The handling of the stricture that Princess Ida was too pedantic exemplifies Professor Hadley's manner:

> Some are displeased with the pedantry, as they call it, of the Princess, and vote her an intolerable blue. It is no wonder, certainly, that one shut out from the ordinary objects of attention and pursuit among her sex, should seek to fill their place by science: especially as a severer mental discipline is an important feature in her favorite scheme. That it should figure in her conversation follows from the same conditions. What has she left to talk of but her studies and her plans?

The other characters, the novel plot, the versification, and the language were also discussed at length. The versatility and freedom with which Tennyson used blank verse was studied in detail. Tennyson had sometimes substituted a trochaic for an iambic foot and had sometimes added an extra syllable at the end of a line. Also, in his language Tennyson had been unorthodox: "He abounds in striking novelties, in words, meanings and constructions seldom or never found elsewhere." This adventurousness in both versification and language, Professor Hadley thought, had proved "happy boldness." The critics who had been startled by the novel design and venture of *The Princess* would see upon a second reading that those properties suited the poem better than any others could.[43]

Soon after these numerous and highly favorable American reviews of *The Princess* during 1848 and early 1849, came the laudatory articles on *The Princess* in the leading British journals.[44] The British critics had undoubtedly been swayed by public opinion. Also, they had probably re-read the poem. Whether the American reviews, some aimed so directly at the British, played any part in the shift can only be conjectured. But at any rate it seems quite clear that if there was any significant influencing of the one group by the other, it went from America to Britain, and not *vice versa.*

III

Tennyson's poems had been set to music in America as early as 1844. In that year on a "pleasant October evening" in the office of the *Knickerbocker,* Lewis Gaylord Clark read "The May Queen" to William R. Dempster, the famous Scotch singer, and upon Clark's suggestion Dempster composed a musical setting for the poem.[45] The cantata in three parts, dedicated to Clark and published by Oliver Ditson of Boston in April, 1845, was tremendously popular.[46] The *Knickerbocker* spoke in December of its "unprecedentedly large sale," and a few months later announced that Dempster had been offered a thousand dollars for the copyright.[47] Dempster sang his cantata in scores of concerts in this country,[48] and other American singers, including the famous Hutchinson family, added it to their repertoire.[49] Already popular,[50] "The May Queen" soon became one of the best known of Tennyson's poems. The reviewer of *The Princess* in Sprague's *American Literary Magazine* in May, 1848, digressed long enough to declare that "at least in this country," "The May Queen" was better known than any other and that "wedded to Dempster's music," it had "made the poet's name familiar to everyone." John Sullivan Dwight, who did not like Dempster, thought that the music hurt the poem:

> He [Dempster] has perpetuated the absurdity of lengthening out a melody to match the whole of Tennyson's "May Queen" —three mortal cantos, of some fourteen stanzas each!—tied for half an hour in a forced marriage with such weakly sentimental sort of melody as you may hear with little variation in all the

concert rooms, find printed on the counter of every music store. It is a mistake, Mr. Dempster! Poetry like that does not need music; and music should not trust to poetry to cover its own nakedness of ideas.[51]

But Dwight was far in the minority. Dempster contributed to Tennyson's reputation in America. Both the cantata and the poem were highly praised for years to come, and in 1848 the famous American composer, I. B. Woodbury, wrote another musical setting for the popular poem.[52]

Tennyson, then, was already known as a writer of songs before the coming of *The Princess,* which was to make him one of the most popular writers of brief lyrics for musical settings. As *The Princess* first appeared, it contained three songs, one of which—"Tears, Idle Tears" (IV, 21–40)—gained immediate and long lasting popularity in America. Scores of magazines and newspapers selected it as an example of Tennyson's best,[53] and even reviewers who found fault with the general structure of *The Princess* were enthusiastic about "Tears, Idle Tears." Quoting Poe as having pronounced the song "unsurpassed by any piece of the same length in the language," one reviewer, probably John Esten Cooke, called it a "gem of uncommon beauty." *The Princess,* he thought, was a unique "mixture of grandeur and puerility," but this little lyric was all grandeur:

There is in many lines, apart from their meaning, a melody of cadence which is the very reflection of mournful thought, and dreamy pondering on past joys. The compression of thought observable in the phrases "divine despair"—"underworld"—and "happy Autumn fields" is also uncommon—and this last image is one on which a page of commentary might be written.[54]

Within a few months after its appearance in America, I. B. Woodbury prepared and published a musical setting entitled "Tears Gentle Tears for the Days that Are No More," [55] and from that garbled beginning, the poem began its career on American music sheets. Several other settings followed Woodbury's, some using "Tears, Idle Tears" and others "The Days that Are No More" as their titles.

Another of the original songs of *The Princess,* "O Swallow, Swallow," (IV, 75–98) also attracted some attention. At least one American reviewer thought it more beautiful than "Tears, Idle Tears," [56] and two early settings for it, one entitled "The Messenger Swallow," were published in Boston.

It was in the third edition of *The Princess* that Tennyson inserted the six songs which are now so widely known. A short rimed lyric was placed at the close of each of the first six Parts of the poem. Usually designated by their first lines, they were, in order: "As thro' the Land at Eve We Went"; "Sweet and Low"; "The Splendor Falls on Castle Walls"; "Thy Voice Is Heard thro' Rolling Drums"; "Home They Brought Her Warrior Dead"; and "Ask Me No More." During the interval between their appearance in London in February, 1850, and their inclusion in an American edition more than three years later, American magazines and newspapers took pleasure in printing them as rarities; [57] therefore, when Ticknor, Reed, and Fields belatedly printed the revised *Princess* in their new edition of *Poems* in late 1853, the songs were not unknown to American readers.

"Sweet and Low," or "The Cradle Song," seems to have been most popular of all. In May, 1851, a musical setting for it by William Vincent Wallace was published in New York, and other settings followed soon afterward. In printing the poem in its "Editor's Table," the *Southern Literary Messenger* for March, 1853, styled it "one of Tennyson's most graceful and musical productions":

Indeed it may be said to sing itself: Mr. Vincent Wallace . . . could add nothing to its melody. Like many other of Tennyson's smaller pieces, it has been leading a precarious life in the corners of newspapers:—we think the readers of the Messenger will thank us for rescuing it from the quickly perishing columns of the daily press.

In 1854, Ferdinand C. Ewer, editor of the *Pioneer,* early California literary magazine, quoted the "exquisite stanzas" of "Sweet and Low" as a lesson to California would-be poets on how to write pure poetry.[58] And in a contest conducted by I. B. Woodbury's *New York Musical Review,* the subscribers selected as their favorite song "Sweet and Low" in the musical setting of Otto Dresel of Boston.[59]

"The Splendor Falls on Castle Walls," or "The Bugle Song," and "Ask Me No More" ranked next to "Sweet and Low" in popularity. Harrison Millard's setting of "Ask Me No More" published in Boston in 1856 sold extensively,[60] and "The Bugle Song," long before it was set to music in America in 1857, was praised as the greatest of lyrics. The *Albion* called it as noble a song "as ever the world [had] heard." [61] Edwin P. Whipple in a fit of irritation over the high praise which had been given to Alexander Smith's *Poems* declared the three stanzas of "The Bugle Song" to be worth more than Smith's whole volume; [62] and in a rare review of the revised *Princess, Graham's Magazine* pronounced the song "perhaps as remarkable a creation of imagination born in melody, as can be found in Tennyson's works." [63]

With the success of these lyrics from *The Princess,* American composers and music publishers began to see similar possibilities in Tennyson's earlier poems. "Airy, Fairy Lilian," "Break, Break, Break," "It Is the Miller's Daughter," "Flow Down, Cold Rivulet," and others were soon set to music. "Break, Break, Break" seems to have been especially popular. Though not attracting particular notice from reviewers of the 1842 *Poems,* its popularity gained steadily. Longfellow recorded in 1851 his pleasure in reciting it aloud while seated alone on the rocks of the Massachusetts coast,[64] and Henry Timrod in 1857 paid homage to it in one of the closest of imitations, "Hark to the Shouting Wind." [65] Several early musical settings for it were published in America.

Many years were yet to come before Tennyson's songs could rival those of Tom Moore and Felicia Hemans in American popularity, but with "The May Queen" and the songs of *The Princess* as extremely successful beginnings, and with the addition of such favorites as "Ring Out, Wild Bells," "Come into the Garden, Maud," and the songs of the *Idylls of the King,* Tennyson was destined to reach the first rank of popularity by the eighteen-sixties.

Chapter IV

RISING FAME: *IN MEMORIAM*

NO ONE HAS EVER STUDIED TENNYSON FOR LONG WITHOUT coming upon the statement that in the year 1850 occurred three of the greatest events in his life: the publication of *In Memoriam,* his marriage, and his appointment as Poet Laureate. From a literary standpoint, the most significant of these was the appearance of *In Memoriam.* It was largely responsible for his receiving the Laureateship, and the publisher's advance payment for *In Memoriam* made his marriage possible. One American, fascinated by the romantic story of Tennyson's long engagement to Emily Sellwood, associated his marriage even more closely with the poem. Twenty years earlier, wrote Thomas Wentworth Higginson, Tennyson had won Miss Sellwood's heart, "but not her head or conscience, for she was very strait in her theology and he very lax in comparison." Years had passed, and she still answered "No," but "then came 'In Memoriam' with its inspiration and its faith, and in one week after its appearance there arrived a letter from the lady, avowing her conscience set at rest at last by that wonderful book, and hinting that all barriers were now thrown down!" [1]

News of Tennyson's plans for *In Memoriam* had reached America as early as 1845. On June 3 of that year, John Forster wrote to Longfellow that Tennyson was thinking "of publishing a set of poems on the death of a friend (Hallam the historian's son)." The poems were to be "a kind of

Inferno and Paradise." Most of the poems, said Forster, had been written for some years; they would make a volume and would be worthy of Tennyson's genius.[2]

In Memoriam was published in London in early June, 1850,[3] and shortly thereafter preparations were under way for an American edition. James T. Fields wrote Evert A. Duyckinck from Boston on June 19, "We have announced *In Memoriam* here and will thank you to insert the accompanying advertisement." [4] Ticknor, Reed, and Fields's large advertisement of *In Memoriam* appeared in Duyckinck's *Literary World* on June 29, and, nearly a month later, the Boston *Daily Evening Transcript* for July 27 announced the new poem as published "today."

Both in London and in Boston, *In Memoriam* was issued anonymously. The title-page gave only the title of the poem, the name of the publisher, and the place and date of publication, and the obverse page bore only the brief inscription,

IN MEMORIAM
A. H. H.
obiit MDCCCXXXIII.

The *Literary World* on June 22 spoke of the "flutter" which had been occasioned in England by the "enigmatic announcement" of *In Memoriam*. But the enigma was short-lived. Even the *Literary World's* early note named Tennyson as the author and Arthur Henry Hallam as the subject. All of Ticknor's advertisements named the author, and few, if any, American reviewers failed to review the poem as Tennyson's. Only rarely did reviewers express any uncertainty as to the authorship or even refer to the fact that Tennyson's name did not appear on the title page. By now Tennyson's name had come to have a strong commercial value, and it is natural that the publishers should have seen to it that the public should know that *In Memoriam* was his.

From the publisher's point of view, the American edition of *In Memoriam* was undoubtedly a success. At least two separate impressions were made in 1850,[5] and others were issued, still apparently from the original plates, every year through 1856. There is no indication, however, that the early sales were sensational, as were those of *The Princess.* No known review referred to a rapid sale of *In Memoriam,* and although information concerning early issues of the two poems is scant, there is reason to believe that the American sales of *The Princess,* at least for the first year, exceeded those of *In Memoriam.* During the period till 1856, there were more issues of *In Memoriam* as a separate poem, but it was, apparently, not until 1856 that *In Memoriam* was included in an American edition of *Poems;* whereas, *The Princess* was included immediately.

A comparison which can be made with more definiteness is that between the sales of the American edition of *In Memoriam* and those of the English edition. There is every reason to believe that the sales in England, where Edward Moxon was having difficulty supplying the demand, far exceeded those in America.[6] Now for the first time the demand for a new Tennyson work in Great Britain completely outdistanced that in America.

As had been the case with Ticknor's former editions, the reviewers highly praised the printing and general appearance of his edition of *In Memoriam.* The book was slightly larger than the first English edition, and the two varied slightly in pagination. As Ticknor, Reed, and Fields advertised it, their edition of *In Memoriam* was uniform with that of *The Princess.*

II

The American public began to hear of *In Memoriam* several weeks before the appearance of Ticknor's first edition.

From scraps of information it had gathered from British newspapers, the *Literary World* tried to describe the poem as early as June 22: " 'In Memoriam' " was "understood to consist of sonnets or elegies." Soon afterward numerous American magazines and newspapers began to print excerpts from the poem,[7] and eclectic magazines reprinted the early reviews from the British weekly periodicals. On July 8 the New York *International Weekly Miscellany* printed a laudatory review of *In Memoriam* from the London *Spectator,* not before, however, notifying its readers in a prefatory paragraph that it did not concur in the high praise.[8] The Boston *Daily Evening Transcript* informed its readers that the British journals were placing the new poem "side by side with the inspirations of Dante, Petrarch, and Shakespeare." [9] And on July 13 the *Literary World* published a lengthy review of its own.

In announcing the publication of Ticknor's edition on July 27, the Boston *Daily Evening Transcript* doubted not that with *In Memoriam* Tennyson's fame would be "increased, even among his admirers, who, to judge from the sale of his famous works, must form a very large audience in America." It was, however, at the hands of Tennyson's American admirers that *In Memoriam* received some of its harshest criticism. The old Tennysonians were divided. Bayard Taylor called it "The first poem which this generation has yet produced." Soon after reading it, he wrote "it has become so vital a part of my nature that if I live at all it will live with me." [10] Charles Sumner, "charmed, touched, and exalted" by *In Memoriam,* felt that he had "read very few poems in any language with equal delight." [11] But Lowell did not care for it,[12] and Emerson considered it the poorest of Tennyson's works:

Tennyson's *In Memoriam* is the commonplaces of condolence among good Unitarians in the first week of mourning. The consummate skill of the versification is the sole merit. The book has the advantage that was Dr. [William Ellery] Channing's fortune, that all the merit was appreciable. He is never a moment too high for his audience. But to demonstrate this mediocrity I was forced to quote those moral sentences which make the fame of true bards . . . and then to ask, Now show me one such line in this book of Tennyson.[13]

Americans generally received *In Memoriam* less favorably than they had any other of Tennyson's works. Contrary to Emerson's feeling, many thought that its meaning was obscure. In his lectures, Henry Reed warned that only repeated reading and constant study could reveal the "wisdom and the beauty of the work." [14] S. S. Cutting's *Christian Review* attributed the extreme obscurity of the verses to their "studied brevity and the partial suppression of the emotion." [15] Another periodical considered *In Memoriam* badly in need of a preface and notes.[16] And the *Southern Literary Messenger,* whose reviewer, probably John Esten Cooke, praised *In Memoriam* highly, regretted that much of its effect was lost because of obscurity:

The great mass of men will never infuse their minds, so to speak, into the mould of the poet's own, and search out the hidden treasures which lie *perdus,* like gems in a great opera . . . a little care might have worked a great improvement in the *In Memoriam.*[17]

Another objection that ran through most of American criticism was that the verses were monotonous. With monotony as its theme, *Brownson's Quarterly Review* gave *In Memoriam* one of the harshest reviews that it received anywhere. The reviewer confessed that he had read only far enough to discover that "harmonious verse and a little namby-pamby sentiment" formed the poem's only merit:

We broke down before reading twenty pages of the volume before us. It is doubtless all our own fault, and owing to our inability to detect or appreciate true poetic gems. In brief words, Tennyson is not a poet to our taste. That he has a poetic temperament, we can believe; that he scatters here and there a real poetic gem in his works, we are not disposed to deny; but to us he is feeble, diffuse, and tiresome. He strikes us as a man of feeble intellect, as wanting altogether in the depth and force of thought indispensable, not to the poetic temperament, but to the genuine poet. He seems to us a poet for puny transcendentalists, beardless boys, and miss in her teens.[18]

Doubtless by the editor, Orestes A. Brownson,[19] this review is a rare and interesting proof that as late as 1850 attacks were still being leveled at Tennyson's admirers, that "peculiar class" now grown to thousands.

Peterson's Magazine of New York, which had been one of Tennyson's earliest and most vigorous sponsors, received *In Memoriam* coolly: "The poems exhibit the characteristic melody, sweetness, and lofty idealism of the author; but have something of monotony, in consequence of being all upon one theme." [20] The *Albion* warned its readers against trying to read the volume at one sitting: the "very subject" was "unavoidably monotonous." [21] Also, the *Southern Quarterly Review,* which did not like *In Memoriam* at all, objected to the monotony of the work:

For the volume before us a few words will suffice. It contains undoubtedly a considerable proportion of excellent verse; sweet fancies and subdued thoughts, in a mournful strain, such as the title might lead us to expect. But the plan of the volume is monotonous,—more than two hundred pages, in verse, upon a single general topic, however diversified by varieties of rhythm, and broken into small pieces, each addressed to some one of the phases of the theme, could scarcely be otherwise. But Mr. Tennyson has not employed a varying rhythm. His verse is not only uniform in measure and structure, but it is one which does not readily commend itself to the ear. Though marked with frequent rests and pauses, the only change which it shows, is in the transition from one sentiment of the same subject to another.[22]

The *American Whig Review* devised a curative formula: "The monotony which superficially meets the reader vanishes as he gets into the wailing mood." As the reader opened the book, he should think of a lost friend—or if among "ye loving and losing," he might think of a cruel sweetheart—who had left him "friendless, lonely, childless, parentless, brotherless, or loveless"; then if in that mood he would read calmly and quietly, he would be comforted, and the monotony would disappear.[23]

American periodicals warmly debated the question whether or not Tennyson's grief in *In Memoriam* was sincere. Could such poignancy of grief last so long a time, they asked; and was not such a feeling between two grown men unmanly and weakly sentimental? Could it be natural and unaffected? One reviewer confessed to a "great doubt of the sincerity of these lachrymal verses"; [24] another thought the grief greatly exaggerated; [25] and the *Democratic Review* in its severe handling of *In Memoriam* dealt Tennyson the hardest blow on this score:

> These poems are, in a word, capricious and fanciful. They do not spring from, nor appeal to, what is deepest and most universal in human nature. The very occasion and circumstances of the volume do not seem to be altogether rational or natural. To lament the departed is a sacred duty, as well as sweet relief. But where no ties of blood have been severed, and the relation is entirely one of sympathy and sentiment, to extend one's grief over a period of from ten to twenty years, and its record over more than two hundred pages, indicates a state of mind with which not the many, but only those of similar idiosyncrasies, will fully sympathize.[26]

Chief among the periodicals which came to Tennyson's defense was the *New Englander*. As it had done for both the *Poems* of 1842 and *The Princess*, it devoted a long and analytical review to *In Memoriam*. One by one it listed the faults that had been found with the poem and then defended Tennyson at every point. The reviewer found *In Memoriam* "a true story of real suffering." Those who thought Tennyson "extravagant" or "hypocritical" did not understand the poem.[27] *Graham's Magazine* was another that had no sympathy with those who called *In Memoriam* "unnatural and unmanly." With most mourners such grief would be unnatural, but with Tennyson it was the natural feeling of a mind and heart in which emotion was always "indissolubly blended with thought." The "great peculiarity" of Tennyson's genius was "intellectual intensity."[28] The New York *Daily Tribune* (August 21, 1850) offered the same argument:

> . . . [The verses of *In Memoriam*] emanate from the sincerest depths of feeling and are embodied in language of thoughtful vigor, sometimes nearly approaching austerity. They are the true utterance of the heart fortified by the severest exercise of the intellect. They breathe the soul of passion, but are clothed in a body so strong and often so rugged, as not to be torn by any storm of emotion. Hence their pervading character is a calmness which impresses you like the imposing grandeur of sculpture.

Harper's Magazine considered Tennyson's "serene tranquility" the best proof of his "sad sincerity." In *In Memoriam* there was "no indulgence in weak and morbid sentiment"; it was free from the "preternatural gloom" which so often made elegiac poetry "an abomination to every healthy intellect." The "tearful bard" was to be praised for not allowing himself to be drowned in his sorrow.[29]

An interesting bit of criticism concerning Tennyson's sincerity was written in a letter from C. C. Felton to Longfellow in 1853.[30] Though never published, it is significant as an instance of one of Tennyson's old adversaries still holding his ground. Felton wrote from Scotland that on a voyage to Glasgow he had chatted with a beautiful Scotch lass. Their conversation turned upon *In Memoriam*, and Felton said, "Parts of it are very sweet: but it is too long drawn: too effeminate, mushy and womanish for a manly friendship." The young lady agreed, and Felton continued with a discourse which, whether serious or not, is amusing:

I do not believe he wrote it from the heart: it was partly from mere fancy, and partly from imitation. I think he must have been fresh from the study of Petrarch's interminable series of Sonnets to Laura, and wishing to do something of the same sort and not having a Laura to bewail— Since Mrs. Tennyson was by his side—happened to remember a young friend and so transferred to his memory, the echo of Petrarch's hopeless passion for Laura.

The similarity between this and Felton's review of the *Poems* of 1842 is striking. There, too, Felton tried to be jocose at Tennyson's expense.

In Memoriam was spared much criticism by virtue of its subject. A mourning for the dead was to be reverenced. The sacred and intensely personal quality of the work raised it above "the region of ordinary criticism." [31] Pointing out faults in the verses was like pointing to the wreath on a dead man's brow and saying "that flower is out of place." [32] Some critics wondered how Tennyson could send such a personal and intimate revelation out into the world: his reluctance was shown by his sending it forth without his name.[33] The *Christian Examiner* worshiped the poem in subdued tones:

It is a book to be read in entire sympathy with its author, and not a volume to be subjected to the stern judgment of those who practise the "ungenial craft." The hard, cold world has nothing to do with such sacred outpourings of sorrow as we here find. They belong to the inner experience of the mourner,—an experience almost too holy for any but one's bosom friends to witness.[34]

As might be expected, the religious periodicals gave *In Memoriam* its highest praise. Congregationalist but more liberal and literary than most of them, the *New Englander* in its long review commended the *"moral purity"* of the poem. No one could read *In Memoriam* without feeling that he had been "in converse with a mind to which pure and elevated thoughts are natural and habitual." Tennyson was leading the way toward a more Christian English poetry:

> There is not a sentence in his writings, which contains an indelicate or ungodly allusion. The change which has come over the poetry of England, in this respect, within the present century, is one of the harbingers of a better day.[35]

Calling *In Memoriam* "the best [book] of its kind which has ever appeared," the Boston *Monthly Religious Magazine* recommended it to all who "cherish the religious sentiment" or long for "that faith in God without which we are as ships without an anchor." [36] Likewise, the *Christian Review* praised Tennyson's reverence for "truth and God" and his revelation in *In Memoriam* that his "strong pillar of consolation" was "the fact of Immortality." [37] Such periodicals found many parallels between *In Memoriam* and the Bible; they liked to compare Tennyson and Hallam's friendship to that of David and Jonathan.[38]

Some of the religious periodicals, however, "born to controversy as surely as man is born to trouble," [39] were not so certain of Tennyson's orthodoxy. The *Christian Register* of Boston was "obliged to pass over" some of the less Christian passages which, it said, "are nothing to us"; [40] and the *New York Recorder,* Baptist weekly, thought that *In Memoriam* placed Tennyson definitely on the side of the agnostics. Tennyson doubted immortality, for he thought that his deceased friend might

> Be blown about the desert dust,
> Or seal'd within the iron hills.

Tennyson knew not; his faith knew not; and he shrieked in his agony:

> . . . what am I,
> An infant crying in the night;
> An infant crying for the light,
> And with no language but a cry.

And in justification of his doubts, he said,

> There is more faith in honest doubt,
> Believe me, than in half the creeds.

The *Recorder* had had its suspicions upon reading "The Two Voices," but now it was certain. Although "his father was a respected clergyman" and although "he was himself educated under Dr. [William] Whewell at Cambridge," Tennyson had become an unbeliever.[41]

Americans found in *In Memoriam* less of the lilting music and airy delicacy which they had praised in Tennyson's former works. The New York *Daily Tribune* (August 21, 1850) missed the "ethereal grace, the sparkling profusion of imagery or the playful dalliance of sentiment which usually gives such charm to the lifesome productions of Tennyson." But Tennyson's followers still found much to admire in the poetry of *In Memoriam.* Oliver Wendell Holmes liked the rime scheme *abba.* Soon after reading *In Memoriam,* he wrote of it to George Ticknor, "It is truly extraordinary what freshness is given to a most commonplace rhythm by a return of that exceptional arrangement of the rhymes occasionally employed by earlier writers." [42] Both R. H. Stoddard and George Henry Boker liked the refined and varied rhythm of *In Memoriam.* Boker wrote to Stoddard in 1850 concerning one whom he called Stoddard's "own dear idol":

> Speaking of Tennyson, is there not a world of beauty in "In Memoriam"? what refinement and exactness of expression! what melody in single lines! what general harmony! what scope and richness! what grand, what tender, what majestic, what childlike varieties in versification! As I live, no man has ever rung such changes on our noble English. . . . Certainly, in all that

pertains to the ART of poetry Tennyson is the first of English poets; but others, Shakespeare, Milton, etc., far excel him in genius. But Tennyson is not dead: what may we not see anon? [43]

The passage of *In Memoriam* most frequently praised for its lyrical beauty was Section CVI beginning "Ring out, wild bells, to the wild sky." Most reviews quoted the passage. Several called it a sequel to "The Death of the Old Year." One magazine printed the two side by side and added illustrations and laudatory comment to form an article entitled "Winter and the New Year." [44] *Graham's Magazine* wrote of "Ring Out, Wild Bells":

> The ringing of the Christmas bells prompts a grand poem, in which the poet rises out of his dirges into a rapturous prophecy of the "good time coming." It is altogether the best of many good lyrics on the same general theme.[45]

Scores of newspapers and magazines printed the passage as an individual poem, many not knowing that it was a part of *In Memoriam*.[46] In 1857 Oliver Ditson of Boston published a musical setting for it entitled "New Year's Bells."

Although a majority of the American reviews of *In Memoriam* mixed unfavorable comment liberally with the favorable, the poem was received in some quarters with superlative praise. When a rare British censure of *In Memoriam* [47] was widely reprinted in America, it provoked more disapproval than approbation. The *Home Journal* termed it an "admirable critical analysis of Tennyson," [48] but the *Albion* thought it "perhaps rather unfair and prejudiced," [49] and a contributor wrote for the *Home Journal* a lengthy reply to the British article. Writing his reply in the form of a letter to the editors of the *Home Journal*, he denounced them for their approval of an attack upon "an almost sacred poem." [50]

One of the most laudatory of American reviews of *In Memoriam* was that in *Sartain's Union Magazine*. In his brief but thoughtful review, the editor, John S. Hart, found not a single fault in the poem:

Here is a small volume which may be read in an hour, and yet one might fill a magazine with observations upon its beauties without exhausting the subject. The world is made richer by such a contribution to its sources of enjoyment. We have felt, in reading, a constant sense of gratitude to the author, increasing at every succeeding page, for having opened to us in this poem such a fresh fountain of delight. The tone of the work is powerful, and yet it is a sorrow so subdued, so chastened, the heart is at once purified and filled with a pervading sense of beauty while listening to the mourner.[51]

Several years after the appearance of *In Memoriam,* criticisms of it became much more favorable than they had been. Definite disapproval became almost taboo, and the highest of praise was soon in order. This change was due not so much to an actual reconsideration of the poem as to the rise of Tennyson and to the superlative praise by the British. As Tennyson neared his height, doubtless there was much more praising of *In Memoriam* than reading of it. Probably many who gave it highest praise had never read it at all. Such descriptions of it as "the greatest elegy ever penned," "the greatest English poem since *Paradise Lost,*" or "the one great poem of the age" became commonplaces of criticism. W. R. Alger's review in 1856 is a good example:

But the costliest offering of words ever laid at this shrine [friendship] is that placed by Alfred Tennyson on the new-made grave of Arthur Hallam. The "In Memoriam" reads, and will a thousand years hence, as though it were "written in star-fire and immortal tears." Victoria's Laureate has herein done for friendship more than Rienzi's did for love, and he shall be crowned for ever with greener bays. . . . The philosophic poet of our own day has built his living lines of reflection and love into a matchless temple of grief, in whose chancel lies the embalmed form of Arthur, the flower of men, lighted by tapers of veneration, bemoaned by voices of wisest thought and sweetest sorrow, to be a shrine for the pilgrims of the heart as long as a single feature remains in the mighty landscape of English literature.[52]

III

Next to America's high praise of the pre-1842 poems, the marked shift in the relationship between British and American criticism of Tennyson upon the appearance of *In Memoriam* is the most significant fact in the history of American Tennyson criticism. Whereas, American critics had excelled the British in praising all of Tennyson's former works, with *In Memoriam* the situation was reversed. Americans liked both the *Poems* of 1842 and *The Princess* better than they did *In Memoriam.* One reviewer of *In Memoriam* devoted much of his time to proving that it was inferior to *The Princess,*[53] and another closed one of the most favorable reviews that *In Memoriam* received in America with a laudatory quotation from an English magazine and the admission that he could not go that far.[54] With *In Memoriam* British critics for the first time greeted a new poem of Tennyson's with immediate and enthusiastic applause.[55] As in America, there was talk of obscurity and monotony, but with a single exception all known reviews in leading British periodicals were favorable.[56] When the London *Times* published its unique unfavorable review,[57] it drew upon itself a concentrated fire of disapproval from the British press.[58]

It is not difficult to understand why the British liked *In Memoriam* best of Tennyson's works. It showed Tennyson in effect following their instructions.[59] They had told him to write upon a great and universal theme—a subject worthy of his powers. They had told him not to waste his genius upon frivolous lyrics, but to make the music subservient to a great purpose. They had said that mere music was not enough, and that they saw in Tennyson the ability to create a poem of epic proportions, a grand expression of his age, if he would only make the attempt. *In Memoriam* conformed to these principles. It had depth, and its theme was universal and sublime.

Americans had given Tennyson no such instructions. They liked his lyric quality and considered it sufficient unto itself. Therefore they had praised his light and airy lyrics. They had not counseled him to write an epic. Some of Tennyson's American admirers liked his poems of 1842 and before better than anything that Tennyson ever wrote afterwards.[60] Then, he was more spontaneous and less constrained by the feeling that he had to have a message for his age. Charles Sumner wrote to Richard Monckton Milnes soon after the 1842 *Poems:*

> I understand that Emerson is afraid that Tennyson, since he published his first volume, has become a "fine gentleman," by which I suppose he means that his free thought and voluntary numbers will be constrained by the conventions of the world.[61]

In Memoriam clearly exemplified the trend away from what Americans had so highly praised. Through 1848 Lowell ranked Tennyson among the greatest of poets; thereafter he liked "Maud," but by the eighteen-sixties he even expressed an aversion for Tennyson.[62] Concerning Poe's high praise of Tennyson one usually mentions as a remarkable circumstance the fact that Poe died before the appearance of *In Memoriam,* but it is entirely possible, and even probable, that Poe, if he had lived, would have liked nothing of Tennyson's as well as he had the *Poems* of 1842 and *The Princess.* Those Americans who had given Tennyson some of his earliest praise, in general, deplored the change which *In Memoriam* evidenced.

Neither what Lowell or Emerson might say nor even the generally slow acceptance of *In Memoriam* in America, however, had much effect upon Tennyson's advancing fame. The year 1850 found a growing popular clamor both in

England and in America for anything that was Tennyson's, and both *In Memoriam* and the Laureateship lent impetus to the advance. As one American periodical in 1850 [63] closed its disapproval of Tennyson, "We think Bryant is a greater poet, and we might refer to others at home and abroad, whom it delights us more to read. But it is unquestionable that Tennyson is the favorite of the hour."

Chapter V

THE POET OF THE AGE

WHEN WORDSWORTH DIED IN APRIL, 1850, A GREAT COMMOTION arose as to who should be the next Poet Laureate. Samuel Rogers refused the honor, numbers of others were considered, and it was given to Tennyson on November 19. Little noise of the commotion reached across the Atlantic. One magazine objected to the consideration of Leigh Hunt.[1] Several were interested in the rumor that as a graceful compliment to the Queen the Laureateship would be bestowed upon a woman.[2] But the matter received little attention. One reviewer of *In Memoriam* did not even know that Wordsworth had been the Laureate. Tennyson, said the reviewer, was about to be offered the Laureateship which had been "unborne since Southey's death." [3]

If the discussion had aroused interest, there can be little doubt as to what its trend would have been. No one was spoken of as the chief of living English poets as often as was Tennyson. When, several months before the appointment, Thomas Holley Chivers wrote for the Macon *Georgia Citizen* that he would "rejoice to see" Tennyson made the next Laureate, he expressed what might safely be called the general American sentiment. Tennyson, Chivers continued, would "dignify the office better than any man that has ever been a Laureate." [4] After the appointment was made, Bayard Taylor, most consistently ardent of Tennysonians, exulted that the title would lose "none of the glory it took from Wordsworth," and literary periodicals spoke of the appointment as being in conformity with their wishes and expectations.[5]

References to Tennyson as the grand representative of his time began much earlier in England than in America. The idea dated back as far as Arthur Hallam's review of *Poems, Chiefly Lyrical* in 1831.[6] Americans never were much concerned over whether Tennyson was or was not the spokesman of his age. Even in the eighteen-forties when Tennyson was in fact more the great leader of living poets to Americans than he was to his own countrymen, American reviewers spoke less of him as a standard bearer than did the British. But a New York reviewer used the idea as a theme for his review of the 1842 *Poems*.[7] Charles A. Bristed in 1845 continued the idea, regretting that contemporary poets were not better so that Tennyson could be leader of a great age and not a mediocre one,[8] and a year later a less known critic declared Almighty God the greatest poet that ever lived, with Milton a close second, and Alfred Tennyson, whose name was soon to be "aromatic in the mouths of men," not far behind.[9] By 1850, whether they called Tennyson the poet of the age in so many words or not, few discussions of contemporary poetry failed to begin by characterizing his work.

This prominence did not mean at all that Tennyson was praised by all of the critics. On the contrary, he sometimes received the blame for all that they did not like in modern poetry. Although their number was decreasing, many critics still harked back to the ages of Byron and Scott or Pope and Dryden, and found nothing in the modern age to praise.

Nowhere was this attitude more strongly entrenched than in the South. In Charleston, South Carolina, Dryden and Pope were the poetic models, and of later poets only Byron received much praise.[10] William J. Grayson represented the strongest of the conservatives: "My select friends [among poets]," he wrote in 1862, "are not of the new schools. I adhere to the old masters and their followers. I believe in Dryden and Pope. . . ." The "sin of modern poetry," Grayson thought, was "exaggeration of sentiment, of passion, of description, of everything." It wanted simplicity and truth. It strove to be deep but ended in obscurity.[11] Though not so conservative, William Gilmore Simms had much the same attitude toward contemporary poets. His *Magnolia, Southern and Western Magazine,* and *Southern Quarterly Review* rarely mentioned Tennyson's poetry and then only to condemn.[12] Henry Timrod, a champion of the new order, wrote of the gentlemen about him "who know Pope and Horace by heart, but who have never read a word of Wordsworth or Tennyson, or who have read them with suspicion, and rejected them with superciliousness." [13]

Charleston was not the only place where such an attitude existed. A few months before his death, Washington Irving confessed that he had never read Tennyson. "A man at my time of life," he said, "makes few new acquaintances with the poets. I read but little of them; and that among the friends of my youth." [14] William Cullen Bryant, of the same generation, had read Tennyson, liked several individual passages,[15] but deplored his and Keats's influence on modern poetry. Contemporary poets showed a dangerous liking for striking novelties, obscure allusions, and "a repulsively abstruse affectation of meaning when there was no meaning." [16] Fitz-Greene Halleck felt the same aversion to the younger poets and attributed their faults to their "ill-luck of having taken Tennyson and Mrs. Browning as models in place of Spenser and Milton." [17] Halleck referred to Tennyson as "facetious" and "too feminine." [18] In his reminiscences of Halleck, Joel Benton wrote that "the era of poetry which began with Tennyson never won his [Halleck's] admiration. He was very tenacious in his dislike of the English Laureate, and thought that he had for thirty years had a most disastrous effect upon English poetry." [19]

Though never as strong as Halleck's, such sentiments were thinly scattered through American magazines and newspapers of the eighteen-fifties. As the watchword of the earlier foes of the Tennysonian school had been "affectation," it had now become "obscurity." An article, "Ancient and Modern Poetry," in the *Home Journal* for March 15, 1856, expressed admiration for the "clear sense and easy flow of Pope" but complained concerning "the poets of the present age—Tennyson, Browning, and others" that "the difficulty of understanding their meaning" destroyed the pleasure which might otherwise be derived from their beauties.

Likewise, in far away California an interesting article entitled "The Age of Modern Poetry" expressed much the same sentiment. That Tennyson's poems were reaching California in the eighteen-fifties is shown by advertisements of Ticknor's editions in California newspapers,[20] but literary criticism in the far West was too much in its infancy then to offer evidence sufficient to indicate a trend for or against Tennyson. This article, however, exemplifies remarkably the yearning for the literary greatness of the past and the dejection over the mediocrity of the present:

> The greatest age of modern poetry, after that of Shakespeare, is to be found in that generation which has just passed away, the sound of the footsteps of whose men yet lingers in our ears. That age saw Byron, Scott, Moore, Wordsworth, Coleridge, Southey, Keats, Shelley, and a score of others, whose works belong to the literature of England alone. To them have succeeded no men who can be considered worthy to tread in their footsteps, or to wear their laurels. The sun of poetry has gone down, and we have but moonlight at the best in its place, with starlight to help us, occasionally. . . . Our age . . . produces no poetry to speak of. The pinch-beck ware of Tennyson hardly makes good the absence of the gold of Byron.[21]

Voiced largely by the older generation, these low estimates of Tennyson and contemporary poetry represented a small minority. Rising to meet their challenge were dozens of younger poets, such as Bayard Taylor, Edmund Clarence Stedman, R. H. Stoddard, Thomas Buchanan Read, George Henry Boker, Henry Timrod, and Paul Hamilton Hayne, who paid homage to Tennyson both in verbal praise and in imitation of his style. Hayne's *Russell's Magazine* (1857–60) championed the cause of Tennyson and the new poetry in Charleston,[22] and Stedman openly acknowledged Tennyson as his master. Through all of Tennyson's poetry, "there runs," said Stedman, "the truest, noblest, broadest, philosophy of the age. He has made me wiser and better." To Stedman, Tennyson was a magnificent reformer of English poetry. If the critics of the old school who, calling Tennyson "finical" and "puerile," ignored him, would read his poems, they would find

> A *Poet,* who dared, at a time when all English poets were running into the most extended and extenuated styles, to prove by his works that the greatest Poet, *other* things being equal, is the greatest *Artist.* Who condensed and finished *everything* he wrote, without injuring it otherwise, and proved that the greater the finish, the greater the poem, for true finish never reduces the strength. . . . He is a Poet who has tried *successfully,* every department of English verse, and is as great as the *greatest* in all.[23]

Evidence that Tennyson was becoming more and more widely considered the greatest living poet is to be found on all sides. Read called Tennyson's poems "divine." [24] Stoddard called him the "sweetest and purest" poet in the English language: Tennyson compressed "more poetry in one line than Pope in five." [25] Tennyson was becoming a standard by which to measure poetic excellence. When wishing to give a poem the highest commendation, reviewers called it worthy "even of Tennyson." [26] In placing him at the head of modern poets, the *Southern Literary Messenger* in November, 1853, praised "the singular congeniality of

Tennyson's poetry with the rising spirit of the time, its harmony with what is apparently to be the tone of sentiment in the coming generation"; and the encomium of another periodical was not extraordinary: "We regard him [Tennyson] as the worthy successor to Coleridge and Wordsworth. . . . We regard him as the fit exponent of the highest civilization of the world. . . . We regard him, in a single word, as pre-eminently *the* poet of our age." [27]

The chief foundation for this exalted position accorded Tennyson was America's love of the early poems. Almost invariably, general reviews of Tennyson's poems in the eighteen-fifties gave much more space to the poems of 1842 than to *The Princess* and *In Memoriam* combined, and although little was known of the discarded pre-1842 poems, some efforts were made to resurrect them.[28] One reviewer in 1855 spoke of "Break, Break, Break," "The Lotos-Eaters," and other early poems as constituting "the greatest epoch of his [Tennyson's] experience"; another, in 1858, declared that the early poems exhibited better than any others the majestic force of Tennyson's genius; and still another felt that although Tennyson had written *The Princess, In Memoriam,* and "Maud," it was by his early short poems that he had "awakened deep echoes in the hearts of the people" and by which he was "best understood." [29]

If newspaper reporters can be trusted, Oliver Wendell Holmes's lecture on Tennyson, in his well known series of lectures on the English poets delivered several times in 1853, mentioned *The Princess* and *In Memoriam* hardly at all.[30] Brief mentions of *In Memoriam* were laudatory, but Holmes saved his time for "Locksley Hall," "Claribel," "Mariana," "The Lady of Shalott," and "The May Queen." Holmes's favorite was "The Lady of Shalott." He thought it fascinating, picturesque, dreamy—all qualities which he found also in other poems of 1842.

Throughout this high American praise of the poems of 1842, one notes the conspicuous absence of several now considered the best of the group. "Morte d'Arthur," for instance, was almost never singled out for comment, and "Ulysses" was rarely praised superlatively. In their stead scores of little poems, oft-quoted and much enjoyed but now barely remembered, ran their course through American newspapers and magazines of the eighteen-fifties.

Ignoring the distinctly English qualities of Tennyson, many American critics labored strenuously to find American traits in his poems. Calling him "the darling of the white-gloved and diamond-ringed society," Holmes felt that Tennyson's great and increasing popularity in America showed that in America the "upper layer of society" was growing; [31] but Holmes's was not the general attitude. "Though he is the poet laureate of England," wrote one reviewer, "Tennyson is by no means the poet of royalty." [32] His poetry's "peculiar applicability to a democratic age" gave it a clear "title to public favor in America." Magazine writers delighted in uncovering passages to prove Tennyson's belief in democracy: "Lady Clara Vere de Vere" showed an "American contempt" for social position; [33] "The Goose" was a plea for the laboring classes; [34] and "The Brook" was proof enough that Tennyson understood "common life" better than "any other famous English poet." [35] A Yale student thought that in its democracy and optimism, Tennyson's poetry was "peculiarly adapted . . . to the American youth of this age," [36] and a particularly imaginative writer was able to see in "Locksley Hall" the "dream of a universal American Empire, gradually absorbing and annexing all the kingdoms of the earth." This empire, said the American, was "vaguely anticipated by Tennyson, and summed up in the striking expression of 'the federation of the world.' " [37]

Americans felt that they had appreciated Tennyson more

readily than had his own countrymen and were proud of the fact. "Tennyson in the old world is beyond his age," wrote one reviewer, "but here, where there is greater freedom of thought, and less allegiance to the blinding influences of *sense,* it is otherwise." By *sense,* explained the reviewer, he meant the "cold, didactic formulas" of the old school of poets. In America an original poet did not have to wait "perhaps a quarter of century" for recognition just because of his "departure from the schools." [38] "The truth is," wrote another reviewer, "that the American Mind is more delicate and sensitive than the English." In support of his statement he declared that the best English poets were "infinitely more extensively read and appreciated in this country than in the land of their birth. Ticknor and Co. sold edition after edition of the poems of Tennyson, while the English edition was a 'drug' in the market." [39]

Such statements are to be found elsewhere,[40] and that Tennyson was selling rapidly cannot be doubted, but in a comparison of sales in America with those in England, one has to consider a factor other than the "American Mind." There was no international copyright law. Ticknor and Company never pirated Tennyson's books, but while Tennyson was demanding the highest of prices from his English publishers, Ticknor was paying much smaller royalties and was selling the books throughout America at less than half their sales prices in London.[41] A listing of the original prices of the American and English first editions will present the contrast graphically: [42]

	American	English
Poems (1842)	$1.50	12 shillings ($3.00)
The Princess	$0.50	5 " ($1.25)
In Memoriam	$0.75	6 " ($1.50)
Maud, and Other Poems	$0.50	5 " ($1.25)

Chambers's Edinburgh Journal printed in 1846 one of the clearest, if exaggerated, early explanations of the situation.

English books in London, said the *Journal,* were available only to the wealthy, while in America they were "distributed throughout every village in the Union," even to "the bar-room and the shanty of the 'far West.' " In consequence, the British authors were better known in the United States than in Great Britain, and more copies of their works were "to be found in a single city there than in the whole country where they were produced." [43]

English authors keenly resented the pirating of their books by American publishers, and that resentment was doubtless an underlying cause of some of the ill-humored English reviews of American works, and in turn, caused some American detractions of the English Laureate in favor of Longfellow and Poe.[44] Upon his several visits to England in the eighteen-fifties, Thomas Buchanan Read noticed the ill feeling in many quarters and once or twice reminded the Englishmen "that several of their head men had made their reputations first in America" and "that it was the echo of their fame created in our country which at last called attention to them in their own." "This," Read said, "they certainly ignore, although it is undeniable both in regard to Carlyle and Tennyson." [45]

Especially in the case of Tennyson, the early American appreciation cannot be ignored. Americans praised him years before they had an edition of his poems. It is true, nevertheless, that the easy availability of his books later and the excellent work of Ticknor and Fields contributed greatly to his American popularity.

Throughout the eighteen-forties and fifties, William D. Ticknor and his associates were the sole authorized American publishers of Tennyson. On March 18, 1856, Tennyson wrote to Ticknor and Fields, "As I have received from you remuneration for my books, it is my wish that with you alone the right of publishing them in America should lie," [46] and Tennyson's wish seems to have been adhered to for several years thereafter.[47] The adherence, however, was no doubt due more to the difficulty of competing with Ticknor than to any consideration for Tennyson's wishes in the matter.

It would be difficult for one to imagine any publisher's receiving higher praise than that accorded Ticknor and Fields. The *Home Journal* (October 7, 1854) entitled an article "Ticknor, Reed and Fields," in praise of their editions of the poets. The *Knickerbocker* proposed a toast to the company: "Success to the MOXONS and MURRAYS of America!" [48] And the "Blue and Gold" pocket edition of Tennyson was considered a sort of crowning achievement. "Immortality in miniature was never more excellently represented." [49] It was almost unbelievable that the complete poems of "one of the truest poets that ever illustrated our language" could now be had for "the price of the last worthless novel." [50] "If," wrote the *Home Journal,* "books had been manufactured in those days when Oberon and Titania were mighty powers in the woodland, when every asphodel and every king's-cup was the *chateau* of a fairy," those books would have been just such beautiful little "claspable tomes" as "Ticknor's miniature Tennyson." [51] When Fields sent his friend, George S. Hillard, a copy, Hillard wrote his verses, "On Receiving a Copy of Tennyson's Poems," which combine the highest praise of Tennyson with that of his American publishers:

When your new Tennyson I hold, dear friend,
Where blue and gold, like sky and sunbeam, blend,—
A fairy tome—of not too large a grasp
For Queen Titania's dainty hand to clasp,—
I feel fresh truth in the old saying wise,
That greatest worth in smallest parcel lies.

. . . .

Thanks to the poet, who to dusty hearts
The balm and bloom of summer fields imparts;

Who gives the toil-worn mind a passage free
To the brown mountain and the sparkling sea;
Who lifts the thoughts from earth, and pours a ray
Of fairy land around life's common way.

And thanks to you, who put this precious wine,
Red from the poet's heart, in flask so fine,
The hand may clasp it, and the pocket hold;—
A casket small, but filled with perfect gold.[52]

II

By the early eighteen-fifties, most of the American anthologies of British poets were including poems of Tennyson. His poetry had appeared in an American anthology as early as 1840, when Fitz-Greene Halleck's *Selections from the British Poets* included "Mariana." A few years later Griswold's *The Poets and Poetry of England in the Nineteenth Century* printed ten of Tennyson's poems along with its already-mentioned depreciatory biographical account of him and devoted more space to him than to Scott, Keats, Coleridge, or Felicia Hemans. Longfellow included "Break, Break, Break" in his group of neglected poems, *The Estray,* in 1847, and when anthologies began to gain in popularity ten years later, all of the most publicized ones including English poems contained specimens from Tennyson. When Joseph William Jenks's *The Rural Poetry of the English Language* left Tennyson out, one reviewer vigorously protested the omission.[53] Evert A. Duyckinck's edition of Willmott's *The Poets of the Nineteenth Century* contained "The May Queen," "Morte d'Arthur," "Edward Gray," "The Goose," and "Break, Break, Break,"[54] and of the forty-three poets represented in Henry Coppee's expensive and richly illustrated *Gallery of Famous English and American Poets,* Tennyson ranked fourth in the amount of space devoted to him.[55]

So varied were the poems of Tennyson selected by the

anthologists that it is difficult to name the favorites. The distribution ranged all the way from "Morte d'Arthur" to "The Goose" and "O Darling Room." As might be expected, the shorter poems predominated. Many of the poems now most common in anthologies were almost ignored. "Morte d'Arthur," "Ulysses," and "The Lady of Shalott" were rare. Surprisingly infrequent were the feminine portraits of the "Lilian" type, which Americans both enjoyed and imitated. If one might hazard a naming of favorites, they seem to have been "The May Queen," "Mariana," "Break, Break, Break," and the rimed songs from *The Princess*.

The most popular kind of anthologies in America from 1840 to 1860 was the gift-books and literary annuals. Composed largely of poetry and prose fiction, their material came predominantly from American writers, but several of the British poets were well represented. Felicia Hemans was far and away the most popular, with Tom Moore, Byron, Wordsworth, and Tennyson vying for the second position.[56] The earliest known American annual to include poems of Tennyson was *Friendship's Offering* for 1842, published in late 1841, which contained "A Fragment" and "No More." Since the annuals especially liked mournful and lugubrious poetry, Tennyson's "Mariana" and verses of its type were popular. One unusually doleful gift-book, *Memory and Hope* for 1851, used *In Memoriam* as its motif: it opened with nine stanzas closely imitating stanzas from *In Memoriam* and closed with a selection from the poem.[57] Another, of a less mournful nature, *The Irving Offering* for 1852, proudly announcing its selections as worthy of the strongest approval of Washington Irving, selected one poem of Tennyson's: "O Darling Room"; and *The Kossuth Offering and Family Souvenir* for the same year, one of the rare annuals to include literary essays, contained an unsigned article, "Tennyson's Lockesley [*sic*] Hall."

Tennyson was represented in several anthologies which gathered together poems on specific subjects. Selections from *In Memoriam* appeared frequently in books of religious verse. Epes Sargent's *The Testimony of The Poets* quoted a long passage from *In Memoriam,*[58] and Stephen G. Bulfinch's *The Harp and the Cross* selected three passages, entitling them "Lazarus and Mary," "God Ruling in All," and "Hope, Doubt, and Trust." *The Poetic Lacon* (1847), a book of aphorisms, contained quotations from Tennyson equal in number to those from the established English poets. Samuel Longfellow and Thomas Wentworth Higginson's *Thalatta: A Book for the Sea-Side,* using as its preface two passages from Tennyson concerning the sea, contained also "Sweet and Low," "Break, Break, Break," and "Ask Me No More"; and Thomas Bulfinch's *Poetry of the Age of Fable* used seven excerpts from Tennyson's classical poems.

School texts containing the work of living authors were not numerous during this period, and many which did exist contained no Tennyson. Nevertheless, Tennyson's poems got an early start in American texts. In 1842 *Perennial Flowers,* a "collection of poetry appropriate for the use of girls in schools" used "The Dying Swan," and in the same year Anna C. Lowell's *Poetry for Home and School* printed four of Tennyson's poems.[59] When Charles D. Cleveland's *English Literature of the Nineteenth Century,* "designed for colleges and advanced classes in schools," appeared in 1851, Tennyson did not appear among its seventy-eight authors, but in its second edition (1853) Tennyson was represented by a biographical account, four short poems, and several passages from *In Memoriam.* Epes Sargent's *Selections in Poetry for Exercises at School and at Home* contained three of Tennyson's poems, and although William H. McGuffey's famous readers seem to have ignored Tennyson till 1857, in that year *McGuffey's New High School Reader* printed parts of "The May Queen," all of

"Break, Break, Break," and a brief biographical account of Tennyson which ranked him "among the first of modern poets." [60]

One of the most popular kinds of school texts in America around 1850 was the book of recitations and exercises in elocution, and Tennyson's poems were frequently used as such exercises. A *Young Ladies' Elocutionary Reader* in 1845 gave "The May Queen" as an "example of *joy,* as expressed in *loud* and *lively* tones," and "New-Year's Eve" as an "example of *pathos,* as expressed in *soft, low, slow,* and *plaintive* tones." [61] A *Juvenile Speaker* gave "The Death of the Old Year" as a "piece for practice," [62] and one of the best known of the elocution books, Epes Sargent's *Intermediate Standard Speaker,* in 1857 printed "The Charge of the Light Brigade" as four paragraphs of prose with instructions concerning articulation, gestures, and posture.

III

The fact that Tennyson was to Americans the pre-eminent poet of the new era is shown nowhere more clearly than in their imitation of his style. As has already been noted, imitation of Tennyson began even before 1842, and thereafter Tennyson's influence upon American poetry grew steadily. The terms "Tennysonism" and "Tennysonianism," coined immediately, soon became everyday expressions with reviewers. In 1852 one wrote, "We do not remember having looked through a book of poems for several years back, without noticing very clearly the influence of Tennyson," [63] and another wrote of a young poet in 1859, "Of course the model is Tennyson, for where is the young poet now that imitates anybody else?" [64] By that time Tennyson had placed his mark upon American poetry more indelibly than had any other living poet.

During the period prior to the *Idylls of the King,* the poems of 1842 were much more widely imitated than were all of Tennyson's later poems combined. It was the singing trochees of "Locksley Hall," the dreamy melody of "The Lotos-Eaters" or "Oenone," and the sprightly liquid notes of "Lilian" or "The Sea-Fairies" that could be traced most clearly through American poetry. Tennyson's influence was definitely in the direction of tuneful music and smooth flowing rhythm. Even in the blank verse of "Ulysses," an early favorite with imitators, it was the rolling, reverberating quality of the lines that was most copied. From Tennyson's 1842 *Poems* dated the great popularity of melodious feminine names and, to some extent, the increasing popularity of brief lyrics written purely for their music.[65]

Despite Poe's violent protestations to the contrary, his and Thomas Holley Chivers' lyrics which have aroused so much controversy concerning plagiarism undoubtedly owed something to Tennyson. The names, Lenore, Annabel Lee, Isadore, and Lily Adair—some used earlier than 1842 and some after—are closely akin to Lilian, Oriana, and Eleanore, and it is difficult to believe that Chivers' "Isadore," whose meter closely resembles that of "Locksley Hall," was written before 1842, the year in which "Locksley Hall" was published.[66] Three of the most quoted stanzas (ll. 119–24) of "Locksley Hall" will be sufficient to call to mind its eight-stress, catalectic, trochaic lines:

For I dipt into the future, far as human eye could see,
Saw the Vision of the world, and all the wonders that would be;

Saw the heavens fill with commerce, argosies of magic sails,
Pilots of the purple twilight, dropping down their costly bales;

Heard the heavens fill with shouting, and there rain'd a ghastly
dew
From the nation's airy navies grappling in the central blue.

Compare "Isadore":

> While the world lay round me sleeping,
> I, alone, for Isadore,
> Patient Vigils lonely keeping—
> Some one said to me while weeping,
> "Why this grief forever more?"
> And I answered, "I am weeping
> For My blessed ISADORE!" [67]

The first two and last two lines of every stanza of "Isadore" fit the "Locksley Hall" cadence exactly, and although the other lines vary it, the resemblance between the two poems is remarkable. The source of the rhythm of Poe's "The Raven" is probably distributed somewhat equally among "Isadore," "Locksley Hall," and poems both English and American which had already copied "Locksley Hall." [68]

Of all of Tennyson's stanza forms, that of "Locksley Hall" was by far the most copied in America through 1860. With its later start, the *In Memoriam* stanza began weakly to rival it in the fifties, but no creation of Tennyson's can be traced so clearly through American poetry as the rhythm of "Locksley Hall" during the twenty years after the publication of the poem.[69] Within a few months after its appearance, Longfellow used the stanza in "The Belfry of Bruges":

> In the market-place of Bruges stands the belfry old and brown;
> Thrice consumed and thrice rebuilded, still it watches o'er the town.
>
> As the summer morn was breaking, on that lofty tower I stood,
> And the world threw off the darkness, like the weeds of widowhood.[70]

Longfellow copied the rhythm again at about the same time in "Nuremberg." [71] Acknowledging that he was imitating poetry of a "rather modern" character, James Gates Percival used it in his "Classic Melodies" of 1843,[72] and in the same year William W. Story wrote "Light and Shadow":

Life is never quite unclouded, nor its circle wholly fair—
But the morn of Hope still creepeth on the shadow of Despair.

Janus-faced, within the Present ever stands the human mind,—
Hope's glad face still gazes forward, Memory's sadly looks behind.[73]

From this beginning the rhythm was taken up by nearly all of the younger poets who were copying Tennyson profusely. Combining the lines into a five-line stanza, Lowell used it to plead for abolition in "The Present Crisis":

When a deed is done for Freedom, through the broad earth's
aching breast
Runs a thrill of joy prophetic, trembling on from east to west,
And the slave, where'er he cowers, feels the soul within him
climb
To the awful verge of manhood, as the energy sublime
Of a century bursts full-blossomed on the thorny stem of time.[74]

The rhythm was a favorite with Thomas Buchanan Read, who used it in his two long poems "Christine" and "Inez" of *Poems* (1847). Note the opening lines of "Christine":

Come my friend, and in the silence and the shadow wrapt apart,
I will loose the golden claspings of this sacred tome—the heart.

By the bole of yonder cypress, under branches spread like eaves,
We will sit where wavering sunshine weaves a romance in the
leaves.[75]

Bayard Taylor used the "Locksley Hall" line in both his *Book of Romances, Lyrics and Songs* and his *Poems of the Orient*. He used it sometimes in three-line stanzas and sometimes in four. "The Birth of the Prophet" has the prophetic tone of the latter part of "Locksley Hall":

For the oracles of Nature recognize a Prophet's birth—
Blossom of the tardy ages, crowning type of human worth—
And by miracles and wonders he is welcomed to the Earth

. . . .

Mighty arcs of rainbow splendor, pillared shafts of purple fire
Split the sky and spanned the darkness, and with many a golden
spire,
Beacon-like, from all the mountains streamed the lambent meteors higher.[76]

Some poets, keeping the rhythm intact, varied the stanza-length greatly and sometimes even the length of the line and the rime scheme. Several poets broke the line where Tennyson placed his pause and thus formed four-line stanzas which seem distinctly derived from "Locksley Hall." [77] The most violent variation which still preserved the Tennysonian rhythm was the change of Tennyson's couplets into *abab* rime. Carefully preserving the pause in the middle of the line and the precise trochees of "Locksley Hall," R. H. Stoddard made that variation in his long poem, "Burden of Unrest":

Thrilling with my youthful longings, which anticipated thee,
Dreams were mine of bridal chambers, and they colored all my
song;
Like the rosy hues of evening, settling yonder on the sea
Blending with the waves, whose motion wafts the dying flame
along.[78]

Chivers did the same thing in "The Queen of My Heart" of *Virginalia:*

If thou art the only Pharos that can light my soul, at even,
When my Bark of Life is wrecking on Times' ocean tempest-
tost,
By what Beacon shall my spirit reach the peaceful Port of
Heaven,
From the Valley of Dark Shadows where so many men are
lost? [79]

The imitators of "Locksley Hall" copied its rhythm in poems upon almost every subject imaginable. Henry B. Hirst used it to make passionate love to his lady; [80] Sarah J. Hale copied it servilely in a rare monologue, "The Lady to Her Falcon"; [81] and William Pembroke Mulchinock of New York created a curiosity in his "The Dying Girl." The poem is the story of Tennyson's "The May Queen" told in "Locksley Hall" verses.[82] Many of the minor poets copied both words and rhythm to the point of palpable plagiarism. Tennyson's prophetic passage concerning universal peace was a favorite. Charles E. Havens' "Bugle Song" is a typical copying of it:

Lo! its echoes dying, dying, down the mystic vale of time,
Tell us that the sword shall cease to be an instrument of crime

And the drum shall be unbeaten, and the trumpet be unblown,
Ev'ry symbol of destruction shall at last be overthrown;

And the banner of our Union, emblem of the reign of love,
Shall be hoisted o'er the ramparts, overshadowed by the Dove.[83]

The lines from "Locksley Hall" describing the time when "the war-drum throbb'd no longer, and the battle-flags were furl'd" are too well known to need quoting.[84]

The *In Memoriam* stanza stands second in popularity among Tennyson stanza-forms copied in America during this period; it was, however, a poor second. Certainly, it did not approach the popularity of that of "Locksley Hall" before 1860. Apparently, nobody used the stanza as Tennyson had—in a lengthy memorial to a lost friend. Americans, who called *In Memoriam* monotonous and too long, made no such attempt, and the well known American poets, many of whom had never admired the poem, made almost no use of the stanza. It was left largely to the underlings to initiate the little flurry of imitations.

In another of its depreciations of Tennyson, Simms's *Southern Quarterly Review* described the imitations which began soon after the appearance of Tennyson's "pretty but very fatiguing collection of small elegiac":

On the instant, the whole swarm of American poetasters found that they had young friends to bewail, and wrote memorials.

Such a lugubrious clamor in lugubrious verse never before annoyed the ears of the public. The notion was—Tennyson is popular. His quaintnesses take. His mysteries are so delicate. His affectations so tickle the young ladies. We have only to Tennysonize in order to share his popularity.[85]

The *In Memoriam* quatrain of four-stress iambics with the rime *abba* is well illustrated in its dignity and lugubriousness by the first three stanzas of the prologue:

> Strong Son of God, immortal Love,
> Whom we, that have not seen thy face,
> By faith, and faith alone, embrace,
> Believing where we cannot prove;
>
> Thine are these orbs of light and shade;
> Thou madest Life in man and brute;
> Thou madest Death; and lo, thy foot
> Is on the skull which thou hast made.
>
> Thou wilt not leave us in the dust:
> Thou madest man, he knows not why,
> He thinks he was not made to die;
> And thou hast made him: thou art just.

Tennyson's claims to originality in the formation of this stanza are not so clear as were those in regard to "Locksley Hall." As has been noted, English poets had used it before him, and American poetry offers several examples of the stanza years before *In Memoriam* was published. Christopher P. Cranch's thirty-eight stanza poem, "The Music of Nature," is a remarkable example of sustained use of the stanza as early as 1836. Some of the stanzas, though the last line is three-stress instead of four, are amazingly close to *In Memoriam:*

> And still I roamed with lightsome heart,
> And from the tones so intermingled,
> Swift-gathering Fancy ever singled
> *One* voice from every part.

And first I heard the mighty ocean
Go thundering to his empire bounds;
A voice of many blended sounds
In sad and wild commotion.[86]

Regardless of these earlier uses of the stanza, however, one can be certain that when the imitations of it began in the eighteen-fifties they had their origin in *In Memoriam*.

John R. Thompson in his poem, "To One in Affliction," used the stanza in much the same way as Tennyson had. The poem seeks to console a father who has lost his son:

Dear friend! if word of mine could seal
The bitter fount of all thy tears,
And, through the future's cloudy years,
Some glimpses of sunshine yet reveal—

That word I might not dare to speak:
A father's sorrow o'er his child
So sacred seems and undefiled,
To bid it cease we may not seek.[87]

Another American followed Tennyson's use of the stanza even more closely in commemoration of the death of James Fenimore Cooper. As to literary merit, the verses follow Tennyson afar off, but the stanza is preserved at all hazards:

A generation dates the taste
For literary joys complete,
From Leatherstocking's wondrous feat—
The joys that saved the hours from waste.

A sound is floating on the night,
Another sound, a hopeful sigh,
Like one whose tears begin to dry—
A recollection of delight.

Awakened by that memory
We see the casket vanish sole:
The spirit it exhaled is whole,
And spreads abroad o'er land and sea.[88]

One of the queerest conglomerations of such memorials to lost friends may be found in an annual for 1851 already referred to: *Memory and Hope*. Compiled in late 1850, the book consisted almost entirely of wailing, lugubrious verses, several imitating *In Memoriam*. It opened with a poetic preface copying in both word and manner the first nine stanzas of the main body of *In Memoriam*. The first stanza is characteristic:

> I hold it as a sacred boon,—
> The memory of the loved and wept;
> And still her vigil Hope hath kept
> Till darkness brightened into noon.

The *In Memoriam* stanza seems to have been a favorite with R. H. Stoddard and Thomas Bailey Aldrich, but apparently neither ever used it as Tennyson did. Stoddard used it several times in his *Songs of Summer*. He taught an Emersonian moral in "Great and Small":

> The insect with its gauzy wings
> Sings and the moth and beetle grim;
> And for the bee—I doat on him,
> And know by heart the tune he sings!
>
> Then learn this truth, the base of all,
> That all are equal, so they fill
> Their proper spheres, and do God's will:
> There is no other Great and Small! [89]

Aldrich's eulogy upon Longfellow preserved the dignity and solemnity of Tennyson's lines:

> Like him of old, whose touch divine
> Drew water from the senseless stone,
> Thy words have drawn a silver tone
> Of music from this heart of mine.
>
> O Poet-soul! O gentle one!
> Thy thought has made my darkness light;
> The solemn Voices of the Night
> Have filled me with an inner tone.[90]

Americans took the greatest of liberties with the stanza, seldom giving it such dignity, and very rarely giving it Tennyson's note of melancholy. William Gibson, minor Boston poet, copied in both word and manner Section CVI of *In Memoriam,* "Ring Out, Wild Bells," and produced a joyful poem, "Christmas Chimes." [91] Grace Greenwood and Julia Ward Howe liked to use the stanza in poems on various subjects, of which the closing stanzas of Grace Greenwood's "Lines I Sent with a Copy of Tennyson's 'In Memoriam' " are characteristic:

> But, friend beloved, well I know
> Thou wouldst be near me when I die,
> Thy soul be last to say good-bye,
> As down the lonely vale I go;—
>
> And then to know through all thy days
> Thou, holding dear my love apart,
> Wouldst think much on my buried heart,
> Were more than volumes of great praise.[92]

At least one magazine writer used the stanza to praise his love,[93] and the Canadian poet, Charles Sangster, combined the *In Memoriam* stanza and tone with the plot of Tennyson's "The Death of the Old Year" to form what a reviewer called one of the queerest mixtures he had ever seen.[94] Could Tennyson have seen all of the American imitations of his poems, probably he would have been least pleased with those of *In Memoriam.*

Of more literary value is a smaller group of imitations of Tennyson's blank verse. Americans generally thought of Tennyson as a lyric poet of singing rimes. Few if any of them attempted such blank verse lyrics as Tennyson's "Tears, Idle Tears." Stoddard in closely copying the theme of that lyric in his three quatrains, "A Phantasy," rimed the second and fourth lines.[95] Henry B. Hirst in an imitation of "Morte d'Arthur" shifted his similar story into couplets.[96] But the Tennysonian blank verse of "Ulysses," *The Princess,* and the rural idylls had a perceptible influence in their almost lyrical intensity, severity of verse-structure, and strict regularity of stress.[97]

The influence of "Ulysses" is especially clear. Lowell's "Prometheus," written in 1843, was indebted to both "Saint Simeon Stylites" and "Ulysses." The following lines strongly remind one of the latter:

> Yes, I am still Prometheus, wiser grown
> By years of solitude,—that holds apart
> The past and future, giving the soul room
> To search into itself,—and long commune
> With this eternal silence;—more a god,
> In my long-suffering and strength to meet
> With equal front the direct shafts of fate,
> Than thou in thy faint-hearted despotism,
> Girt with thy baby-toys of force and wrath.
>
> . . . .
>
> Each hath his lonely peak, and on each heart
> Envy, or scorn, or hatred, tears lifelong
> With vulture beak; yet the high soul is left;
> And faith, which is but hope grown wise, and love
> And patience which at last shall overcome.[98]

Even closer to the blank verse of "Ulysses" is Lowell's later poem, "Columbus":

> Here am I; for what end God knows, not I;
> Westward still points the inexorable soul;
> Here am I, with no friend but the sad sea,
> The beating heart or this great enterprise
> Which without me, would stiffen in swift death;
> This have I mused on, since mine eye could first
> Among the stars distinguish and with joy
> Rest on that God-fed Pharos of the north,
> On some blue promontory of heaven lighted
> That juts far out into the upper sea.[99]

Henry Timrod's "Arctic Voyager" is another poem greatly indebted to "Ulysses":

> This, and worse,
> I suffered—let it pass—it has not tamed
> My spirit nor the faith which was my strength,
> Despite of waning years, despite the world
> Which doubts, the few who dare, I purpose now—
> A purpose long and thoughtfully resolved,
> Through all its grounds of reasonable hope—
> To seek beyond the ice which guards the Pole,
> A sea of open water; for I hold,
> Not without proofs, that such a sea exists,
> And may be reached, though since this earth was made
> No keel hath ploughed it. . . .[100]

Probably no American poet was more strongly stirred by Tennyson's blank verse than the minor Kentucky poet, William Ross Wallace, one of whose few distinctions was the fact that Poe praised him highly.[101] In the wake of "Ulysses" came several blank verse monologues in which great leaders and travelers recounted their experiences. Wallace wrote ones for Washington, Wordsworth, and Daniel Boone. In all three he leaned heavily on "Ulysses" and, especially in the last, coolly paraphrased:

> I must away: for action is my life;
> And it is base to triumph in a Past,
> However big with mighty circumstance,
> Danger full-faced and large heroic deed,
> If yet a future calls. It calls to me.
> What if some seventy years have thinned this hair,
> And dimmed this sight, and made the blood roll on
> Less riotous between the banks of life?—
> This heart hath vigor yet. . . .
>
> . . . .
>
> Yes! Surely I must go, and drink anew
> The splendor that is in the pathless woods,

And wear the blue sky as a coronal,
And bid the torrent sound my conquering march,
And ponder far away from all that mars
The everlasting wonder of the world,
And with each dewy morning wake and feel
As though that world, so fresh, so beautiful
With sunrise and the mist, had just been made.[102]

Lowell, Timrod, and Wallace all call instantly to mind Tennyson's ringing lines:

I cannot rest from travel; I will drink
Life to the lees. All times I have enjoy'd
Greatly, have suffer'd greatly, both with those
That loved me, and alone; on shore, and when
Thro' scudding drifts the rainy Hyades
Vext the dim sea.[103]

No other blank verse poem of Tennyson's left its mark as distinctly as did "Ulysses." Thomas Bailey Aldrich prefaced his poem, "The Three Conceits," with a prologue which he acknowledged to have modeled after that of *The Princess.*[104] Julia Ward Howe's long poem, "Rome," suggests *The Princess* on nearly every page, and her "Wherefore" used bits of narrative material from "Morte d'Arthur" in its story of the passing glory of the Hungarian patriot, Louis Kossuth.[105] Rural idylls such as William Ellery Channing's "Edward and Margaret," "The Friends," and "The Sexton's Story,"[106] Alfred B. Street's blank verse poems in *Drawings and Tintings,*[107] and Stoddard's "Arcadian Idyl"[108] remind one of Tennyson's "Dora," "The Gardener's Daughter," or "Love and Duty," but the connection is intangible. It is extremely difficult to distinguish such an influence from that of Wordsworth or others.

Sometimes American poets imitated specific poems of Tennyson in subject, manner, and wording. Timrod and Stoddard wrote such imitations of "Break, Break, Break." Note Timrod's "Hark to the Shouting Wind":

Hark to the shouting Wind!
Hark to the flying Rain!
And I care not though I never see
A Bright blue sky again.

There are thoughts in my breast to-day
That are not for human speech;
But I hear them in the driving storm,
And the roar upon the beach.

And oh, to be with that ship
That I watch through the blinding brine!
O Wind! for thy sweep of land and sea!
O Sea! for a voice like thine!

Shout on, thou pitiless Wind,
To the frightened and flying Rain!
I care not though I never see
A calm blue sky again.[109]

Thomas Buchanan Read wrote two obvious imitations of "The Lady of Shalott." Anyone who remembers Tennyson's nine-line stanza, its refrain, and the dreamy atmosphere of the poem will instantly recognize them in "The Maid of Linden Lane":

While you sit as in a trance,
Where the moon-made shadows dance,
From the distaff of Romance
  I will spin a silken skein:
Down the misty years gone by
I will turn your azure eye;
You shall see the changeful sky
Falling down or hanging high
Over the halls of Linden Lane.

. . . .

Ah, yes, lightly sing and laugh—
Half a child and woman half;
For your laughter's but the chaff
  From the melancholy grain;
And, ere many years shall fly,

Age will dim your laughing eye,
And like me you'll totter by;
For remember, love, that I
Was the Maid of Linden Lane.[110]

Others copied "The Lady of Shalott" almost as servilely,[111] and "The Ballad of Oriana" was another favorite with imitators, especially among the minor poets. Henry B. Hirst's "Eleanore" and William Pembroke Mulchinock's "Aileen Aroon" are puerile copies of it:

I am lone without thy love,
Eleanore,
And my life with grief is wove,
Eleanore;
While the scorn thy glances dart
Makes a winter in my heart,
Eleanore! [112]

Oh! but my step is weak,
Aileen, aroon!
Wan and pale is my cheek,
Aileen, aroon!
Come o'er the ocean tide,
No more to leave my side,
Come, my betrothed bride,
Aileen, aroon! [113]

"The Death of the Old Year," several imitations of which have already been mentioned, was another favorite. Hirst wrote three separate versions of it.[114] Lowell acknowledged "Sir Galahad" as the inspiration for his "The Vision of Sir Launfal," and the "Prelude to Part First" of "The Vision" is very close to Tennyson's "The Sleeping Palace." [115] "The Talking Oak" was several times borrowed bodily, notably in parts of Story's "The Mistake"; [116] "The May Queen" was copied in poems which sound like parodies;[117] "A Farewell" was also frequently imitated—once by a Virginian who set out to "improve" it,[118] and even the songs to the owl had their imitators.[119]

Though fewer post-1842 poems were thus closely copied, several imitations of the songs of *The Princess* have been found,[120] and Julia Ward Howe, James Barron Hope, and the Alabama poet, A. B. Meek, reproduced "The Charge of the Light Brigade." Of the three reproductions, Mrs. Howe's "Balaklava" is the poorest poem and the closest imitation:

> They gave the fatal order, Charge!
> And so, the light Brigade went down,
> Where bristling brows of cannon crown
> The front of either marge.
>
> Traced all in fire we saw our way,
> And the black goal of Death beyond—
> It was no moment to despond,
> To question, or to pray.
>
> Firm in the saddle, stout of heart,
> With plume and sabre waving high,
> With gathering stride and onward cry,
> The band was swift to start.[121]

In a rare imitation of the "Ode on the Death of the Duke of Wellington," John Esten Cooke commemorated the death of Elisha Kent Kane, the arctic explorer,[122] and Stoddard in "The Serenade of Ma-Han-Shan" wrote one of the earliest apparent imitations of the later widely copied song, "Come into the Garden, Maud." [123]

More important than stanza forms, themes, or verbal echoes in Tennyson's influence upon American poets are his tunes and musical language. It was Tennyson's intoxicating music that made Bayard Taylor fearful of its contagion, and its contagion is well shown by the mark that it placed upon the work of the younger poets. That mark is evasive, and yet certain. Often without being able to put his finger upon a particular spot to call an echo, the reader can yet feel the Tennysonian tune as he reads. The American poems which show this influence most distinctly may be divided into the two groups used in studying the pre-1842 influence, those of the "Mariana" and of the "Lilian" type.

Most important are the poems in the dreamy, mournful vein of "Mariana" and "Oenone." Alice Cary has caught their language and music in her "The Daughter":

> Often the harmless flock she sees
> Lying white along the grassy leas,
> Like lily-bells weighed down with bees,
> Sometimes the boatman's horn she hears
> Rousing from rest the plowman's steers,
> Lowing untimely to their peers.
> And now and then the moonlight snake
> Curls up its white folds, for her sake,
> Closer within the poison brake.
> But still she keeps her lonesome way,
> Or if she pauses, 'tis to say
> Some word of comfort, else to pray.
> For 'tis a blustery night withal,
> In spite of star or moonlight's fall,
> On the two whipperwill's sweet call—[124]

William W. Story's "Night-Watch" has the Tennysonian flavor even more distinctly:

> On the wall the shadow sleepeth,
> And the dreary wind is sighing,
> Whispering restlessly it creepeth,
> Now uprising, and now dying,
> Through the leaves, and through the vine
> That around the window twine,
> While my silent watch I keep—
> Sleep, beloved! sleep! [125]

Thomas Bailey Aldrich's "Maud Allinggale" and George H. Boker's "I Sit Beneath the Sunbeam's Glow" might almost pass for parodies of "Oenone":

> The wind was toying with her hair,
> As on the turret top she stood;

Her gaze was on the bending wood,
And in her eyes a dim despair.
Moaning Oenone, sad and pale,
Sweet Psyche when her love had gone
Were not more tearful or forlorn
Than Maud of Allinggale.[126]

I sit beneath the sunbeam's glow,
Their golden currents round us flow,
Their mellow kisses warm my brow,
But all the world is dreary.
The vernal meadow round me blooms,
And flings to me its soft perfumes,
Its breath is like an opening tomb's
I'm sick of life, I'm weary.[127]

No poem of the group had a more contagious music and atmosphere than that of "The Lotos-Eaters." Several lines from its first stanza exemplify its mood and manner:

In the afternoon they came unto a land
In which it seemed always afternoon.
All round the coast the languid air did swoon,
Breathing like one that hath a weary dream.
Full-faced above the valley stood the moon;
And, like a downward smoke, the slender stream
Along the cliff to fall and pause and fall did seem.

It is easy to see how this languid, dreary mood could cast a spell upon a young poet. Whether consciously or unconsciously, Story was under the spell in his "The Island Home":

Dallied we here, and loitered there,
There was no hurry to be gone,
Silken soft was the murmurous air,
Pleasant the beams of the rising sun,—
In and out of many a cove,
Anchored beside a shady shore,
Drooping the sail and bending the oar,
Day after day thus idly wore,—
This was the life we used to love.[128]

Paul Hamilton Hayne's variation of the meter in "The Realm of Rest" destroyed the drowsy mood, but the tune and the language are still Tennysonian:

> Within the realm that Nature boundeth,
> Are those balmy shores of peace,
> Where no passion-torrent soundeth,
> And no storm-wind seeks release?
> Rest they 'mid the waters golden,
> Of some strange untravelled sea,
> Where low, Halcyon winds have stolen,
> Lingering round them slumbrously? [129]

In "The Sea-Fairies," "The Merman," and "The Mermaid," Tennyson somewhat combined the atmosphere of "The Lotos-Eaters" and the sprightliness of his feminine portraits, and the combination was popular with American imitators.[130] William Ellery Channing almost plagiarized "The Sea-Fairies" in his "To My Companions":

> Ye heavy-hearted Mariners
>   Who sail this shore,
> Ye patient, ye who labor,
>   Sitting at the sweeping oar,
> And see afar the flashing Sea-gulls play,
> On the free waters, and the glad bright day,
> Twine with his hand the spray,
>   From out your dreariness,
> I speak for I am yours
>   On these gray shores.[131]

Bayard Taylor's "The Waves" reminds one of both "The Sea-Fairies" and "The Mermaid":

>   Children are we
>   Of the restless sea,
> Swelling in anger or sparkling in glee;
>   We follow our race,
>   In shifting chase
> Over the boundless ocean-space!
> Who hath beheld where the race begun?

Who shall behold it run?
Who shall behold it run? [132]

From the beginning, Americans greatly admired Tennyson's light and airy lines to "Lilian," "Madeline," "Margaret," "Rosalind," and "Kate." Lowell might be said to have begun the American imitations of these feminine portraits, and from his beginning before 1842, they were never lacking in imitators. Stoddard's series of "Portraits" in his *Foot-Prints* are, everyone, echoes of Tennyson, and, strangely enough, Stoddard used Tennyson's names and gave to the different names the characteristics which Tennyson had given them.[133] "Kate" is

Light—as every Kate is light—
A fickle and coquetish thing:
Very changeable in mind,
Coy, inconstant as the wind,
Now a smile and then a pout,
Now a sigh and then a shout!
Passionate and loving—cold,
Gentle, and a blisterer bold;
Varying—take her every way,
Kate is like an April day;
Shades and brightness, sun and shower,
Everything within an hour.

In "Isabel"—the name of Tennyson's pensive portrait—Stoddard described a lady calm and dignified:

Very, very fair is she,
Flower of all the family.
Fair—but let the truth be told—
Isabel is somewhat cold.
Stately and reserved and nice,
Prim and studied and precise;
Very dignified in mien
Lofty—too much like a Queen.

Stoddard's "Portraits" are fitting examples of the scores of "laughing, prattling, sportive" Sallies, "dreamy-eyed" Lillyans, "hoping, fearing" Lily Lees, and "ever roving, ever loving" Cora Lyles that flitted through the pages of American gift-books and magazines in the eighteen-forties and fifties.[134] Few of the group had any literary merit, but they form one of the most reliable means for measuring Tennyson's influence, for Tennyson's feminine portraits are probably more distinctly his than any others of his shorter poems.

With all of these imitations of Tennyson, there grew up a sort of caricatured Tennysonian language. Imitators tended to copy especially Tennyson's eccentricities and mannerisms of speech. In making that point concerning William Ellery Channing, Poe wrote one of the best explanations of what was meant by "Tennysonisms" in diction. He listed compound epithets, the Biblical *eth* verbal ending, present tenses used as past, peculiarly used prepositions, and eccentric pronunciations. The imitators, said Poe, had adopted and exaggerated Tennyson's "characteristic defect, having mistaken it for his principal merit." [135] This defect, the *Literary World* called "the exquisitely far-fetched in poetic expressions," [136] and Cornelius C. Felton thought that Tennyson was the worst of men for Americans to copy for "with much genius and an exquisite ear for musical rhythm, [he] has also a Titanian fondness for quaint and dainty expressions, affected turns, and mawkishly effeminate sentiment; and . . . would be the worst model, therefore, not only for a young poet to imitate, but even to read; so contagious are the vices of his manner." [137]

Probably Lowell was reprimanded for his "Tennysonism" more than any other American poet of the period, but it was the obscure and little noticed versifiers who bore the stamp of Tennyson most clearly. It would be difficult to imagine a book's being more Tennysonian than Mulchinock's *Ballads and Songs,* Hirst's *The Coming of the Mammoth and Other Poems,* or William Wallace's *Meditations in America and Other Poems.* Even a casual glance through these books will show Tennyson's mannerisms, exaggerated and perverted, on almost every page. The work of Taylor, Stoddard, Story, Read, or Timrod was above these, but they exhibited much "Tennysonism." When reviewers used their coined words, "Tennysonism" and "Tennysonianism," they usually referred to matters of language, but, as has been seen, the most Tennysonian poets of America showed their "Tennysonism" in almost every conceivable way.

IV

Several Americans came to know Tennyson personally during the years in which he was becoming a celebrity. Literary Americans, and many who were not literary, journeyed to England with their predominant aim the meeting of famous English literary figures. Since Tennyson lived a rather secluded life and since he had a distaste for Americans collectively, American travelers had much difficulty gaining an audience with him unless they were well armed with letters of introduction. This inaccessibility of Tennyson made him, all the more, prize game for the celebrity-seekers and in turn led to the annoyances which Tennyson suffered from Americans in later years when, armed with spy-glasses, tourists tracked him to his most secluded haunts, and New York reporters, notebook in hand, climbed the trees in his garden to overhear his conversation.

Thomas B. Read wrote in 1860 of a Boston artist who had remained in London for months trying in vain to get Tennyson and Carlyle to sit for portraits.[138] Read himself went to London several times in the eighteen-fifties for the purpose of painting Tennyson's portrait, and it was with the greatest difficulty that he finally gained his end.[139] On one visit, Read wrote, Tennyson talked "so disrespectfully" of America that he was on the verge of "letting him [Tennyson] alone severely." [140]

Tennyson took no pains to hide his poor opinion of America. James Fenimore Cooper, one of the first Americans with whom he came in contact, stirred his resentment,[141] as Cooper had stirred that of most Englishmen, and Tennyson shared the general English feeling that Americans were uncultured. When in 1858 Americans wanted to buy Thomas Woolner's bust of him, Tennyson blocked the trade with specific instructions to Woolner not to let it go to America,[142] and Tennyson is said to have remarked years later that the only thing he ever wanted to see in America was the grave of Edgar Allan Poe.[143] Nevertheless, the little noticed poem of 1852, "Hands All Round," toasted England's "gigantic daughter of the West," [144] and Tennyson's feeling was more kindly to Americans individually than to them collectively. To American poets who visited him he was quite cordial.[145]

One of the first Americans to share Tennyson's hospitality was Emerson. On his second visit to England in 1848, Emerson met Tennyson at the home of Coventry Patmore and later visited Tennyson in his own house. Emerson has graphically described his first impression of Tennyson:

> I was contented with him, at once. He is tall, scholastic-looking, no dandy, but a great deal of plain strength about him, and though cultivated, quite unaffected; quiet, sluggish sense and strength, refined, as all English are, and good-humored. . . . There is in him an air of general superiority, that is very satisfactory. He lives very much with his college set,—Spedding, Brookfield, Hallam, Rice, and the rest,—and has the air of one who is accustomed to be petted and indulged by those he lives with, like George Bradford. Take away Hawthorne's bashfulness, and let him talk easily and fast, and you would have a pretty good Tennyson.

Neither at Coventry Patmore's nor at Tennyson's home did Emerson have much opportunity to talk with Tennyson; therefore, Emerson was eagerly anticipating another visit as he passed through London again a month later, but then Tennyson was in Ireland.[146]

No American enjoyed a more pleasant visit with Tennyson in the eighteen-fifties than the Massachusetts poet, Frederick Goddard Tuckerman. During the three days which Tuckerman spent in Tennyson's home, Farringford, on the Isle of Wight, in January, 1855, he and Tennyson had long and interesting talks in Tennyson's little smoking attic.[147] Tennyson recited his poems, and the two discussed them together. As a farewell gift, Tennyson gave Tuckerman the original manuscript of "Locksley Hall," an act which Tuckerman spoke of as "a favour of which I may be justly proud, as he says he has never done such a thing in his life before, for anybody." [148] Several letters and gifts passed between Tennyson and Tuckerman following the visit,[149] and upon hearing of Tuckerman's death in 1873, Mrs. Tennyson wrote of him to his sister, "He must ever retain one of the foremost places among American guests who have done honour to their country and whom it is good for us to have known." [150]

In June, 1857, Bayard Taylor made the first of his series of visits to Tennyson. Thackeray had written a letter of introduction for him, and Tennyson received him cordially. Taylor spent two days at Farringford. He and Tennyson took a long walk along the chalk cliffs of the island, and they talked pleasantly together for many hours. In a letter to George H. Boker, Taylor described his visit:

We smoked many a pipe together, and talked of poetry, religion, politics, and geology. I thought he seemed gratified with his American fame; he certainly did not say an unkind word about us. He had read my Oriental poems and liked them. He spoke particularly of their imagery and conscientious finish. I need not tell you that his verdict is a valuable one to me. Our intercourse was most cordial and unrestrained, and he asked me, at parting, to be sure and visit him every time I came to England. His wife is one of the best women I ever met with, and his two little boys, Hallam and Lionel, are real cherubs of children.

Taylor was particularly impressed by "the delightful family circle." He thought that Tennyson was "fortunate and happy in his family relations" and that "with his large and liberal nature, his sympathies for what is true and noble in humanity, and his depth and tenderness of feeling," he deserved to be so.[151]

Many American travelers were overjoyed to get a mere glimpse of Tennyson. One saw in Cheltenham "a very remarkable looking man . . . whose expression seemed entirely unlike anything he had seen in England, in its ideality and intensity." The American did not know who the man was, but when later he learned that Tennyson was at Cheltenham at that precise time, he was "quite sure" that he had seen the great poet and was delighted.[152] The vivacious and effusive Madame Octavia Walton LeVert of Mobile, Alabama, fluttered over meeting Tennyson at a reception. He had, she thought, a "poetic face, over which lingers a soft shade of sadness."[153] Hawthorne saw Tennyson momentarily at a Manchester arts exhibition in 1857 and was overjoyed to have seen him.[154] Hawthorne ran to get his wife so that she, too, might see Tennyson, and together they feasted their eyes upon "this one poet of our day," but they never met him.

The record which Hawthorne has left of his fleeting glimpse of Tennyson is interesting. He thought Tennyson "the most picturesque figure, without affectation" that he had ever seen:

He seemed as if he did not see the crowd nor think of them, but as if he defended himself from them by ignoring them altogether; nor did anybody but myself cast a glance at him. . . . There was an entire absence of stiffness in his figure; no set-up in him at all; no nicety or trimness; and if there had been it would have spoilt his whole aspect. Gazing at him with all my eyes, I liked him well, and rejoiced more in him than in all the other wonders of the exhibition.

Hawthorne also heard Tennyson's voice, "a bass voice, but not of resounding depth; a voice rather broken as it were, and ragged about the edges, but pleasant to the ear." In his greeting of friends, Tennyson "betrayed his shy and secluded habits," and Hawthorne "was indescribably sensible of a morbid painfulness in him, a something not to be meddled with." Hawthorne wished to see more of Tennyson, would have liked to "smoke a cigar with him," but was much too shy to seek an introduction. When James T. Fields later told Tennyson of the incident, Tennyson regretted that Hawthorne had not introduced himself. "I am sure," said Tennyson, "I should have been glad to meet a man like Hawthorne anywhere." [155]

Emerson, Tuckerman, Taylor—these began the long procession of American literati who in later years visited Tennyson and enjoyed talking with him and hearing him recite his poems. Fields, Longfellow, Lowell, Holmes, and scores of others formed the procession and were cordially received. As Tennyson wrote Thackeray in reply to Thackeray's letter introducing Bayard Taylor, ". . . my 'castle' was never yet 'barricaded & entrenched' against good fellows." [156] With few exceptions the American literary figures proved "good fellows." Many of them confessed that they approached Farringford and Aldworth, Tennyson's later home, as pilgrims to the shrine of the first poet of their time.

Chapter VI

THE DIVIDED REACTION TO *MAUD, AND OTHER POEMS*

THE FIRST VOLUME OF POEMS WHICH TENNYSON PUBLISHED after his becoming Poet Laureate did little to strengthen his position as the grand representative of the age. *Putnam's Magazine* noted a strong public sentiment that in the title-poem, "Maud," Tennyson was "recreant to the hope and humanity of the age." [1] Nevertheless, the volume, *Maud, and Other Poems,* received superlative praise in several quarters. Thomas R. Lounsbury, as a student at Yale, wrote in 1858 that "no work, published within the last twenty years, has been the subject of more contradictory opinions than the Maud of Tennyson." [2] Few criticisms of the poem were moderate: the critics were either strong in approval or harsh in disapproval.

Through an arrangement with Tennyson, Ticknor and Fields received proof sheets of *Maud, and Other Poems* nearly two months before the publication of the English edition.[3] Ticknor and Fields announced their edition as "in press" as early as June 15, 1855,[4] and on July 31, the Boston *Daily Evening Transcript* announced that the book would be published "in advance of its appearance in England, in a few days." Apparently, Ticknor and Fields planned to get ahead of the London publisher, but they missed that by several days. On August 2, Edward Moxon advertised his edition in the London *Times* as "just published," and Ticknor and Fields's long expected edition was finally issued on August 18.[5]

Several days before the official date of publication, Ticknor and Fields sent advance sheets of the poems to several of their friends and reviewers.[6] The Boston *Daily Evening Transcript* reviewed the book on July 31 "from leaves in the rough proof." Bayard Taylor received the book in some form by August 6 for review in the New York *Tribune*,[7] and extracts from, and fragmentary descriptions of, the poems were floating about in newspapers and magazines weeks before the book appeared.[8] Referring to the wide publicity which it had already received, Bayard Taylor assured James T. Fields on August 6 that the book would "sell immensely." [9]

The first American edition numbered three thousand copies, and there is ample proof that it sold well.[10] Within less than a month of the first publication, two thousand more copies were printed, and by March, 1856, two more new impressions had been issued. The poems of *Maud, and Other Poems* were included in Ticknor and Fields's one- and two-volume editions of *Poems* in 1856, and in all of their later editions of complete *Poems.* The poems as published in 1855 underwent only one significant revision—that of the third London edition of 1856 in which several additions were made to "Maud." This final text of the poems appeared in America first in Ticknor and Fields's "Blue and Gold" pocket edition of *Poetical Works* in 1857.

Maud, and Other Poems consisted of eight poems: "Maud," "The Brook," "The Letters," "Ode on the Death of the Duke of Wellington," "The Daisy," "To the Rev. F. D. Maurice," "Will," and "The Charge of the Light Brigade." The "Ode on the Death of the Duke of Wellington" and "The Charge of the Light Brigade" had appeared earlier,[11] and numerous magazines and newspapers had already presented them to the American public.[12] Both appeared in *Maud, and Other Poems* greatly revised. Also, the title-poem was not entirely new. Tennyson had contributed to a London annual, *The Tribute,* in 1837 some "Stanzas" ["Oh! that 'twere possible"] which formed the nucleus of "Maud." [13] Much revised, the "Stanzas" became Section XXIV of "Maud" as it appeared in 1855. A portion of the "Stanzas" had appeared in America in 1845 when Charles Astor Bristed, then a student at Cambridge University, sent them to the *Knickerbocker,*[14] from which they were copied by several other magazines and newspapers.[15] In its unfavorable review of *Maud, and Other Poems,* the *Knickerbocker* proudly remembered that "the very best thing in the volume" had appeared in its pages ten years earlier, and regretted that in spite of that kernel of excellence, the book would not increase the number of Tennyson's admirers in America.[16]

II

It is doubtless true that "Maud" tended to diminish rather than to increase the number of Tennyson's admirers, but many of his most enthusiastic admirers greeted the new poem with even greater applause than that which they had accorded earlier works. Both the Boston *Daily Evening Transcript* and the New York *Daily Tribune* in their early reviews (July 31, August 7, 1855) were laudatory. Noting that "Maud" contained "lines of great power and beauty," the *Transcript* quoted many of the "most beautiful passages" to show Tennyson's exquisite fancy and striking originality. And the *Tribune* gave the poem higher praise than it had accorded *In Memoriam:*

> Tennyson has been silent too long. . . . But his tongue has lost nothing of its strange enchantment. He yet speaks in those weird and mystic tones which weave a resistless spell around the imagination, even when they fail to present a lucid concep-

tion to the intellect. The poem which gives its name to this volume is a deep rhythmical tragedy. Over the whole scene rests a somber, lurid light, relieved at intervals by bursts of tender rapture, but not sufficient to overcome the prevailing blood-red tone of the representation. In keeping with the rapid transitions of sentiment, the verse often changes from extreme ruggedness of diction to a soft and liquid flow of exquisite sweetness and grace, preserving the measure from monotony and the reader from satiety. None of Tennyson's former poems are more elaborately constructed, or show more of the dainty artifices of composition, in which he takes such a genial delight. Some of these peculiarities are indulged in to excess, creating a conspicuous mannerism, especially in the use of sonorous alliterations, and the sudden contrasts between an almost prosaic homeliness of expression, and language of singularly rich and melting melody.

Tennyson's American admirers who had praised his early poems so highly gave "Maud" its highest praise. They saw in it a return to the melody and pure music of the earlier period. Several who had deplored Tennyson's change in *In Memoriam* praised "Maud" highly. Lowell thought "Maud" "wonderfully fine—the antiphonal voice to 'In Memoriam.' " He "tried to read it aloud, but broke down in the middle in a subdued passion of tears." [17] Years later Lowell pronounced "Maud" the "strongest and most characteristic" of Tennyson's poems.[18] Emerson, too, gave high praise: "When I read 'Maud' then I say, Here is one of those English heads again such as in the Elizabethan days were rammed full of delightful fancies. What colouring like Titian, colour like the dawn." [19] And Edward Everett Hale, writing for the *North American Review* its first review of Tennyson, called "Maud" a "charming rosary, strung of beads, very unlike one another, of playful or sad, or meditative poetry, always poetry, and always natural, fresh, true, and new." [20]

A little group of Tennyson's admirers gained their first impressions of "Maud" during a pleasant afternoon in beautiful Lawton's Valley, near Newport, Rhode Island. Longfellow, George William Curtis, Thomas Gold Appleton (Longfellow's brother-in-law), and Julia Ward Howe were of the party. Appleton wrote, "We are all charmed with Tennyson's new poem," [21] and Longfellow described the afternoon in his journal:

> We all went to pass the afternoon in Lawton's Valley with the Howes. Strolled down into the deep green gorge by the mill-stream, and seated by the ruins of the old mill, Curtis read to us Tennyson's new poem, Maud. Very beautiful, though there is in parts a spirit of ferocity which I do not like. But the loves of the hero and heroine are exquisitely drawn, and the songs delicious.[22]

Julia Ward Howe also pleasantly remembered the reading:

> Tennyson has a marvelous feeling for the music of words and phrases. You feel their music even apart from their sense. And I shall always hear the murmur of running water through the lines, when I read them again. How perfect an accompaniment the brook made to the poem. . . .[23]

Several reviewers noted in "Maud" a return to Tennyson's earlier manner. Finding "traces of an earlier and youthful treatment in 'Maud,' " *Putnam's Magazine* wrote, "The subtle melody, the dainty word-choosing, and the sonorous alliteration, belong to a youthful period, and a youth which we hope may be immortal." [24] And the *Knickerbocker* thought that the echoes of "Tennyson's earlier muse" formed the poem's only merit.[25]

These traces of melodious music were found especially in the songs, the only portion of "Maud" to receive consistent praise. They were published again and again as extracts in newspapers and magazines, and American musical settings for "Come into the Garden, Maud" and "Go Not, Happy Day" appeared almost immediately after their publication. In reviewing J. C. D. Parker's popular setting for

"Come into the Garden, Maud," *Dwight's Journal of Music* praised the song more than the setting:

It was rather a dangerous matter, to attempt to render Tennyson's dainty verses into music. Because the words are perfect *without* music; or rather they *are* music; and because this dainty poet has the daintiest admirers, and who can so catch his tone, his spirit as to hope to suit these? We only wonder therefore that the composer has succeeded so well.[26]

Several reviewers refused to quote "Come into the Garden, Maud," on the grounds that it was too well known,[27] and they were unanimous in praise of it. In its extremely unfavorable review of "Maud," the *Southern Literary Messenger* considered the song "proof that Tennyson has not lost the gift of poesy," [28] and the New York *Daily Times* thought that the songs constituted the greatest beauties of the poem: "Birds in the High Hall-garden" was a "charming lyric of quaint simplicity," and "Come into the Garden, Maud" was "not surpassed by any of Mr. Tennyson's previous efforts." [29]

Frederick Goddard Tuckerman and George William Curtis praised the lyric quality of "Maud." Doubtless thinking of its extreme irregularity of versification, Tuckerman wrote, ". . . it seems to me that only poets can fully appreciate and enjoy the singular beauty of 'Maud' "; [30] and Curtis declared that because of its music "Maud" had become "already a household word":

Tennyson's diocese is large, and is composed of those who have a sensitive appreciation of the subtlest charm of poetry. . . . Now comes "Maud," a passionate love poem, full of burning social protest and indignation. It came in the summer, and young men and maidens hailed it as the best flower of the year. In lonely, pleasant places—in the shadow of hills, and on the sea-shore, the penetrant music of the poem made its way.[31]

Upon reading this article of Curtis's concerning the new poem which was "moving polite youth in the East," William Dean Howells was led to buy a copy of "Maud," the first poem of Tennyson's that he ever read, and thus, said Howells, "I first became acquainted with the poet who at once possessed himself of what was best worth having in me." [32] Writing years later, Howells described his sensations:

> Of course, "Maud" seemed to me the finest poem I had read, up to that time, . . . I did not like all parts of it equally well, and some parts of it seemed thin and poor (though I would not suffer myself to say so then), and they still seem so. But there were whole passages and spaces of it where divine and perfect beauty lifted me above life. I did not fully understand the poem then; I do not fully understand it now, but that did not and does not matter; for there is something in poetry that reaches the soul by other avenues than the intellect.

Intoxicated by "Maud," Howells sought other poems of Tennyson, and from that point, he said, "This great poet opened to me a whole world of thinking and feeling, where I had my being with him in that mystic intimacy which cannot be put into words." [33]

Very soon after the publication of "Maud" it became clear that the poem was to receive some of the harshest criticism that had ever been dealt out to Tennyson, and his supporters began to square off for the battle. The Boston *Daily Evening Transcript* wrote, "It has been very severely handled in many quarters, but we are not disposed on that account to abate our admiration of the poem in any particular. . . . Maud is eminently a favorite of ours." [34] And the Editor of the Easy Chair, noting that the public had labeled the poem "a failure," staunchly held his ground, "We sit in our Chair and believe in 'Maud' still." [35]

"Maud" took Tennyson's readers by surprise. Accustomed to his tranquil unconcern about social and political matters, they were astonished by this violent arraignment of contemporary society. Apparently, most readers failed to dissociate the hero of "Maud" from the author, and this failure led to their attributing the actions and thoughts of a man on the verge of insanity to Tennyson himself.

With the single exception of the songs, every portion and every quality of "Maud" received severe handling from some quarter. The plot was "fevered and forced," lacking both coherence and truth.[36] In both plot and versification, the poem was "a bungling hotch-potch." [37] The characters, "too shadowily defined," were both unnatural and "diseased." [38] The style was "harsh and hard," lacking "the sensuousness, the harmony, the satisfying completeness and rounded grace, so characteristic of Tennyson in his ordinary poetic moods." [39] The tone was too morbid and melancholy. The poem should have been named not "Maud" but "Maudlin." [40] It presented a "false view of life, its obligations, and its duties." [41] The "whole sentiment of the poem" ignored "the nobler and purer feelings of humanity." The hero of the poem lived "his life of selfish desire and selfish enjoyment . . . without one thought of anything better, nobler than himself—the summit of creation": he worshiped nothing; he reverenced nothing.[42]

The religious periodicals unanimously condemned the "distrustful, irreligious character" of "Maud." The *Christian Examiner* declared, "Notwithstanding some clever points made by Mr. Tennyson, enough that is puerile, distempered, and audacious goes philandering and blustering through the pages of 'Maud' to thin very seriously the bays of the English Laureate." [43] The *Theological and Literary Journal* of New York thought that "Maud" tended to "debase the morals" and "pervert and degrade" the taste of young readers.[44] And the *Ladies' Repository,* a "monthly periodical devoted to literature and religion," after a long account of its former pleasures in reading Tennyson and its faithfulness to him, expressed its keen disappointment in "Maud":

> How our own heart leaped for joy when it learned that "Maud" was in press, and how eagerly we seized the first volume which came to the booksellers' shelves. Alas! the remembrance of its impression is painful—is very unpleasant; and now that it is announced another volume is soon to be given us [*Idylls of the King*], we know not whether to look forward hopefully or to anticipate another tribute to the "spirit of the age," which gloats over tales of war and incidents of the horrible kind.[45]

Various uncomplimentary definitions were coined for "Maud" by its critics. The *Albion* called it "a morbid, misanthropical, autobiographical, episodical tale, relieved by gushes of genuine and exquisite poetry." [46] Liking the *Albion's* definition, the *Home Journal* (September 15, 1855) quoted it as "a gem of a little deep-souled sentence" and continued its own denunciation of "Maud" by assuring its readers that "our New York poet Stoddard (who is the most like what the critics represent Tennyson to be) would write you a hundred times better volume of poems, for a hundred dollars in six days." The *Southern Literary Messenger* called "Maud" "a morbid, splenetic, fragmentary effusion, in which false philosophy is embodied in vicious verse—quite unworthy in all respects of Mr. Tennyson." The *Messenger's* reviewer, possibly its editor, John R. Thompson, could not believe that the poem was "favorably regarded even by Tennyson himself."

No known review of "Maud," American or British, was more severe than that in the *Southern Literary Messenger:*

> If this extraordinary compound of mysticism and misanthropy had not appeared with the name of the English Laureate on the title page, we should have been certain that it had its origin in one of two exceptional conditions of the mind—either that it came from some unhappy lunatic, whose poetic faculty had been disordered and now vibrated discordantly, "like sweet

bells jangled, out of tune and harsh," or that it was the production of some wag, who designed an attempt on the critics by endeavoring to palm off nonsense on them for profound philosophy. Though occasionally we discover a passage of genuine and exquisite poetry, worthy of the author of Locksley Hall, the stuff so greatly preponderates, that we are tempted one hundred and odd times (there being so many pages in Ticknor and Field's [*sic*], edition of it) before getting at the conclusion, to throw Maud out of the window and take to some more sensible and healthful reading. And the reader is the more provoked with the performance, because he is left in a painful state of indecision, after having accomplished its perusal, as to which deserves the greater amount of censure, the story itself, or the manner in which it is told.[47]

The year that *Maud, and Other Poems* was published, 1855, saw also the publication of Longfellow's *Hiawatha* and Whitman's *Leaves of Grass*. To these two American volumes, Tennyson's was frequently compared, usually to its disadvantage. In one of his anonymous reviews of his own works, Walt Whitman reviewed the *Leaves of Grass* and *Maud, and Other Poems* side by side, contrasting them to the disparagement of the latter. Tennyson, he said, was the poet of aristocracy, while Whitman was the poet of democracy. The one harmonized with and represented English life: Tennyson's poems were "a natural growth" of the "present phases of high life in Great Britain." But the other represented America, as Tennyson could not, for "what very properly fits a subject of the British crown may fit very ill an American freeman":

He [Tennyson] is the bard of ennui and of the aristocracy and their combination into love. This love is the old stock love of playwrights and romancers, Shakspeare the same as the rest. It is possessed of the same unnatural and shocking passion for some girl or woman, that wrenches it from its manhood, emasculated and impotent, without strength to hold the rest of the objects and goods of life in their proper positions. It seeks nature for sickly uses. It goes screaming and weeping after the facts of the universe, in their calm beauty and equanimity, to note the occurrence of itself, and to sound the news, in connection with the charms of the neck, hair, or complexion of a particular female.

"Poetry, to Tennyson," said Whitman, "is a gentleman of the first degree, boating, fishing and shooting genteelly through nature, admiring the ladies, and talking to them in company with that elaborate, half-choked deference that is to be made up by the terrible license of men among themselves." Tennyson's "effusions" were filled "from top to toe" with the "spirit of the burnished society of upper class England." Whitman never got around to specific mention of "Maud" or any other poem in the volume, but he closed his estimate of Tennyson with the significant admission, "It remains to be distinctly admitted that this man is a real poet, notwithstanding his ennui and his aristocracy." [48]

One periodical reviewed *Maud, and Other Poems* and *Leaves of Grass* together under the title, "The Assembly of Extremes." The reviewer found in the two books, apparently so "unlike, at first thought," the "most striking likenesses." The one was "refined in its Art . . . delicate in its structure, and consummate in its subtlety of expression"; while the other was "rough and rude" in comparison. But both were morbid, and both were "defiant of laws which attempt to regulate forms, and those which *should* regulate essences":

Maud is irreligious through mental disease, produced by excess of sentimental action—"Leaves of Grass," through irregularly-developed mental action and insufficiency of sentiment. A calmer perception of Nature would have corrected in Tennyson that feeling which looks upon sorrow as the only thing poetic, and serenity and holy trust, as things to which Love has no alliance, while a higher seeing of Nature would have shown Walt Whitman that all things in Nature are not alike beautiful.[49]

In the comparisons of *Hiawatha* and *Maud, and Other Poems,* more dissimilarity than similarity was pointed out.

Soon after the publication of *Maud, and Other Poems,* Tennyson received an anonymous letter which he enjoyed repeating:

> Sir—I used to worship you, but now I hate you. I loathe and detest you. You beast! So you've taken to imitating Longfellow.
>
> Yours in aversion,[50]

But most critics saw no such similarity. The tendency to disparage Tennyson in favor of Longfellow was particularly evident in comparisons of *Hiawatha* and "Maud." The *Home Journal* (March 8, 1856) pronounced *Hiawatha* far superior to "Maud." O. Prescott Hiller of Boston contrasted in his travel book the "feeble praise" given "Maud" and what he termed the "universal admiration" accorded *Hiawatha,* and concluded that Longfellow was the greater poet.[51] And Charles Eliot Norton wrote that "no two poems could be more in contrast" than these. Portions of "Maud," Norton thought, were "of most exquisite and touching beauty," but "as a whole," it was a "sad, morbid, painful picture of a man's mind." [52]

Graham's Magazine drew a contrast of a different sort. "Maud," it said, was much the superior poem. While Longfellow was dabbling with "the sequestered romance of savage life," Tennyson was dealing with "the great war and ways of the world, with all its hypocrisies, rogueries and falsehoods." An "earnest and bitter piece of mundane philosophy," "Maud" exemplified the fact that British poets wrote "of passing questions and historical events with more directness and earnestness" than did the American. "Even Tennyson, who [had] always lived so much in a quaint region of his own, between Fairy Land and the Georgian Era," was now coming out upon the field of action and reality. The "emphatic war-note" in "Maud," with its appeal for "war on the most deadly scale, rather than the cheateries and rascalities of social life," was highly commendable: "We are sorry it is not an American poet who sings in that fine frenzy." [53]

Americans' love for Tennyson was strikingly shown in the attitude of his admirers who were disappointed in "Maud." In his letter to Fields, Bayard Taylor tried hard to conceal his disappointment: there were "delicious things in the book"; it was "not an advance on Tennyson's former books, neither a falling off, and perhaps we should not ask more." [54] Stoddard had to confess that he wished Tennyson had not written "Maud." [55] But others devised ingenious apologies. Stedman explained, "He wrote it in a hurry, and published it, because the English people were expecting something of him, and *no poet writes well to order.*" [56] Edward Everett Hale disliked the closing stanzas glorifying war, but he could account for them. The greater part of "Maud," he said, must have been written years earlier. Then as time passed and a poem was needed, Tennyson drew it out again, and saw in it some exquisite passages: " 'Certainly they are worth publishing,' we imagine him saying to himself;—and so there is hurried on a clumsy postscript about the Russian war, and the whole is sent to press." [57]

Though not nearly so favorable, Americans' reception of "Maud" resembled their reaction to *The Princess* in their determination to accept the poem for what it was. The Editor of the Easy Chair declared, "We thought 'Maud' a lovely poem, and did not think it necessary to state that it was not 'Paradise Lost,' nor anything else which it was not." [58] In the face of the stupid criticisms, Tennyson, thought Curtis, must be "feeling very much as a rose would feel if it were wondered whether a rose could ever be a dahlia." [59] Hale rather angrily questioned the harsh critics. After describing the beautiful music and imagery of the poem, he asked,

Have we—if we study our rights carefully,—have we any right to ask more than this? Has any one promised us that "Maud" shall have a beginning, middle, and end? Has any one promised us that it should have a finished *denouement?*

"For ourselves," Hale concluded, "we are gratified with what we have; and will not complain that we have no more." [60]

This attitude had characterized all of the American criticism of Tennyson, and it was distinctly American. The British critics never treated Tennyson thus. They had refused to give *The Princess* such a hearing, and they refused again with "Maud." [61] The American reception of "Maud" seems to have been more favorable than the British. In fact, of reviews in the most prominent American periodicals the favorable outnumbered the unfavorable almost two to one. The same could hardly be said of the British.[62]

"Maud" is frequently referred to as the most persecuted of Tennyson's major poems.[63] Tennyson thought of it so, and he received many consoling messages from his friends. Among the comforters were James T. Fields and Frederick Goddard Tuckerman. Fields wrote his regrets for the "stupid" criticisms,[64] and Tuckerman reassured Tennyson that they would not affect his fame:

The newspapers are loud, but the poet holds it ["Maud"] to his heart in silence. I have seen the attack in *Blackwood,* . . . [It is] strange that people because they cannot appreciate or rightly understand a subject, abuse the treatment of it, which may be (and in this case is) wholly in keeping. . . . As for affecting your fame however or influencing the motions of the masses by a magazine article, a man might as well stand upon the sea-shore in a flood-tide and attempt to put the waves back with a pitchfork. . . .[65]

Tuckerman's description of the irresistible advance of Tennyson's fame proved true, but for years to come, some of Tennyson's most enthusiastic supporters omitted from their strong approval of his work the one poem, "Maud."

III

Reviewers of *Maud, and Other Poems* gave nearly all of their attention to the title-poem, with only brief glances at the other poems in the volume. The "Ode on the Death of the Duke of Wellington" and "The Charge of the Light Brigade," however, had occasioned some discussion before *Maud, and Other Poems* appeared. The original 1852 version of the "Ode" was rather hostilely received by the British periodicals,[66] and the American, taking their cue from the British, reviewed it harshly too. The American periodicals usually contented themselves with reprinting the British reviews, but in rare instances they wrote original opinions. The *Southern Literary Gazette* thought that the "Ode" was "marked by a studied plainness of language which in some passages degenerates into prosaism—a fault not often attributable to the author of the Princess."[67] The Boston *Daily Evening Transcript* (December 4, 1852) thought the passage concerning Admiral Nelson "in an odd style for a funeral ode." Many lines in the poem, said the *Transcript,* "certainly would be called doggerel" if anyone but Tennyson had written them: the "Ode" would not "add much to Mr. Tennyson's poetical reputation." Nevertheless, American reviewers found some things to their liking. The *Southern Literary Gazette,* along with its condemnation, noted several "suggestive felicities of expression" worthy of Tennyson. *To-Day: A Boston Literary Journal,* probably referring to the death of Zachary Taylor on July 9, 1850, thought the "Ode" of special interest to Americans because it was "not inappropriate to the loss which our own nation has recently sustained."[68] And *Putnam's Magazine* came to Tennyson's defense:

> . . . the almost unvarying opinion of the critics is, that it [the "Ode"] is not equal to the occasion. But who ever wrote an oc-

casional ode or an occasional oration that took the palm? Occasions are only golden moments to mediocrities. Your man of genius must take his own time and way of doing things. Yet there are passages in Tennyson's Ode, that relish of the butt of Canary, which is his laureate salary.[69]

The original version of "The Charge of the Light Brigade" was criticized even more severely by the British press than that of the "Ode" had been, but Americans liked the poem from the beginning. Several weeks before its publication, the London correspondent of the New York *Daily Tribune,* having heard rumors that Tennyson was to write some war poems in praise of English valor, feared that Tennyson was not equal to the task:

England wants a poet who shall attend her in the great struggle that she has just entered upon. But Tennyson is not the man. His mind dwells in a region too serene. He cannot set the blood dancing, and make the soul rush to arms. He is not a voice to be heard above the raging of the storm. He cannot stir the wild Beast of Passion in the blood; and he lacks the fire that shall make it leap, like lightning, from its lair. He is a Poet of Peace, not of War.

Then, when "The Charge of the Light Brigade" appeared, the *Tribune* reprinted the "thrilling lyric" as a "splendid refutation" of its correspondent's statement.[70]

Apparently, the only significant objections raised by Americans to the poem concerned its subject-matter, the commemoration of a disasterous charge of the British cavalry in the Battle of Balaclava, October 25, 1854, in the Crimean War. In a general condemnation of occasional poems, William J. Grayson wrote that "even Tennyson could make nothing of Balaklava's celebrated charge of the six hundred"; [71] and *Graham's Magazine* felt that "a bloody blunder—an insane and ghastly charge proving the disgraceful generalship of the British leaders" was a poor subject for poetry.[72] Frederick G. Tuckerman told Tennyson of his objection to the line "Someone had blunder'd," and others also disliked that line.[73]

The American periodicals which reprinted "The Charge of the Light Brigade" were highly pleased with it. They thought it a vigorous and stirring war lyric. The preface to the poem in *Peterson's Magazine* is typical:

> Tennyson, in the following poem, has proved that he can write in the bold, Homeric strain, demanded by such a theme, quite as well as in what has hitherto been considered his peculiar vein. No similar lyric in the language surpasses this. Campbell's "Battle of the Baltic" seems artificial beside its stern and terrible grandeur.[74]

The Boston *Daily Evening Transcript* printed just as high an estimate. It would "be at a loss to pick out of Tennyson's poems anything which stamps him more as a true poet than the 'Charge of the Light Brigade.'" Anyone whose heart did not "beat more bravely to this glowing strain," was not "made of the stuff that would have ridden with the 'Noble six hundred!'" [75]

In an attempt to placate the British critics, Tennyson almost re-wrote the poem for its inclusion in *Maud, and Other Poems*. The line, "Someone had blunder'd," was deleted, and the poem was considerably shortened.[76] This new version, the American periodicals considered greatly inferior to the original. *Peterson's Magazine* thought the poem had been "spoiled," and the New York *Daily Times* referred to it as "completely emasculated and deprived of all that rough vigor which palpitated in every verse on its first appearance." [77]

Except for "The Brook," the remaining poems of *Maud, and Other Poems* received little more than what might be termed perfunctory praise. "The Brook," however, gave reviewers genuine pleasure. Hale spoke of it as "a charming little idyl." [78] Another, comparing it to "The Gardener's Daughter," declared it "a triumph both of the Tennysonian blank verse, which is as marked as the Miltonic, and of the Tennysonian melody." [79] And in his disappointment with "Maud," Stedman thought that "The Brook" redeemed the whole volume.[80] With its narrative blank verse and its little rimed song, "I Come from Haunts of Coot and Hern," "The Brook" was as characteristically Tennysonian as anything in the volume and was, naturally, admired by the lovers of the orthodox Tennyson. It represented better than any other poem in the volume the kind of Tennysonian poetry which was destined to give Tennyson his tremendous popularity among the educated and uneducated alike in the years just ahead.

CONCLUSION: A LOOK AHEAD

THE YEAR 1859, WITH THE PUBLICATION OF THE FIRST OF the *Idylls of the King,* ushered in a new era in the reputation of Tennyson. One must not assume for a moment that the cool reception given "Maud" marked the beginning of a reaction against Tennyson. With the coming of the *Idylls,* Tennyson's fame reached heights which it had never before known. Bayard Taylor wrote that after the publication of the first *Idylls,* it became almost "a heresy" to question Tennyson's absolute perfection.[1] And Longfellow wrote of the reception of the *Idylls,* "I believe there is no discordant voice on this side of the water." [2]

With the coming of the *Idylls* and the tremendous applause with which they were greeted, Tennyson's reputation in America became more nearly parallel with that in Great Britain than it had been in the earlier period. Criticisms were less distinctly American. Doubtless the critics were arriving at their estimates as independently as they had earlier, but the trend toward uniformity was the natural result of the nearer approach to the acme of acclaim.

From 1859 Tennyson began to assume more than ever before his position as the people's poet. Previously he had been read and admired most by the intellectuals. *In Memoriam* and "Maud" could not be called popular poems. But such poems as the *Idylls* and the tremendously popular *Enoch Arden* were. Ticknor and Fields sold eleven thousand copies of their first edition of the *Idylls* within the first month after its publication, and the editions of *Enoch Arden* were too numerous and their sale too rapid for accurate recording.[3] Professor A. C. Bradley wrote in his essay, *The Reaction against Tennyson,* "It was the four *Idylls of the King* published in 1859 that opened to him the heart of the public and began that immense popularity which he never saw diminished." Tennyson's rise was somewhat contemporaneous with the "popular culture" movement for universal reading and universal education in America, and one American wrote in 1892, "As a force in the popular culture of the country Tennyson's influence has been greater than that of any other English poet." [4]

Throughout Tennyson's life, he received his greatest praise for the lyrical qualities of his poetry. He was the skillful metrist, the perfect poetic artist. Even in the midst of their highest praise of Tennyson, critics disparaged his inventive powers. He was, wrote a reviewer of *Tiresias, and Other Poems,* the decorator and not the architect.[5] His manner and not the matter counted for most. With the emphasis thus placed upon the lyrics, Tennyson's early poems retained their high relative position among his works, and when Americans thought of Tennyson, the poems of 1842 were among the first to come to their minds. Stedman wrote in 1875 of the 1842 *Poems,* "At the present day, were this volume to be lost, we possibly should be deprived of a larger specific variety of Tennyson's most admired poems than is contained in any other of his successive ventures." [6]

During the height of Tennyson's fame from 1859 to his death in 1892, the American criticisms did not consist entirely of praise. The apostate Lowell and other intellectuals reviewed harshly the simpler and more popular poems, and one American book of criticism in 1877 headed its chapter on Tennyson, "An Over-rated Poet." [7] The historical dramas received especially severe criticism. They were not dramatic, said some critics; they lacked unity and tragic power. Also, several reviewers professed to find in *Demeter and Other Poems* (1889) and the other later volumes signs of old age and failing genius. But these criticisms were but slight eddies in the steady flow of Tennyson's fame, which faltered little till after his death. Probably no poet who has ever lived enjoyed more fame during his lifetime than did Tennyson.

Soon after his death, however, the reaction began. Taylor had written in 1877, "There are, at present, signs of the beginnings of such a reaction, and we need not be surprised if (as in Byron's case) it should swing past the line of justice, and end by undervaluing, for a time, many of the poet's high and genuine qualities." [8] Taylor's prophecy has now been fulfilled, and possibly even now Tennyson's reputation has not reached its nadir, but the sinking gained little momentum till the close of the Victorian period. Hamilton W. Mabie wrote in the year of Tennyson's death that Tennyson then had more readers and admirers in America than in England and that he was considered by Americans the greatest of English poets.[9] Whether the reaction against Tennyson began earlier in England than in America is difficult to say, but on both sides of the Atlantic it came when to like Tennyson was to be mid-Victorian, and to be mid-Victorian was to be antiquated. Tennyson rose and fell with his age.

APPENDICES

Appendix A

AMERICAN EDITIONS OF TENNYSON'S POEMS, 1827–1858

In descriptions of the editions, references are given only for those facts which are not documented in the notes to the chapters. Information referred to as from the records of the Houghton Mifflin Company is taken from the detailed accounts of Ticknor's Tennyson editions prepared for me by the Houghton Mifflin Company and included in a communication of September 21, 1940. The company states that the information was gathered from Ticknor's "sheet stock records," "old cost book records," and annual sales catalogues. With each edition listed is given the name of a library which owns a copy. The Library of Congress is always named if a copy is there.

I. Complete Poems

POEMS. By Alfred Tennyson. In two volumes. Vol. I. [II.] Boston: William D. Ticknor. MDCCCXLII.

First American edition. Issued July 7, 1842. The edition consisted of from 1500 to 2000 copies. In size, contents, and collation, the edition was an exact reproduction of the London edition of 1842. For the contents of the volumes, see Wise, *op. cit.*, I, 80-86. The published price was $1.50. A copy is in the Harvard College Library.

Leaf: 6¾ x 4½ inches. *Pagination:* Vol. I: vii, 233 pages; Vol. II: vii, 231 pages.

POEMS. By Alfred Tennyson. In two volumes. Vol. I. [II.] Boston: William D. Ticknor and Co. MDCCCXLVI.

The poems included in this edition were the same as those of the 1842 edition. A copy is in the Library of Congress.

Leaf: 6¾ x 4½ inches. *Pagination:* Vol. I: vii, 231 pages; Vol. II: vii, 231 pages.

POEMS. By Alfred Tennyson. In two volumes. Vol. I. [II.] A New Edition, Enlarged. Boston: William D. Ticknor and Co. MDCCCXLVIII.

To the poems of the 1842 edition, this edition added "The Princess," from the first London edition of 1847. A copy is in the Princeton University Library. Many later impressions of this edition were issued: 1849 (Duke University Library), 1851 (Boston Public Library), 1852 (University of Virginia Library), 1853 (University of Pennsylvania Library). Of three 1849 impressions seen in the preparation of this work, one (Harvard College Library) had a portrait of Tennyson tipped in facing the title-page of Volume I and not included in the pagination. All later impressions seen contained the tipped in portrait.

Leaf: 7 x 4½ inches. *Pagination:* Vol. I: vii, 264 pages; Vol. II: vii, 278 pages.

POEMS. By Alfred Tennyson. In two volumes. Vol. I. [II.] A New Edition. Boston: Ticknor, Reed, and Fields. MDCCCLIV.

The contents of this edition differed from the contents of the 1848 edition only in variations in the text of "The Princess." The version of "The Princess" included in this edition was that of the fourth London edition. Previously, all American printings of "The Princess" had been from the first London edition. For variations between the two London editions, see Wise, *op. cit.*, I, 99–103. This was the first American edition to include the famous intercalary songs of "The Princess." Volume I contained a tipped in portrait of Tennyson opposite the title-page. A copy is in the Harvard College Library.

Leaf: 6¾ x 4½ inches. *Pagination:* Vol. I: vii, 264 pages; Vol. II: vii, 293 pages.

POEMS. By Alfred Tennyson. In two volumes. Vol. I. [II.] A New Edition. Boston: Ticknor and Fields. MDCCCLIV.

This edition added eight poems to the contents of the previous edition of the same year. Tennyson's dedication, "To the Queen," was prefaced to Volume I, and "The Sea-Fairies," "The Deserted House," "Edwin Morris; or, The Lake," "To ——, After Reading a Life and Letters," "To E. L., on His Travels in Greece," "Come Not, When I Am Dead," and "The Eagle" were inserted at the end of the first volume. A copy is in the Library of Congress. A later impression of this edition was issued with imprint 1855 (Harvard College Library). Volume I contained a portrait of Tennyson opposite the title-page.

Leaf: 7 x 4½ inches. *Pagination:* Vol. I: x, 280 pages; Vol. II: vii, 293 pages.

THE POETICAL WORKS OF ALFRED TENNYSON, POET LAUREATE. Complete in One Volume. Boston: Ticknor and Fields. MDCCCLVI.

This was the first of Ticknor and Fields's famous "Blue and Gold" pocket editions of the poets. In addition to the poems of the second 1854 edition, this edition contained "In Memoriam" and all of the poems of *Maud, and Other Poems* (see below). The version of "Maud" was that of the first London edition. The edition contained a portrait of Tennyson. The records of the Houghton Mifflin Company indicate that five impressions of this edition totaling 9200 copies were issued in 1856. Some impressions contained George S. Hillard's verses, "On Receiving a Copy of Tennyson's Poems." The published price was seventy-five cents. A copy is in the Harvard College Library.

Leaf: 5½ x 3⅜ inches. *Pagination:* vii, 518 pages. The blue binding and gold edges of the volume gave the edition its name.

POEMS. By Alfred Tennyson, Poet Laureate. In two volumes. Vol. I. [II.] A New Edition. Boston: Ticknor and Fields. MDCCCLVI.

This was advertised as the "Cabinet" edition. The poems included were the same as those of the first "Blue and Gold" edition. Printed in the front of Volume I was Tennyson's letter of March 18, 1856, to Ticknor and Fields expressing his wish that with them alone should rest the right of publishing his poems in America. Volume I contained opposite its title-page a portrait of Tennyson. A copy is in the Boston Public Library. A later impression of this edition was issued with the imprint 1857 (Library of Congress).

Leaf: 7⅛ x 4½ inches. *Pagination:* Vol. I: vii, 494 pages; Vol. II: vii, 448 pages.

THE POETICAL WORKS OF ALFRED TENNYSON, POET LAUREATE. Complete in One Volume. Boston: Ticknor and Fields. MDCCCLVII.

This was the second "Blue and Gold" pocket edition of Tennyson's poems. It contained a portrait of Tennyson and George

S. Hillard's poem, "On Receiving a copy of Tennyson's Poems." This edition differed from the first "Blue and Gold" edition only in variations in the texts of "The Princess" and "Maud." "The Princess" was reprinted from the fifth London edition, which represents the final text of the poem, and "Maud" was reprinted from the third London edition. For variations between these and former editions, see Wise, *op. cit.*, I, 102–03, 131–32. A copy is in the Harvard College Library. The records of the Houghton Mifflin Company list many impressions issued in 1857, 1858, 1859, and 1860. A copy bearing the imprint 1858 is in the University of Virginia Library.

Leaf: 5½ x 3⅜ inches. *Pagination:* vii, 524 pages.

II. Individual Works

THE PRINCESS; A MEDLEY. By Alfred Tennyson. Boston: William D. Ticknor and Co. MDCCCXLVIII.

First American Edition. Issued February 9, 1848. It was a reprint of the first London edition of *The Princess* (1847). The American edition differed slightly in size and pagination from the English. The published price was fifty cents. A copy is in the Library of Congress. References to later 1848 impressions of this edition have been seen.

Leaf: 7 x 4½ inches. *Pagination:* 168 pages.

THE PRINCESS; A MEDLEY. By Alfred Tennyson, Poet Laureate. A New Edition. Boston: Ticknor and Fields. MDCCCLV.

This edition was a reprint of the fourth London edition. For variations between the fourth and former editions, see Wise, *op. cit.*, I, 102. A copy is in the Boston Public Library.

Leaf: 7 x 4½ inches. *Pagination:* 151 pages.

IN MEMORIAM. Boston: Ticknor, Reed, and Fields. MDCCCL.

First American edition. Issued July 27, 1850. It was a reprint of the first London edition of 1850. The American edition differed slightly in size and pagination from the English. The fact that some copies bearing the imprint 1850 were printed by Metcalf & Co. of Cambridge, while others were printed by Hobart & Robbins of Boston, indicates that there were at least two separate impressions in 1850. The published price was seventy-five cents. Two copies are in the Library of Congress, one by each printer. Many later impressions of this edition were issued: 1851 (University of Pennyslvania Library), 1852 (Harvard College

Library), 1854 (Harvard College Library), 1855 (Yale University Library), and 1856 (Harvard College Library).

Leaf: 7⅛ x 4½ inches. *Pagination:* 216 pages.

MAUD, AND OTHER POEMS. By Alfred Tennyson, D. C. L., Poet Laureate. Boston: Ticknor and Fields: MDCCCLV.

First American edition. Issued August 18, 1855. The first impression consisted of 3000 copies. It was a reprint of the first London edition of 1855. The American edition differed slightly in size and pagination from the English. The volume contained eight poems: "Maud," "The Brook; an Idyl," "The Letters," "Ode on the Death of the Duke of Wellington," "The Daisy," "To the Rev. F. D. Maurice," "Will," and "The Charge of the Light Brigade." The published price was fifty cents. A copy is in the Library of Congress. The records of the Houghton Mifflin Company list two later impressions of the edition in 1855, the first of 2000 copies and the second of 2400 copies, and one impression of 1000 copies in 1856. A copy bearing the imprint 1856 is in the Library of Congress.

Leaf: 7 x 4½ inches. *Pagination:* 168 pages.

III. Sheet Music *

ASK ME NO MORE

Ask Me No More. Tennyson's celebrated song of the Coquette. Music by Harrison Millard. Boston. Published by Oliver Ditson, Washington St. [Four agents.] Copyright 1856 [deposited June 17]. Plate number: 8423. 5 pages, 13⅜ x 10 inches.

"To Miss Georgia E. Wood, N. York"

A copy is in the Library of Congress.

THE BEGGAR MAID

The Beggar Maid. Tennyson. Music by Thompson Lennig. Boston. Oliver Ditson. Without plate number. 5 pages (?), 14 x 10 inches.

No complete copy of this piece has been found. One sheet, pages 3 and 4, is in the Library of Congress. This is probably

* The dates doubtfully assigned to the undated sheets for which no copyright records have been found have been arrived at by use of the plate numbers, the addresses of the publisher, and the names and addresses of his agents. The assigning of these dates has been largely the work of Messrs. Herbert S. Smith and Everett B. Tewksbury of the Music Department of the Boston Public Library, whose assistance I gratefully acknowledge.

one of the earliest settings for Tennyson's poems published in America. No copyright record has been found.

Break, Break, Break

Florence. A Collection of [12] Songs. The Poetry by Longfellow, Tennyson and Others. Music by F[rancis]. Boott. . . . [No. 8] O Well for the Fisherman's Boy, or Break, Break. Boston. Published by Oliver Ditson & Co., Washington St. [Four agents.] Copyright 1857 [deposited June 4]. Plate number: 14144. 5 pages, 14 x 10¾ inches.

A copy is in the Library of Congress.

Song of the Brook

The Brook. Words by Tennyson. Music by Dolores [Ellen Dickson]. Boston. Published by Oliver Ditson & Co., 277 Washington St. [Five agents.] [1857–1860 (?)] Without plate number. 5 pages, 14 x 10¾ inches.

A copy is in the collection of Mr. J. Francis Driscoll of Brookline, Massachusetts.

Come into the Garden, Maud

Come into the Garden, Maud. Serenade from Tennyson's Maud. Set to Music by J. C. D. Parker. Boston. Published by Oliver Ditson & Co., Washington St. [Four agents.] Copyright 1855 [deposited Nov. 17]. Plate number: 7879. 7 pages, 14 x 10¾ inches.

A copy is in the Harvard College Library.

Tennyson's Come into the Garden Maud for mezzo-soprano voice with Piano accompaniment composed by Otto Dresel. Boston, Russel & Fuller, 291 Washington St. Copyright 1858. Plate number: 3214. 5 pages, 14 x 10¾ inches.

"To Miss S. G. Gay"

Some copies bear the imprint: Boston, Russell & Tolman, 201 Washington St.

Two copies, one with each imprint, are in the collection of Mr. J. Francis Driscoll.

Come into the Garden, Maud. Serenade from Tennyson's Maud. Set to Music . . . by John Blockley. Boston. Published by Oliver Ditson & Co., 277 Washington St. [Four agents.] [1858 (?)] Plate number: 18923. 7 pages, 14 x 10¾ inches.

A copy is in the collection of Mr. J. Francis Driscoll.

A Farewell

Flow Down, Cold Rivulet. A Farewell, written by Alfred Tennyson. Music by William R. Dempster. Boston. Published by Oliver Ditson, 115 Washington St. [Four agents.] Copyright 1852 [deposited Oct. 7]. Plate number: 5073. 5 pages, 14 x 10¾ inches.

A copy is in the Library of Congress.

Go Not, Happy Day

Go Not Happy Day! The words from Alfred Tennyson's New Poem of Maud. The Music by Alice Foster. Boston. E. H. Wade, 197 Washington St. [1855–1856 (?)] Without plate number. 7 pages, 14 x 10¾ inches.

A copy is in the Harvard College Library.

It Is the Miller's Daughter

Songs of the South— A collection of Songs and Duetts. Composed by Chas. J. Merz. . . . It Is the Miller's Daughter. Tennyson. Boston. Published by Oliver Ditson & Co., Washington St. [Four agents.] Copyright 1857. Plate number: 14073. 5 pages, 13½ x 10 inches.

A copy is in the collection of Mr. J. Francis Driscoll.

The May Queen

The May Queen, Cantata in Three Parts. Poetry by Alfred Tennyson, music composed and most cordially dedicated to his friend Lewis Gaylord Clark Esq. of New York by William R. Dempster. Part First. . . . Part Second. . . . Part Third. . . . [The title-page contained brief summaries of the three parts.] Boston. Published by Oliver Ditson, 115 Washington St. Copyright 1845 [Part First was deposited on April 9, 1845, and Parts Second and Third on March 2, 1846]. Without plate number. 29 pages, 14 x 10¾ inches.

Slight variations in the ornamented border of the title-page show that several separate impressions were made in 1845. Also copies have been found with the imprint 1846. The cantata was sold as a whole, and also each part was sold separately. A copy is in the Library of Congress. A copy with the 1846 imprint is in the Harvard College Library.

The May Queen. By Alfred Tennyson. The Music by I. B. Woodbury. Part First. . . . Part Second. . . . Part Third. . . . [The title-page contained brief summaries of the three parts.] New York, Firth, Pond & Co., 1 Franklin Sq. [One agent.] Copyright 1848 [deposited Nov. 16]. Plate number: 254. 9 pages, 12½ x 10 inches.

"To the Rev. Ralph Hoyt"

A copy is in the Harvard College Library.

O Swallow, Swallow

The Dulciana. A collection of Favorite Duetts . . . The Messenger Swallow. . . . Composed by John Blockley. Boston. Published by Oliver Ditson & Co., 277 Washington St. [Five agents.] [1855 (?)] Plate number: 8536. 7 pages, 13 x 10¾ inches.

A copy is in the Harvard College Library.

Ring Out, Wild Bells

Florence. A collection of [12] Songs. The Poetry by Longfellow, Tennyson and Others. Music by F[rancis]. Boott . . . [No. 7] The New Year's Bells. Boston. Published by Oliver Ditson & Co., Washington St. [Four agents.] Copyright 1857 [deposited June 4]. Plate number: 14144. 5 pages, 14 x 10¾ inches.

A copy is in the Library of Congress.

The Splendor Falls on Castle Walls

Bugle Song. Words by Tennyson. Music by S. D. S. Boston. Published by Oliver Ditson, Washington St. [Four agents.] Copyright 1857 [deposited Sept. 16]. Plate number: 8901. 5 pages, 14 x 10½ inches.

A copy is in the Library of Congress.

Sweet and Low

Cradle Song. Words by Alfred Tennyson. Music by Wm. Vincent Wallace. New York. Published by William Hall & Son, 239 Broadway. [Four agents.] Copyright 1851 [deposited May 1]. Without plate number. 8 pages, 13½ x 10½ inches.

A copy is in the Boston Public Library.

Cradle Song. "Sleep and rest, Sleep and rest, Father will come to thee soon." By Wm. Vincent Wallace. New York. Published by William Hall & Son, 239 Broadway. [Four agents.] Copyright 1851 [deposited July 15]. Plate number: 1086. 5 pages, 13½ x 10½ inches.

"Dedicated to Madame F. Lablache"

Transposed in C for Soprano.

A copy is in the Library of Congress.

Sweet and Low. Ballad by Alfred Tennyson. Music by J[ohn]. Blockley. Boston. Published by Oliver Ditson, 115 Washington St. [Five agents.] [1854 (?)] Plate number: 7663. 5 pages, 12½ x 10 inches.

A copy is in the Harvard College Library.

The Favorite Ballads of Wm. Vincent Wallace arranged for the Spanish Guitar. . . . No. 9. Cradle Song. Arranged by Charlie C. Converse. Composed by W. V. Wallace. New York. Published by William Hall & Son, 239 Broadway. [One agent.] Copyright 1855 [deposited Jan. 20]. Plate number: 3141. 5 pages, 13½ x 10½ inches.

A copy is in the Library of Congress.

The New York Musical Review. Prize Songs. . . . No. 1. Sweet and Low. [Composed by] Otto Dresel. Boston. Nathan Richardson at the Musical Exchange, 282 Washington St. Copyright 1855 [deposited Nov. 16]. Without plate number. 5 pages, 14 x 10¾ inches.

First published in the *New York Musical Review and Gazette*, VI, 392–93 (Nov. 17, 1855).

A copy is in the Harvard College Library.

Tears, Idle Tears

Tears Gentle Tears for the Days that Are No More. Words from Tenneyson's [*sic*] Poem "The Princess." Music by I. B. Woodbury. New York. Published by William Hall & Son, 239 Broadway. Copyright 1848 [deposited Dec. 9]. Plate number: 263. 5 pages, 13¼ x 10⅜ inches.

"Inscribed to Mrs. Jamieson of Hartford Ct."

A copy is in the Harvard College Library.

Tears, Idle Tears. Poems set to Music. Cavatina. . . . Words by Tennyson. Music by P. O. Bassvecchi. Charleston, South Carolina, Geo. F. Cole. Imprint 1856. Without plate number. 11 pages, 14¼ x 10¾ inches.

Apparently, Geo. F. Cole did not copyright the piece. The incomplete and only existing records of South Carolina copyrights for 1856 do not list it. The piece was copyrighted and republished by Firth, Pond & Co. of New York in 1857 [deposited Aug. 7]. The New York records of copyright describe it as a "Cavatina, sung with great applause by a distinguished Lady Amateur, at the Grand Concert of the Calhoun Monument Association on May 4th, 1856. Composed for and dedicated to Miss S. F. Elmore of S. C.—By P. O. Bassvecchi." A copy (Geo. F. Cole, 1856) is in the Boston Public Library.

The Days that Are No More. Song. . . . The Poetry by Tennyson. The Music by Jacques Blumenthal. Boston. Published by Oliver Ditson & Co., 451 Washington St. [Three agents.] [1857(?)] Plate number: 29128. 7 pages, 12 x 10¾ inches.

A copy is in the Harvard College Library.

Appendix B

TENNYSON ITEMS IN AMERICAN LITERARY ANNUALS AND GIFT-BOOKS, 1827–1858

The following list is compiled almost entirely from the large collections of literary annuals and gift-books in the Library of Congress, the American Antiquarian Society, and the Harvard College Library. With each item is listed a library which owns a copy of the annual. The Library of Congress is always given if the annual is there. When an item is an extract from a poem, the line references are to the present editions of the poem rather than to the rare earlier versions. In no case is there significant textual variation. The items are arranged chronologically by the dates of the annuals. An effort has been made to determine the year *for* which each annual was issued. When a date was included in the title of the annual, that date is given. When both copyright and imprint dates are known and the former is a year earlier than the latter, the imprint date is given as the year for which the annual was issued. When such a date cannot be determined, the copyright date (marked *cop.*) is given. The twelve items marked by asterisks, all of which I later saw, were contributed by Professor Bradford A. Booth of the University of California at Los Angeles from his unpublished index of American annuals.

* "A Fragment" ["Where is the Giant of the Sun, which stood"], *Friendship's Offering* for 1842 (Boston: E. Littlefield), pp. 218–19. Library of Congress.

* "No More," *Friendship's Offering* for 1842, p. 307. Library of Congress.

"The Miller's Daughter," [lines 215–46: "Look thro' mine eyes with thine. . . ."], *The Album of Love* for 1846, p. 65. American Antiquarian Society.

"Sonnet" ["But were I loved as I desire to be"], *The Album of Love* for 1846, p. 89. American Antiquarian Society.

"To J. S.," *The Album of Love* for 1846 (Boston: Elias Howe), p. 56. American Antiquarian Society.

* "Love Thou Thy Land, with Love Far-brought," *Friendship's Gift* for 1848 (Boston: John P. Hill), pp. 210–13. The stanzas were given the title "Freedom." Library of Congress.

The Princess [Part VII, ll. 243–71: "The woman's cause is man's; they rise or sink. . . ."], *The Marriage Offering* for 1848 (Boston: William Crosby and H. P. Nichols), p. 200. The lines were given the title "Woman." American Antiquarian Society.

"Love Thou Thy Land, with Love Far-brought," *The Lady's Gift* for 1849 (Nashua, N. H.: Charles T. Gill), pp. 210–13. The stanzas were given the title "Freedom." American Antiquarian Society.

* "Lilian," *The Present* for 1850 (Manchester, N. H.: Robert Moore), pp. 150–51. Library of Congress.

"The Miller's Daughter" [lines 215–46: "Look thro' mine eyes with thine. . . ."], *The Album of Love* for 1850 (New York: Leavitt & Company), p. 65. This annual is an exact reprint of the Boston *Album of Love* for 1846. American Antiquarian Society.

"Sonnet" ["But were I loved as I desire to be"], *The Album of Love* for 1850, p. 89. American Antiquarian Society.

"To J. S.," *The Album of Love* for 1850, p. 56. American Antiquarian Society.

In Memoriam [Section V, ll. 1–12: "I sometimes hold it half a sin. . . ."], *Memory and Hope* for 1851 (Boston: Ticknor, Reed & Fields), p. 244. Boston Athenaeum.

* "The Poet's Song," *The Forget-Me-Not* for 1851 (New York: Cornish, Lamport & Co.), p. 203. American Antiquarian Society.

The Princess [Part VII, ll. 243–71: "The woman's cause is man's; they rise or sink. . . ."], *The Ladies' Wreath* for 1851 (New York: J. M. Fletcher & Co.), p. 249. The lines were given the title "The Sphere of Woman." Library of Congress.

* "Break, Break, Break," *The Woodbine* (Philadelphia: Lind-

say & Blakiston, cop. 1851), p. 201. The stanzas were given the title "Remembrance." Library of Congress.

* "Come Not, When I Am Dead," *Gems of Beauty* for 1852 (Boston: Phillips, Sampson & Co.), p. 79. American Antiquarian Society.

* "Come Not, When I Am Dead," *The Keepsake* for 1852 (New York: John C. Riker), p. 121. Harvard College Library.

* *In Memoriam* [Section XCIV, ll. 1–16: "How pure at heart and sound in head. . . ."], *The Talisman, An Offering of Friendship* for 1852 (Philadelphia: Hogan & Thompson), p. 60. Library of Congress.

"Love and Death," *The Gift of Affection* for 1852 (New York: Leavitt & Company), p. 91. American Antiquarian Society.

"Mariana," *The Gift of Affection* for 1852, p. 91. American Antiquarian Society.

"O Darling Room," *The Irving Offering* for 1852 (New York: Leavitt & Company), p. 154. Library of Congress.

"Tennyson's Lockesley [*sic*] Hall," [Anonymous critical essay], *The Kossuth Offering and Family Souvenir* for 1852 (New York: Mark H. Newman & Co.), pp. 38–41. Library of Congress.

* "Come Not, When I Am Dead," *The Gift Book of Gems* for 1853 (Boston: Phillips, Sampson & Co.), p. 79. Library of Congress.

"Love and Death," *Poetry of the Affections* for 1853 (New York: Leavitt & Allen), p. 72. American Antiquarian Society.

"Mariana," *Poetry of the Affections* for 1853, p. 91. American Antiquarian Society.

"The Poet's Mind," *The Ladies' Diadem: A Token of Friendship* for 1853 (New York: Bunce and Brothers), p. 195. Library of Congress.

"The Sleeping Beauty," *The Ladies' Diadem: A Token of Friendship* for 1853, p. 260. Library of Congress.

"Circumstance," *The Young Lady's Cabinet of Gems* for 1854 (Boston: Kelley & Brother), p. 129. American Antiquarian Society.

"The Gardener's Daughter" [lines 33–47: "Not wholly in the busy world, nor quite . . ."], *The Young Lady's Cabinet of Gems* for 1854, p. 136. The stanzas were given the title "The Garden." American Antiquarian Society.

"The Gardener's Daughter" [lines 209–20: "There sat we down

upon a garden mound . . ."], *The Young Lady's Cabinet of Gems* for 1854, p. 136. The stanzas were given the title "The Trio." American Antiquarian Society.

* "Mariana," *The Hyacinth* for 1854 (Philadelphia: Henry F. Anners), p. 147. Columbia University Library.

The Princess [Part IV, ll. 21–40: "Tears, idle tears . . ."], *Heart-Songs: A Book for the Gift-Season* for 1856 (Boston: Crosby, Nichols, and Co.), pp. 90–91. Library of Congress.

* "Recollections of the Arabian Nights," *The Oriental Annual* (New York: Leavitt & Allen, [cop. 1857]), pp. 70–75. Library of Congress.

Appendix C

REVIEWS OF TENNYSON'S POEMS IN AMERICAN MAGAZINES AND NEWSPAPERS, 1827–1858

Except in rare cases, only reviews or articles devoted entirely to Tennyson are included in this index. The few listed reviews and articles not concerned primarily with Tennyson contain especially significant Tennyson criticism. No attempt is made here to record every reference to Tennyson. The complete files of some two hundred magazines, including all of any literary significance, have been searched in the preparation of this index. Also, numbers of newspapers have been checked, but only two, the Boston *Daily Evening Transcript* and the New York *Daily Tribune,* have been searched for the entire period. References for the assignment of authorship for anonymous reviews are given only when the assignments have not been explained in notes to the chapters. In order that some idea may be had of the variation in the number of Tennyson reviews from year to year, the reviews are grouped chronologically by years and arranged chronologically within each year.

1832

Museum of Foreign Literature and Science, XXI, 128–38 (August). Review of *Poems, Chiefly Lyrical.* From *Blackwood's Edinburgh Magazine* [XXXI, 721–41 (May, 1832)]. [Christopher North.]

1833

Select Journal of Foreign Periodical Literature, II, 106–21 (July). Review of *Poems* (1833). From London *Quarterly Review* [XLIX, 81–96 (April, 1833)]. [John Wilson Croker.]

1834

Museum of Foreign Literature and Science, XXIV, 257–58 (March). "Alfred Tennyson" [Brief article]. From London *Athenaeum* [No. 316, p. 772 (Nov. 16, 1833)].

1836

Western Messenger, II, 323–25 (December). Review of *Poems, Chiefly Lyrical.* [James Freeman Clarke.]

1837

Every Body's Album, II, 232 (March). Brief notice of *Poems, Chiefly Lyrical* and *Poems* (1833).

1838

Christian Examiner, XXIII, 305–27 (January). Review of *Poems, Chiefly Lyrical* and *Poems* (1833). J. S. D. [John Sullivan Dwight.]

1840

Burton's Gentleman's Magazine, VI, 100–03 (February). Review of Longfellow's *Voices of the Night* [Poe's accusation of Longfellow as a plagiarist of Tennyson]. Edgar A. Poe.

1841

Dial, II, 135 (July). "Tennyson's Poems." [Margaret Fuller.]

News-Gong, A Literary Intelligencer, I (December.) Comment upon Tennyson's poems under "English Literary Intelligence." Evert A. Duyckinck. Not seen in the preparation of this work; no copy is known to exist.

1842

Arcturus, III, 235–38 (February). "The Poems of Tennyson." Evert A. Duyckinck.

Brother Jonathan, II, 213 (June 18). Brief notice of *Poems* (1842).

Boston *Daily Evening Transcript,* July 7. Brief notice of *Poems* (1842).

New York *Evening Post for the Country,* July 8. Review of *Poems* (1842).

New York *Daily Tribune,* July 12. Brief notice of *Poems* (1842). From New York *Evening Post* [July 8].

Boston *Daily Courier,* July 12. Review of *Poems* (1842).

Boston *Morning Post,* July 12. Review of *Poems* (1842).

New York *Evening Post for the Country,* July 12. "Poems by Alfred Tennyson."

Boston *Daily Times,* July 14. Review of *Poems* (1842).

New World, V, 48 (July 16). Review of *Poems* (1842).

New York *Weekly Tribune,* July 16. Brief notice of *Poems* (1842). From New York *Evening Post* [July 8].

Brother Jonathan, II, 325 (July 16). Review of *Poems* (1842).

New World, V, 63 (July 23). Review of *Poems* (1842).

Democratic Review, XI, 215 (August). Review of *Poems* (1842).

Knickerbocker, XX, 208 (August). Review of *Poems* (1842) in "Editor's Table."

Boston *Daily Evening Transcript,* August 15. Review of *Poems* (1842).

Graham's Magazine, XXI, 152–53 (September). Review of *Poems* (1842). [Rufus W. Griswold.]

Orion, I, 395 (September). Brief notice of *Poems* (1842).

Southern Literary Messenger, VIII, 612 (September). Review of *Poems* (1842).

Boston Miscellany of Literature and Fashion, II, 140 (September). Review of *Poems* (1842).

Dial, III, 273–76 (October). "A Review of the Poems of Alfred Tennyson." [Margaret Fuller.]

Lady's World of Fashion, II, 114–17 (October). Review of *Poems* (1842). C.

Boston *Daily Advertiser,* October 10. Brief notice of *Poems* (1842). From New York *Evening Post* [July 8].

Christian Examiner, XXXIII, 237–44 (November). Review of *Poems* (1842). C. C. F. [Cornelius C. Felton.]

Knickerbocker, XX, 582 (December). Brief notice of *Poems* (1842) in "Editor's Table" [Largely excerpts from *Christian Examiner,* XXXIII, 237–44 (November)].

1843

Philadelphia *Saturday Museum* (January 28). Review of Rufus W. Griswold's *The Poets and Poetry of America.* [Edgar Allan Poe(?).] Used in Poe's *Works,* XI, 220–43; no copy of *Museum* available.

Dial, III, 517–18 (April). "Europe and European Books." [Ralph Waldo Emerson.]

New York *Daily Tribune,* April 17. "Wordsworth and Tennyson." From *Dial* [III, 517–18 (April)]. R. W. Emerson.

Albion, 4th Ser., II, 242 (May 20). Review of *Poems* (1842). From *Edinburgh Review* [LXXVII, 373–91 (April, 1843)]. [James Spedding.]

1844

Democratic Review, XIV, 62–77 (January). "Tennyson's Poems." [Fanny Kemble Butler.] See Bobbé, *op. cit.,* p. 188.

Knickerbocker, XXIII, 291–93 (March). Comment upon "The May Queen" in "Editor's Table."

Southern Literary Messenger, X, 240–46 (April). Review of *Poems* (1842). [Henry Charles Lea.]

Democratic Review, XV, 580 (December). "Marginalia." Edgar A. Poe.

Christian Parlor Magazine, I, 231–33 (December). "Tennyson's Poems."

1845

New Englander, III, 57–66 (January). Review of *Poems* (1842). [Luzerne Ray.]

Broadway Journal, I, 195–96 (March 29). Comment upon Longfellow's plagiarizing Tennyson in "Critical Notices." [Edgar Allan Poe.]

———, I, 348 (May 31). "Literary Gossip."

Knickerbocker, XXV, 487–88 (June). Comment upon "My Early Love."

———, XXV, 534–40. (June). Review of *Poems* (1842). C. A. B. [Charles Astor Bristed.]

American Whig Review, II, 45–48 (July). Review of Rufus W. Griswold's *The Poets and Poetry of England in the Nineteenth Century.* [Edwin P. Whipple.]

Broadway Journal, II, 26 (July 19). "Alfred Tennyson." [Edgar Allan Poe.]

Columbian Lady's and Gentleman's Magazine, IV, 91–93 (August). "Thoughts on the Poets—Tennyson." Henry T. Tuckerman.

Godey's Lady's Book, XXXI, 120–23 (September). "Marginal Notes—No. II." Edgar A. Poe.

Knickerbocker, XXVI, 288 (September). Comment upon "My Early Love" in "Editor's Table."

Eclectic Magazine of Foreign Literature, Science and Art, VI, 205–17 (October). Review of *Poems* (1842). From *British Quarterly Review* [II, 46–71 (August, 1845)].

Broadway Journal, II, 322 (November 29). Brief notice of *Poems* (Ticknor's 2nd edition). [Edgar Allan Poe.]

1846

Christian Parlor Magazine, III, 29 (May). "Tennyson's Poetry."

Albion, 4th Ser., V, 325 (July 11). "Past and Present Condition of British Poetry." From *Fraser's Magazine* [XXXIII, 708–18 (June, 1846)].

Littel's Living Age, X, 164–80 (July 25). *Ibid.*

Eclectic Magazine of Foreign Literature, Science and Art, VIII, 499–508 (August). *Ibid.*

New York Illustrated Magazine of Literature and Art, II, 241–44 (September). "Tennyson." H. H. Clements.

1847

Eclectic Magazine of Foreign Literature, Science and Art, XI, 144 (May). "Poetry of Tennyson." [Thomas Noon Talfourd(?).] The *National Magazine* (I, 434, Nov., 1852) borrowed the same article and headed it "Scraps from Sergeant Talfourd."

———, XI, 161–68 (June). "Alfred Tennyson." From *Tait's Edinburgh Magazine,* N. S., XIV, 229–34 (April, 1847). George Gilfillan.

Albion, 4th Ser., VI, 568 (November 27). "On the Poetry and Poets of the Age."

1848

Boston *Daily Evening Transcript,* February 9. Brief notice of *The Princess.*

Boston *Daily Chronotype,* February 10. Brief notice of *The Princess.*

———, February 11. Review of *The Princess.*

Boston *Daily Atlas,* February 11. Review of *The Princess.*

Boston *Daily Evening Transcript,* February 11. Review of *The Princess.*

Literary World, III, 28 (February 12). Review of *The Princess.* C. B. F.

New York *Daily Tribune,* February 14. Review of *The Princess.*

Albion, 4th Ser., VII, 95–96 (February 19). Review of *The Princess.*

Daguerreotype, II, 80–84 (February 26). Review of *The Princess.* From London *Examiner* [No. 2084, pp. 20–21 (Jan. 8, 1848)].

Literary World, III, 61–62 (February 26). Review of *The Princess.*

Massachusetts Quarterly Review, I, 256–59 (March). Review of *The Princess.* [James Russell Lowell.]

Democratic Review, XXII, 287 (March). Brief notice of *The Princess.*

Holden's Dollar Magazine, I, 185 (March). Review of *The Princess.*

Eclectic Magazine of Foreign Literature, Science and Art, XIII, 289–95 (March). "Alfred Tennyson." From *Hogg's Weekly Instructor* [VI, 281–84 (Dec. 25, 1847)].

Albion, 4th Ser., VII, 113 (March 4). Review of *The Princess.* Excerpts from London *Athenaeum* [No. 1053, pp. 6–8 (Jan. 1, 1848)]. [J. Westland Marston.] See Marchand, *op. cit.,* p. 277.

Littell's Living Age, XVI, 441–45 (March 4). Review of *The Princess.* From London *Examiner* [No. 2084, pp. 20–21, Jan. 8, 1848)].

Harbinger, VI, 158 (March 18). Review of *The Princess.* J. S. Dwight.

Peterson's Magazine, XIII, 155 (April). Review of *The Princess.*

Graham's Magazine, XXXII, 300 (May). Review of *The Princess.*

American Literary Magazine, II, 275–81 (May). Review of *The Princess.*

American Whig Review, VIII, 28–39 (July). "A Talk about the Princess." Charles A. Bristed.

Boston *Daily Evening Transcript,* September 4. Review of *Poems* (London, 1848).

Home Journal, September 23. Brief notice of *The Princess.*

Albion, 4th Ser., VII, 463 (September 23). Review of *Poems* (Boston, 1848).

Illustrated Monthly Courier, I, 78–79 (November 1). Review of *The Princess.* [Henry B. Hirst(?).]

1849

Yale Literary Magazine, XIV, 112–21 (January). "A Frolic with Tennyson" [Review of *The Princess*]. [F. M. Finch.] See Table of Contents of Vol. XIV.

New Englander, VII, 193–215 (May). Review of *The Princess.* [James Hadley.]

Southern Literary Messenger, XV, 292–96 (May). "Marginalia." Edgar A. Poe.

Graham's Magazine, XXXIV, 363–64 (June). "Fifty Suggestions." Edgar A. Poe.

Eclectic Magazine of Foreign Literature, Science and Art, XVII, 169–82 (June). Review of *The Princess* and *Poems* (London, 1848). From *Blackwood's Edinburgh Magazine* [LXV, 453–67 (April, 1849)].

1850

Eclectic Magazine of Foreign Literature, Science and Art, XIX, 66–90 (January). "Tennyson, and the Schools of Poetry." From *Edinburgh Review* [XC, 388–433 (Oct., 1849)]. [Aubrey de Vere.] See Tennyson's *Memoir,* I, 256.

Christian Parlor Magazine, VI, 145–48 (March). "Alfred Tennyson."

Literary World, VI, 622 (June 22). Brief notice of *In Memoriam.*

International Weekly Miscellany, I, 34 (July 8). Review of *In Memoriam.* Largely from London *Spectator* [XXIII, 546 (June 8, 1850)].

Literary World, VII, 30–31 (July 13). Review of *In Memoriam.*

Littell's Living Age, XXVI, 167–70 (July 27). Review of *In Memoriam.* From London *Examiner* [No. 2188, pp. 356–57 (June 8, 1850)].

———, XXVI, 170–71 (July 27). Review of *In Memoriam.* From London *Spectator* [XXIII, 546 (June 8, 1850)].

American Whig Review, XII, 176–81 (August). "A Few Words about Tennyson." P.

Macon *Georgia Citizen,* August 2. "Valley of Diamonds." Dr. T[homas]. H[olley]. Chivers.

Christian Register, XXIX, 122 (August 3). Review of *In Memoriam.*

Albion, 4th Ser., IX, 381 (August 10). Review of *In Memoriam.*

Boston Weekly Museum, III, 69 (August 10). Review of *In Memoriam.*

Home Journal, August 10. Review of *In Memoriam.*

New York *Daily Tribune,* August 21. Review of *In Memoriam.*

Home Journal, August 31. "The Poetic Principle." Edgar A. Poe.

Graham's Magazine, XXXVII, 198–99 (September). Review of *In Memoriam.*

Christian Examiner, XLIX, 289–90 (September). Review of *In Memoriam.* [C. C. Smith.]

Democratic Review, XXVII, 204–07 (September). Review of *In Memoriam.* S. E. B.

Harper's Monthly Magazine, I, 570 (September). Brief notice of *In Memoriam.*

Peterson's Magazine, XVIII, 134 (September). Brief notice of *In Memoriam.*

Eclectic Magazine of Foreign Literature, Science and Art, XXI, 144 (September). Review of *In Memoriam.* Excerpts from *Westminster Review* [LIII, 572–73 (July, 1850)].

Savannah (Georgia) *Morning News,* September 4. Brief notice of *In Memoriam.*

Holden's Dollar Magazine, VI, 631 (October). Review of *In Memoriam.*

Sartain's Union Magazine of Literature and Art, VII, 231–39 (October). "The Poetic Principle." Edgar A. Poe.

———, VII, 256 (October). Review of *In Memoriam.* [Prof. John S. Hart.] See Index to Vol. VII.

Brownson's Quarterly Review, VII, 539–40 (October). Review of *In Memoriam.* [Orestes A. Brownson(?).]

Nassau Literary Magazine, X, 62–65 (October). Review of *In Memoriam.* B.

Eclectic Magazine of Foreign Literature, Science and Art, XXI, 209–18 (October). Review of *In Memoriam.* From London *Prospective Review* [VI, 306–31 (August, 1850)].

New Englander, VIII, 598–615 (November). Review of *In Memoriam.* [Increase N. Tarbox.]

Southern Literary Messenger, XVI, 686–91 (November). Review of *In Memoriam.* E. C. [John Esten Cooke(?).]

Southern Quarterly Review, XVIII, 535–36 (November). Review of *In Memoriam.*

Literary World, VII, 458 (December). "Music in Prose and

Poetry. With a New Poem by Tennyson" [Comment upon "The Bugle Song"]. From *Fraser's Magazine* [XLI, 644–45 (June, 1850)].

1851

Democratic Review, XXVIII, 49–54 (January). "Shelley and Tennyson." B.

Christian Review, XVI, 36–50 (January). Review of *In Memoriam* and *Poems* (Boston, 1849). [George P. Fisher.]

Christian Parlor Magazine, VII 7 (January). Review of *In Memoriam.*

New York Recorder, VI, 181 (February 12). "Infidelity in England" [Third in a series of articles on the subject, this article dealing primarily with Tennyson]. C. B. W.

Literary World, VIII, 195–96 (March 8). An outline for the study of *In Memoriam.* H. W. P.

Boston *Daily Evening Transcript,* March 11. "Religious Tendencies of Modern English Literature." From *New York Recorder* [VI, 181 (Feb. 12)].

Southern Literary Messenger, XVII, 252 (April). Comment upon Tennyson's sonnets in "Editor's Table." [John R. Thompson.] See Jackson, *op. cit.,* p. 108.

International Magazine, III, 182–83 (May). "Has There Been a Great Poet in the Nineteenth Century?" Largely from *Eclectic Review* [5th Ser., I, 408–10 (April, 1851)].

North American Miscellany and Dollar Magazine, II, 126–31 (May 17). "Alfred Tennyson and His Poems." From *Eliza Cook's Journal* [IV, 353–55 (April 5, 1851)].

American Whig Review, XIII, 534–44 (June). "Death-Verses: A Stroll through the Valley of the Shadow of Death with Tennyson. . . ." [Review of *In Memoriam*]. J. S.

1852

Literary World, X, 11–12, 48–49 (January 3 and 17). "The Poetry of Sorrow" [Review of *In Memoriam*]. From London *Times* [Nov. 28, 1851].

Albion, 4th Ser., XI, 51–52 (January 31). "The Poetry of Sorrow." From London *Times* [Nov. 28, 1851].

Yale Literary Magazine, XVIII, 133 (February). "The Mission of Modern Poetry." T.

Albion, 4th Ser., XI, 61–62 (February 7). "The *Times* and the

Poets." From *Tait's Edinburgh Magazine* [N. S., XIX, 18–21 (Jan., 1852)].

Home Journal, February 14. "Mind and Money-Making" [Excerpts from and comment upon "The Poetry of Sorrow," London *Times,* Nov. 28, 1851].

———, February 28. Review of *In Memoriam.* Signed "New Hampshire."

Boston Weekly Museum, IV, 303 (February 28). Review of *In Memoriam.* [Largely from *Home Journal,* February 14.]

———, IV, 315 (March 13). Review of *In Memoriam.* From *Home Journal,* Feb. 28, 1852.

Literary World, X, 204–206 (March 20). "The *Times* and Tennyson." From *Tait's Edinburgh Magazine* [N. S., XIX, 18–21 (Jan., 1852)].

American Whig Review, XV, 520–23 (June). "Recollections of Poets Laureate—Tennyson."

Methodist Quarterly Review, XXXIV, 358–60 (July). "Tennyson's Credence in the Future."

National Magazine, I, 434 (November). "Poetry of Tennyson." Under general heading "Scraps from Sergeant [Thomas Noon] Talfourd." Same article, unsigned, appeared in *Eclectic Magazine of Foreign Literature, Science and Art,* XI, 144 (May, 1847).

To-Day: A Boston Literary Journal, II, 365–66 (November 27). Review of *Ode on the Death of the Duke of Wellington.*

Albion, 4th Ser., XI, 585 (December 4). Review of *Ode on the Death of the Duke of Wellington.* From London *Times* [Nov. 15, 1852].

Boston *Daily Evening Transcript,* December 4. "Tennyson on Wellington."

Literary World, XI, 374 (December 11). Review of *Ode on the Death of the Duke of Wellington.* From London *Times,* Nov. 15, 1852.

Southern Literary Gazette, II, 284–85 (December 18). Review of *Ode on the Death of the Duke of Wellington.*

———, II, 296–97 (December 25). Comment upon the London *Times's* criticism of Tennyson.

1853

Putnam's Monthly Magazine, I, 108 (January). Review of *Ode on the Death of the Duke of Wellington.*

Littell's Living Age, XXXVI, 62–63 (January 8). Review of *Ode on the Death of the Duke of Wellington.* From London *Times* [Nov. 15, 1852].

Literary World, XII, 102–03, 169 (February 5 and 26). Comment upon Poe's alleged plagiarizing of Tennyson.

Southern Literary Messenger, XIX, 184–89 (March). Comment upon "Sweet and Low" in "Editor's Table." [John R. Thompson(?).] See Jackson, *op. cit.,* p. 117.

New York *Daily Times,* March 25. Review of *Ode on the Death of the Duke of Wellington.*

Monthly Religious Magazine, X, 150–58 (April). Review of *In Memoriam.* F.

Literary World, XII, 290–91 (April 9). Review of *Ode on the Death of the Duke of Wellington.* Largely from London *Athenaeum* [No. 1323, pp. 280–81 (March 5, 1853)].

Boston *Daily Evening Transcript,* April 20. Report of a lecture by Oliver Wendell Holmes on Tennyson and Browning.

Littell's Living Age, XXXVII, 441–43 (May 14). Review of *Ode on the Death of the Duke of Wellington.* From London *Athenaeum* [No. 1323, pp. 280–81 (March 5, 1853)].

New York *Daily Times,* June 7. A comparison of Alexander Smith and Tennyson under heading "Literary and Critical."

Littell's Living Age, XXXVIII, 2 (July 2). "Tennyson's Oriana." Signed "A Borderer."

Home Journal, August 20. "Tennyson on Woman's Rights."

Graham's Magazine, XLIII, 336 (September). Review of *Poems* (Boston, 1854).

Southern Literary Messenger, XIX, 649–58 (November). Review of *In Memoriam* and *Poems* (Boston, 1849).

1854

National Magazine, IV, 15–17 (January). "Winter and the New Year" [Critical article upon "The Death of the Old Year" and "Ring Out, Wild Bells"].

Putnam's Monthly Magazine, III, 678–79 (June). Brief notice of *In Memoriam.*

New York *Daily Tribune,* June 8. "Art and Literature in London. From Our Own Correspondent."

Yale Literary Magazine, XIX, 298–99 (July). "Wordsworth and Tennyson." W. W.

New York *Daily Tribune,* July 22. Review of *Poems* (London, 1853).

Eclectic Magazine of Foreign Literature, Science and Art, XXXIII, 73 (September). "Tennyson."

1855

Yale Literary Magazine, XX, 136–43 (January). Review of *In Memoriam.* B.

Pioneer; or, California Monthly Magazine, III, 28–34 (January). "The Poems of Alfred Tennyson." Charles E. Havens.

Boston *Daily Evening Transcript,* January 16. "Tennyson's Battle Ode" [Review of "The Charge of the Light Brigade"]. Signed "Philo-Tennyson."

New York *Daily Tribune,* February 20. "Literature in London . . . From Our Own Correspondent."

Peterson's Magazine, XXVII, 252 (March). Review of "The Charge of the Light Brigade" in "Editor's Table."

Graham's Magazine, XLVI, 276–77 (March). Review of "The Charge of the Light Brigade" in "Editor's Table."

Boston *Daily Evening Transcript,* March 15. "[Alexander] Smith and the Poet Laureate."

Pioneer; or, California Monthly Magazine, III, 279–80 (June). Review of "The Charge of the Light Brigade" in "Editor's Table." [Ferdinand C. Ewer (?).]

Albion, 4th Ser., XIV, 346 (July 21). Brief notice of *Maud, and Other Poems.* [From London *Leader,* June 23, 1855.]

Home Journal, July 31. Brief notice of *Maud, and Other Poems.*

Boston *Daily Evening Transcript,* July 31. Review of *Maud, and Other Poems.*

New York *Daily Tribune,* August 7. Review of *Maud, and Other Poems.*

Boston *Daily Evening Transcript,* August 22. "Tennyson's Famous Battle Ode" [Brief notice of "The Charge of the Light Brigade"].

Eclectic Magazine of Foreign Literature, Science and Art, XXXVI, 616–28 (September). "The Poetry of Alfred Tennyson." From *Hogg's Instructor* [V, 1–14 (July, 1855)]. Gerald Massey.

Putnam's Monthly Magazine, VI, 318 (September). Review of *Maud, and Other Poems.*

Albion, 4th Ser., XIV, 417 (September 1). Review of *Maud, and Other Poems.*

Saturday Evening Post, September 8. Review of *Maud, and Other Poems.*

Home Journal, September 15. Review of *Maud, and Other Poems.*

Littell's Living Age, XLVI, 54–57 (September 15). Review of *Maud, and Other Poems.* From London *Examiner* [No. 2479, pp. 483–84 (Aug. 4, 1855)].

———, XLVI, 57–61 (September 15). Review of *Maud, and Other Poems.* From London *Spectator* [XXVIII, 813–14 (Aug. 4, 1855)].

Bibliotheca Sacra, XII, 851 (October). Brief notice of *Maud, and Other Poems.*

Harper's Monthly Magazine, XI, 701–06 (October). Review of *Maud, and Other Poems* in "Editor's Easy Chair." [George William Curtis.]

Putnam's Monthly Magazine, VI, 382–92 (October). "Alfred Tennyson."

American Phrenological Journal, XXII, 90–91 (October). "An English and an American Poet" [Comparison of *Maud, and Other Poems* and Whitman's *Leaves of Grass*]. [Walt Whitman.]

Graham's Magazine, XLVII, 360–61 (October). Brief notice of *Maud, and Other Poems* in "Editor's Table."

Southern Literary Messenger, XXI, 638–39 (October). Review of *Maud, and Other Poems.* [John R. Thompson(?).]

North American Review, LXXXI, 544–46 (October). Review of *Maud, and Other Poems.* [Edward Everett Hale.]

Graham's Magazine, XLVII, 371–72 (October). Review of *Maud, and Other Poems.*

Littell's Living Age, XLVII, 51–59 (October 6). Review of *Maud, and Other Poems.* From *Blackwood's Edinburgh Magazine* [LXXVIII, 311–21 (Sept., 1855)].

Home Journal, October 13. "Fusion of Authors and Publishers" [Largely excerpts from review of *Maud, and Other Poems, Blackwood's Edinburgh Magazine,* LXXVIII, 311–21 (Sept., 1855)].

———, October 20. "Indecent Poetry" [Article upon "Fatima"].

———, October 20. "More about 'Maud.' "

Home Journal, October 27. "Value of Half an Hour" [Letter to editors of *Home Journal* concerning "Maud."] Y.

Knickerbocker, XLVI, 525–26 (November). Review of *Maud, and Other Poems.*

Peterson's Magazine, XXVIII, 307–09 (November). "Tennyson's Maud." Jeremy Short.

Genius of the West, IV, 347–48 (November). Review of *Maud, and Other Poems* in "Editor's Tableau."

New York *Daily Times,* November 13. Review of *Maud, and Other Poems.*

Home Journal, December 15. "Idlewild Evening Lamp" [Comment upon *The Princess, In Memoriam,* and *Maud, and Other Poems*]. [Largely excerpts from *Edinburgh Review,* CII, 498–519 (Oct., 1855).]

Boston *Daily Evening Transcript,* December 19. Review of *Maud, and Other Poems.* W.

1856

Crayon, III, 30–32 (January). Review of *Maud, and Other Poems* in "Studies among the Leaves."

Christian Examiner, LX, 133–40 (January). Review of *Maud, and Other Poems.*

Harper's Monthly Magazine, XII, 262 (January). Review of *Maud, and Other Poems in* "Editor's Easy Chair." [George William Curtis(?).]

Graham's Magazine, XLVIII, 71 (January). Comment upon "Maud" in "Editor's Table."

Southern Literary Messenger, XXII, 97–100 (February). "Tennyson's Portraiture of Woman." Cecilia.

Independent, VII, 48 (February 7). "Contemporary Poets" [Review of *Maud, and Other Poems*].

Littell's Living Age, XLIX, 349 (May 10). "Tennyson and Jeremy Taylor."

National Magazine, VIII, 562–63 (June). "Tennyson and Longfellow." Excerpts from *Blackwood's Edinburgh Magazine* [LXXIX, 125–38 (Feb., 1856)].

Albion, XV, 285 (June 14). Brief notice of first "Blue and Gold" edition of Tennyson's *Works.*

New York *Daily Tribune,* June 20. Brief notice of first "Blue and Gold" edition of Tennyson's *Works.*

Christian Examiner, LXI, 151 (July). Brief notice of first "Blue and Gold" edition of Tennyson's *Works.*

North American Review, LXXXIII, 104–32 (July). "The Literature of Friendship" [Review of *In Memoriam*]. W. R. Alger.

Putnam's Monthly Magazine, VIII, 98 (July). Brief notice of first "Blue and Gold" edition of Tennyson's *Works.*

Home Journal, August 16. "The English Poet-Laureate."

San Francisco *Daily Evening Bulletin,* August 25. "The Lotus-Eater."

Knickerbocker, XLVIII, 307–08 (September). Brief notice of first "Blue and Gold" edition of Tennyson's *Works* in "Editor's Table."

Graham's Magazine, XLIX, 275 (September). Brief notice of first "Blue and Gold" edition of Tennyson's *Works.*

Arthur's Home Magazine, VIII, 180–81 (September). Review of first "Blue and Gold" edition of Tennyson's *Works.*

Crayon, III, 314–16 (October). Comment upon *Maud, and Other Poems* in "Country Correspondence."

Putnam's Monthly Magazine, VIII, 371–80 (October). "What Is Poetry?" [Comment upon Tennyson's diction.]

National Magazine, IX, 408–15 (November). "Alfred Tennyson." [R. H. Stoddard.] See Table of Contents of Vol. IX.

Southern Literary Messenger, XXIII, 470–71 (December). Comment upon "A Farewell" in "Editor's Table." [John R. Thompson(?).] See Jackson, *op. cit.,* p. 130.

1857

Albion, 4th Ser., XXXV, 177 (April 11). "Woolner's Bust of Tennyson." From "London Paper, March 14."

Russell's Magazine, I, 179, 181–82 (May). Comment upon "Maud" and *In Memoriam* in "Editor's Table."

Yale Literary Magazine, XXII, 358–61 (August). "The Beauties of Maud." D. G. B. [D. G. Brinton.] Brinton was one of the editors of the August number: see XXII, 334.

1858

New York *Daily Times,* January 28. "Alfred Tennyson and Opium." H.

Presbyterian Quarterly Review, VI, 656–63, 681–85 (March). "Tennyson."

Russell's Magazine, II, 500–01 (March). "Isabel, A Portrait."

Boston *Daily Evening Transcript,* March 18. "Tennyson." Excerpts from *Presbyterian Quarterly Review* [VI, 656–63, 681–85 (March, 1858)].

Ladies' Repository, XVIII, 420–23 (July). Review of *Maud, and Other Poems.* O. J. Victor, Esq.

Yale Literary Magazine, XXIV, 79–84 (November). "Locksley Hall." C. C. C.

———, XXIV, 89–98 (December). "Tennyson's Maud as a Work of Art." T. R. L. [Thomas R. Lounsbury.] Lounsbury was one of the editors of the December number: see XXIV, 89.

BIBLIOGRAPHY

BIBLIOGRAPHY

Only those works actually referred to in the book are listed in this bibliography. The American editions of Tennyson, the gift-books, and the articles and reviews listed in the appendices are not re-named here.

I. Works of Tennyson

Poems by Two Brothers. London: W. Simpkin and R. Marshall, 1827.

Poems, Chiefly Lyrical. London: Effingham Wilson, 1830.

Poems. London: Edward Moxon, 1833.

Poems, two volumes. London: Edward Moxon, 1842.

The Princess: a Medley. First, third, fourth, and fifth editions. London: Edward Moxon, 1847, 1850, 1851, 1853.

In Memoriam. London: Edward Moxon, 1850.

Ode on the Death of the Duke of Wellington. London: Edward Moxon, 1852.

Maud, and Other Poems. First and third editions. London: Edward Moxon, 1855, 1856.

Select Poems of Alfred Tennyson, ed. William J. Rolfe. Boston: J. R. Osgood and Company, 1885.

The Works of Alfred Tennyson, twelve volumes, ed. William J. Rolfe. Boston: Estes and Lauriat, 1895–1898.

The Poetic and Dramatic Works of Alfred Lord Tennyson, ed. William J. Rolfe. Student's Cambridge Edition. Boston and New York: Houghton Mifflin Company, 1898.

II. Articles and Reviews

Announcement of *Poems by Two Brothers.* London *Daily Chronicle,* April 27, 1827.

Review of *Poems by Two Brothers. Gentleman's Magazine,* XCVII, Supplement to Part I, 609 (June, 1827).

Editorials on Alfred and Charles Tennyson. *Tatler,* February 24, 26, March 1, 3, 1831. [Leigh Hunt.]

"On Some of the Characteristics of Modern Poetry and on the Lyrical Poems of Alfred Tennyson." *Englishman's Magazine,* I, 616–28 (August, 1831). [Arthur Henry Hallam.]

Review of *Poems* (1842). *Examiner,* No. 1791, pp. 340–41 (May 28, 1842). [John Forster (?).]

———. *Tait's Edinburgh Magazine,* N. S., IX, 502–08 (August, 1842).

———. *Quarterly Review,* LXX, 385–416 (Sept., 1842). [John Sterling.]

———. *Westminster Review,* XXXVIII, 371–90 (Oct., 1842). R. M. M. [Richard Monckton Milnes].

"Lays of the Would-Be Laureates." *Tait's Edinburgh Magazine,* N. S., X, 273–76 (May, 1843). Bon Gaultier [William Edmondstone Aytoun and Theodore Martin].

"Puffs and Poetry." *Tait's Edinburgh Magazine,* N. S., X, 649–54 (Oct., 1843). Bon Gaultier.

"Diffusion of Books." *Chambers's Edinburgh Journal,* N. S., VI, 198–200 (Sept. 19, 1846).

Review of *The Princess. Athenaeum,* No. 1053, pp. 6–8 (Jan. 1, 1848).

———. *Howitt's Journal,* III, 28–29 (Jan. 8, 1848).

———. *Spectator,* XXI, 41–42 (Jan. 8, 1848).

———. *Gentleman's Magazine,* N. S., XXIX, 115–31 (Feb., 1848).

———. *Quarterly Review,* LXXXII, 427–53 (March, 1848).

———. *Eclectic Review,* 4th Ser., XXIII, 415–23 (April, 1848).

———. *Sharpe's London Magazine,* VI, 139–41 (April, 1848).

Review of *Poems* (London, 1848) and *The Princess. North British Review,* IX, 43–72 (May, 1848).

Announcement of *In Memoriam.* London *Times,* June 8, 1850.

Review of *In Memoriam. Tait's Edinburgh Magazine,* N. S., XVII, 499–505 (August, 1850).

———. *North British Review,* XIII, 532–55 (August, 1850).

"Tennyson." *Fraser's Magazine,* XLII, 245–55 (Sept., 1850). [Charles Kingsley.]

"Our Weekly Gossip" [Article upon Tennyson's becoming Poet Laureate]. *Athenaeum,* No. 1204, p. 1218 (Nov. 23, 1850). [Henry F. Chorley.]

Review of *Ode on the Death of the Duke of Wellington. Athenaeum,* No. 1308, p. 1263 (Nov. 20, 1852).

———. *Literary Gazette,* No. 1870, pp. 852–53 (Nov. 20, 1852).

Review of *Speeches by the Right Hon. Thomas Babington Macaulay.* London *Morning Chronicle,* August 27, 1853.

Review of *Maud, and Other Poems. Athenaeum,* No. 1449, pp. 893–95 (August 4, 1855).

———. *Bentley's Miscellany,* XXXVIII, 262–65 (Sept., 1855).

———. *Dublin University Magazine,* XLVI, 332–40 (Sept., 1855).

———. *Westminster Review,* N. S., VIII, 597–601 (Oct., 1855).

———. *National Review,* I, 377–410 (Oct., 1855).

Review of *Enoch Arden and Other Poems. North American Review,* XCIX, 626 (Oct., 1864). James Russell Lowell.

———. *North American Review,* C, 305–07 (Jan., 1865).

"Tears—Idle Tears." *Land We Love,* III, 470–75 (Oct., 1867). Colonel J. T. L. Preston.

"Some Reminiscences of Fitz-Greene Halleck." *Frank Leslie's Illustrated Newspaper,* XXV, 243 (Jan. 4, 1868). Joel Benton.

"Fitz-Greene Halleck." *Putnam's Monthly Magazine,* N. S., I, 231–47 (Feb., 1868). Evert A. Duyckinck.

"Literary Gossip" [Poe and Tennyson]. *Athenaeum,* No. 2473, p. 395 (March 20, 1875).

"Reminiscences of a Poet-Painter." *Lippincott's Magazine,* XIX, 307–21 (March, 1877). John R. Tait.

"Tennyson." *International Review,* IV, 397–408 (May, 1877). Bayard Taylor.

"Fitz-Greene Halleck." *North American Review,* CXXV, 60–67 (July, 1877). Bayard Taylor.

"Tennyson and Washington Irving." *Notes and Queries,* 5th Ser., XII, 65 (July 26, 1879). D. Barron Brightwell.

Review of *Tiresias and Other Poems. Atlantic Monthly,* LVII, 423–26 (March, 1886). George E. Woodberry.

"The Influence of Tennyson in America." *Review of Reviews,* American Edition, VI, 553–56 (Dec., 1892). Hamilton W. Mabie.

"A Child of the College." *Atlantic Monthly,* LXXVIII, 758–68 (Dec., 1896). Thomas Wentworth Higginson.

"Who Was Chivers?" Boston *Daily Evening Transcript,* April 24, 1897. Warfield Creath Richardson.

"The Poe-Chivers Papers." *Century Magazine,* LXV, 435–47, 545–58 (Jan. and Feb., 1903). George E. Woodberry.

"Longfellow's Letters to Samuel Ward." *Putnam's Monthly,* III, 38–43, 165–71, 301–08 (Oct., Nov., Dec., 1907). Henry Marion Hall.

"The Centenary of 'The Quarterly Review.'" *Quarterly Review,* CCX, 731–84; CCXI, 279–324 (April and July, 1909).

"Thomas Buchanan Read." *University of Pittsburgh Bulletin,* XXIX, 1–4 (Jan., 1930). I. C. Keller.

"Poe's 'Nevermore': A Note." *American Literature,* VII, 439–52 (Jan., 1936). Robert S. Forsythe.

"Richard Henry Stoddard's Chinese Poems." *American Literature,* XI, 417–38 (Jan., 1940). William Purviance Fenn.

"Notes and Queries" [Article upon Croker's review of *Poems* of 1833]. *Colophon,* New Graphic Ser., I, 95–96 (Feb., 1940).

"Longfellow and His Authorized British Publishers." *PMLA,* LV, 1169–79 (Dec., 1940). Clarence Gohdes.

III. Miscellaneous Works

Aldrich, Thomas Bailey. *The Bells: A Collection of Chimes.* New York: J. C. Derby, 1855.

Armstrong, Margaret. *Fanny Kemble, A Passionate Victorian* New York: The Macmillan Company, 1938.

Arvin, Newton (ed.). *The Heart of Hawthorne's Journals.* Boston and New York: Houghton Mifflin Company, 1929.

Barhydt, D. Parish. *Life. A Poem.* New York: Wm. Holdridge, 1851.

Beaty, John O. *John Esten Cooke, Virginian.* New York: Columbia University Press, 1922.

Blodgett, Harold. *Walt Whitman in England.* Ithaca, N. Y.: Cornell University Press, 1934.

Bobbé, Dorothie. *Fanny Kemble.* New York: Minton, Balch & Company, 1931.

Boker, George H. *The Podesta's Daughter and Other Miscellaneous Poems.* Philadelphia: A. Hart, 1852.

Bon Gaultier [William Edmondstone Aytoun and Theodore Martin]. *The Book of Ballads.* New York: J. S. Redfield, 1852.

The Book of Pearls. New York: D. Appleton & Co., 1849.

The Book of the Boudoir. Boston: Phillips, Sampson, and Company, [cop. 1853].

The Boudoir Annual. Boston: Phillips & Sampson, 1846.

Bradley, A. C. *The Reaction against Tennyson.* Oxford: University Press, 1917.

Bradley, Edward Sculley. *Henry Charles Lea.* Philadelphia: University of Pennsylvania Press, 1931.

The Brilliant, A Gift-Book for 1850. New York: Baker & Scribner.

Brownson, Orestes A. *Works,* twenty volumes, ed. Henry F. Brownson. Detroit: T. Nourse, 1882–1887.

Broughton, Leslie Nathan (ed.). *Wordsworth & Reed, The Poet's Correspondence with His American Editor, 1836–1850, and Henry Reed's Account of His Reception at Rydal Mount, London and Elsewhere in 1854.* Ithaca, N. Y.: Cornell University Press, 1933.

Bulfinch, Stephen G. (ed.). *The Harp and the Cross.* Boston: American Unitarian Association, 1857.

Bulfinch, Thomas (ed.). *Poetry of the Age of Fable.* Boston: Tilton & Co., 1857.

Butler, Frances Kemble. *Journal by Frances Anne Butler.* London: J. Murray, 1835.

———. *Records of a Girlhood.* New York: H. Holt and Company, 1879.

Cain, Henry Edward. *James Clarence Mangan and the Poe-Mangan Question.* Washington, D. C.: Privately printed, 1929.

Caldwell, Howard H. *Poems.* Boston: Whittemore, Niles & Hall, 1858.

Campbell, Killis. *The Mind of Poe and Other Studies.* Cambridge, Mass.: Harvard University Press, 1933.

Cardwell, Guy Adams, Jr. *Charleston Periodicals, 1795–1860.* Unpublished Ph.D. thesis, University of North Carolina, 1936.

Cary, Alice. *Lyra, and Other Poems.* New York: Redfield, 1852.

———. *Poems.* Boston: Ticknor and Fields, 1855.

Casseday, Ben (ed.). *The Poetic Lacon, or, Aphorisms from the Poets.* New York: D. Appleton & Co., 1847.

Channing, William Ellery. *Poems.* Boston: C. C. Little and J. Brown, 1843.

———. *Poems.* Boston: J. Munroe and Company, 1847.

Channing, William H. (ed. with others). *Memoirs of Margaret Fuller Ossoli,* two volumes. Boston: Phillips, Sampson and Company, 1852.

Chivers, Thomas Holley. *Eonchs of Ruby.* New York: Spalding & Shepard, 1851.

———. *Virginalia; or Songs of My Summer Nights.* Philadelphia: Lippincott, Grabo & Co., 1853.

Cleveland, Charles D. (ed.). *English Literature of the Nineteenth Century*. First and second editions. Philadelphia: E. C. & J. Biddle, 1851 and 1853.

Coates, Reynell (ed.). *Leaflets of Memory*. Philadelphia: E. H. Butler & Co., 1846.

Coleridge, Samuel Taylor. *Specimens of the Table Talk of the Late Samuel Taylor Coleridge*. London: J. Murray, 1852.

Conway, Moncure Daniel. *Emerson at Home and Abroad*. Boston: James R. Osgood and Company, 1882.

Cooke, George Willis. *A Bibliography of James Russell Lowell*. Boston and New York: Houghton, Mifflin and Company, 1906.

———. *An Historical and Biographical Introduction to Accompany The Dial,* two volumes. Cleveland: The Rowfant Club, 1902.

Coppee, Henry (ed.). *A Gallery of Famous English and American Poets*. Philadelphia: E. H. Butler & Co., 1859.

Cozzens, Frederic S. *Fitz-Greene Halleck. A Memorial*. New York: The Trow & Smith Book Manuf'g. Co., 1868.

Cranch, Christopher P. *The Bird and the Bell, with Other Poems*. Boston: James R. Osgood and Company, 1875.

———. *Poems*. Philadelphia: Carey and Hart, 1844.

Curtis, George William. *Early Letters of George William Curtis to John S. Dwight,* ed. George Willis Cooke. New York and London: Harper & Brothers, Publishers, 1898.

Cushing, William. *Index to the North American Review*. Cambridge, Mass.: Press of John Wilson and Son, 1878.

———. *Index to the Christian Examiner*. Boston: J. S. Cushing, 1879.

Damon, S. Foster. *Thomas Holley Chivers, Friend of Poe*. New York and London: Harper & Brothers, Publishers, 1930.

Davis, William Augustus. *Biographical Notice of Charles Stearns Wheeler*. Boston: J. Munroe and Company, 1843.

Derby, J. C. *Fifty Years among Authors, Books and Publishers*. New York: G. W. Carleton & Co., 1884.

Emerson, Ralph Waldo. *Complete Works,* twelve volumes, ed. Edward Waldo Emerson. Cambridge, Mass.: Printed at the Riverside Press, 1903.

———. *Journals,* ten volumes, ed. Edward Waldo Emerson and Waldo Emerson Forbes. Boston and New York: Houghton Mifflin Company, 1909–1914.

Emerson, Ralph Waldo. *Letters,* six volumes, ed. Ralph L. Rusk. New York: Columbia University Press, 1939.

Fields, James T. *Yesterdays with Authors.* Boston: James R. Osgood and Company, 1872.

The Forget-Me-Not for 1856. New York: Leavitt & Allen.

Foster, H. C. (ed.). *An Excursion among the Poets.* Richmond, Va.: H. C. Foster, 1854.

Fuller, S. Margaret. *Papers on Literature and Art.* New York: Wiley and Putnam, 1846.

The Garland: or, Token of Friendship. New York: Leavitt & Allen, 1855.

The Gem: A Literary Annual. London: W. Marshall, 1831.

Gibson, William. *A Vision of Faery Land, and Other Poems.* Boston: J. Munroe and Company, 1853.

Godwin, Parke. *A Biography of William Cullen Bryant with Extracts from His Private Correspondence,* two volumes. New York: D. Appleton and Company, 1883.

Gohdes, Clarence. *The Periodicals of American Transcendentalism.* Durham, N. C.: Duke University Press, 1931.

Grayson, William J. *Autobiography,* ed. Robert Duncan Bass. Unpublished Ph.D. thesis, University of South Carolina, 1933.

Greenwood, Grace [Mrs. Sara Jane Lippincott]. *Poems.* Boston: Ticknor, Reed, and Fields, 1851.

Griswold, Rufus W. *Passages from the Correspondence and Other Papers of Rufus W. Griswold.* Cambridge, Mass.: W. M. Griswold, 1898.

———. (ed.). *The Poets and Poetry of America to the Middle of the Nineteenth Century.* Philadelphia: Carey and Hart, 1850.

———. *The Poets and Poetry of England in the Nineteenth Century.* Philadelphia: Carey & Hart, 1845.

Hadley, James. *Essays Philological and Critical.* New York: Holt & Williams, 1873.

Hale, Edward Everett. *James Russell Lowell and His Friends.* Boston and New York: Houghton, Mifflin and Company, 1899.

———. *Lights of Two Centuries.* New York and Chicago: A. S. Barnes & Company, 1887.

Hale, Susan. *Life and Letters of Thomas Gold Appleton.* New York: D. Appleton and Company, 1885.

Hall, S. C. (ed.). *The Book of Gems,* three volumes. London and Paris: Fisher, Son & Co., 1840.

Halleck, Fitz-Greene (ed.). *Selections from the British Poets,* two volumes. Harper's Family Library, No. CXII. New York: Harper & Brothers, 1840.

Hansen-Taylor, Marie, and Scudder, Horace E. *Life and Letters of Bayard Taylor,* two volumes. Boston: Houghton, Mifflin and Company, 1884.

Hawthorne, Hildegarde. *The Poet of Craigie House.* New York and London. D. Appleton-Century Company, 1936.

Hayne, Paul Hamilton. *Poems.* Boston: Ticknor and Fields, 1855.

Hewitt, Mary E. *Songs of Our Land, and Other Poems.* Boston: William D. Ticknor & Company, 1846.

Heywood, J. C. *How They Strike Me, These Authors.* Philadelphia: J. B. Lippincott & Co., 1877.

Higginson, Thomas Wentworth. *Letters and Journals,* ed. Mary Thatcher Higginson. Boston and New York: Houghton Mifflin Company, 1921.

———. *Studies in History and Letters.* Boston and New York: Houghton, Mifflin and Company, 1900.

Hiller, O. Prescott. *English and Scottish Sketches. By an American.* London: William White, 1857.

Hirst, Henry B. *The Coming of the Mammoth, The Funeral of Time, and Other Poems.* Boston: Published by Phillips & Sampson, 1845.

———. *The Penance of Roland, A Romance of the Peine Forte et Dure, and Other Poems.* Boston: Ticknor, Reed, and Fields, 1849.

Hope, James Barron. *Leoni Di Monota: and Other Poems.* Philadelphia: J. B. Lippincott & Co., 1857.

Horne, R. H. *A New Spirit of the Age.* New York: Harper & Brothers, 1844.

Howe, Julia Ward. *Passion-Flowers.* Boston: Ticknor, Reed, and Fields, 1854.

———. *Words for the Hour.* Boston: Ticknor and Fields, 1857.

Howells, William Dean. *My Literary Passions.* New York: Harper & Brothers, 1895.

Howitt, William. *Homes and Haunts of the Most Eminent British Poets.* New York: Harper & Brothers, 1847.

Jackson, David K. *The Contributors and Contributions to The*

Southern Literary Messenger. Charlottesville, Va.: The Historical Publishing Co., Inc., 1936.

Jenks, Joseph William (ed.). *The Rural Poetry of the English Language*. Boston: J. P. Jewett and Company, 1856.

Johnson, Laura Winthrop. *The Life and Poems of Theodore Winthrop, Edited by His Sister*. New York: H. Holt and Company, 1884.

Lauvrière, Emile. *L'Étrange vie et les étranges amours d'Edgar Poe*. Paris: Desclee de Brouwer & Cie, Editeurs, 1934.

Lenox Library Short-Title Lists. New York: Privately Printed, 1887.

LeVert, Madame Octavia Walton. *Souvenirs of Travel,* two volumes. Mobile, Ala.: S. H. Goetzel and Company, 1857.

Longfellow, Henry Wadsworth. *Complete Writings,* eleven volumes. Boston and New York: Houghton, Mifflin and Company, 1904.

——— (ed.). *The Estray: A Collection of Poems*. Boston: W. D. Ticknor & Co., 1847.

Longfellow, Samuel. *Life of Henry Wadsworth Longfellow,* three volumes. First and second editions. Boston: Ticknor and Company, 1886; and Boston and New York: Houghton, Mifflin and Company, 1891.

———, and Higginson, Thomas Wentworth (eds.). *Thalatta: A Book for the Sea-Side*. Boston: Ticknor, Reed & Fields, 1853.

Lounsbury, Thomas R. *The Life and Times of Tennyson*. New Haven, Conn.: Yale University Press, 1915.

Lowell, Anna C. (ed.). *Poetry for Home and School*. Boston: S. G. Simpkins, 1843.

Lowell, James Russell. *Class Poem*. Cambridge, Mass.: Cambridge Press: Metcalf, Torry, and Ballou, 1838.

———. *Complete Writings,* sixteen volumes. Cambridge, Mass.: Printed at the Riverside Press, 1904.

———. *Poems,* ed. Edmund M. Ashe. New York: Frederick A. Stokes Company, Publishers, 1894.

———. *A Year's Life*. Boston: C. C. Little and J. Brown, 1841.

Lowry, Henry F., and Rusk, Ralph Leslie (eds.). *Emerson-Clough Letters*. Cleveland: The Rowfant Club, 1934.

Lytton, Edward George Earle Lytton Bulwer-. *The New Timon, A Romance of London*. London: H. Colburn, 1846.

McGuffey, William H. (ed.). *McGuffey's New High School Reader*. Cincinnati: Sargent, Wilson & Hinkle, 1857.

Mangan, James Clarence. *Poems,* ed. D. J. O'Donoghue. Dublin: O'Donoghue & Co., 1903.

Marchand, Leslie A. *The Athenaeum, A Mirror of Victorian Culture*. Chapel Hill: University of North Carolina Press, 1941.

Meek, A. B. *Songs and Poems of the South*. New York: S. H. Goetzel & Co., 1857.

Morse, John T., Jr., *Life and Letters of Oliver Wendell Holmes,* two volumes. Cambridge, Mass.: Printed at the Riverside Press, 1896.

Mott, Frank Luther. *A History of American Magazines,* three volumes. Cambridge, Mass.: Harvard University Press, 1938–1939.

Mowatt, Anna Cora. *Fashion; or, Life in New York. A Comedy in Five Acts*. London: W. Newbery, 1850.

Mulchinock, William Pembroke. *Ballads and Songs*. New York: T. W. Strong, 1851.

Mumby, Frank A. *The House of Routledge, 1834–1934*. London: G. Routledge & Sons, 1934.

Nicolson, Harold. *Tennyson, Aspects of His Life, Character, and Poetry*. Boston and New York: Houghton Mifflin Company, 1925.

Nixon, Herman Clarence. *Alexander Beaufort Meek*. Auburn, Ala.: Alabama Polytechnic Institute Press, 1910.

Norton, Charles Eliot (ed.). *The Correspondence of Thomas Carlyle and Ralph Waldo Emerson,* two volumes. Boston: J. R. Osgood and Company, 1883.

———. *Letters,* two volumes, ed. Sara Norton and M. A. De Wolfe Howe. Boston and New York: Houghton Mifflin Company, 1913.

Percival, James Gates. *The Dream of a Day and Other Poems*. New Haven, Conn.: Printed and Published by S. Babcock, 1843.

Perennial Flowers, A Collection of Poetry Appropriate for the Use of Girls in Schools. Boston: Munroe and Francis, 1843.

Phillips, Mary E. *Edgar Allan Poe, The Man,* two volumes. Philadelphia: The John C. Winston Co., 1926.

Pierce, Edward L. *Memoir and Letters of Charles Sumner,* four volumes. Boston: Roberts Brothers, 1877–1893.

Poe, Edgar Allan. *Complete Works,* seventeen volumes, ed. James A. Harrison. New York: T. Y. Crowell & Company, 1902.

———. *Poems,* ed. Killis Campbell. Boston, New York, etc.: Ginn and Company, 1917.

———. *The Raven, and Other Poems.* New York: Wiley and Putnam, 1845.

———. *Tamerlane and Other Poems. . . .* Reproduced in facsimile from the edition of 1827 with an introduction by Thomas Ollive Mabbott. New York: Columbia University Press, 1941.

The Poets and Poetry of America, A Satire by Lavante. Philadelphia: W. S. Young, 1847. Second edition, ed. Geoffrey Quarles. New York: Benjamin and Bell, 1887.

Pope-Hennessy, Una. *Edgar Allan Poe, A Critical Biography.* London: Macmillan and Co., Limited, 1934.

Powell, Thomas. *The Living Authors of England.* New York: D. Appleton, 1849.

Pyre, J. F. A. *The Formation of Tennyson's Style.* Madison, Wis.: University Press, 1921.

Ralli, Augustus. *Guide to Carlyle,* two volumes. London: G. Allen & Unwin, Ltd., 1920.

Read, Thomas Buchanan (ed.). *The Female Poets of America.* Philadelphia: E. H. Butler & Co., 1848.

———. *Lays and Ballads.* Philadelphia: George S. Appleton, 1849.

———. *Poems.* Boston: W. D. Ticknor & Company, 1847.

Records of a Lifelong Friendship: Ralph Waldo Emerson and William Henry Furness. Boston and New York: Houghton Mifflin Company, 1910.

Reed, Henry. *Lectures on English Literature, from Chaucer to Tennyson.* Philadelphia: Parry & McMillan, 1855.

Reid, T. Wemyss. *The Life, Letters, and Friendships of Richard Monckton Milnes,* two volumes. New York: Cassell Publishing Company, 1891.

Russell, Francis T. *The Juvenile Speaker.* New York: Harper & Brothers, 1847.

Russell, William and Anna U. *Introduction to the Young Ladies' Elocutionary Reader.* Boston: J. Munroe and Company, 1845.

Sangster, Charles. *The St. Lawrence and the Saguenay, and*

Other Poems. New York: Miller, Orton & Mulligan, 1856.
Sargent, Epes (ed.). *International Standard Speaker*. Philadelphia: C. Desilver, 1857.
———. *Selections in Poetry for Exercises at School and at Home*. Philadelphia: C. Desilver, 1855.
———. *The Testimony of the Poets*. Boston: B. B. Mussey & Co., 1854.
Scott, Leonora Cranch. *The Life and Letters of Christopher Pearse Cranch*. Boston and New York: Houghton Mifflin Company, 1917.
Scudder, Horace Elisha. *James Russell Lowell,* two volumes. Cambridge, Mass.: Printed at the Riverside Press, 1901.
Stedman, Edmund Clarence. *Victorian Poets*. Boston: James R. Osgood and Company, 1875.
Stedman, Laura, and Gould, George M. *Life and Letters of Edmund Clarence Stedman,* two volumes. New York: Moffat, Yard and Company, 1910.
Stewart, Allegra. *A Comparison of Lowell and Tennyson*. Unpublished Master's Essay, Columbia University, 1923.
Stoddard, Richard Henry. *Foot-Prints*. New York: Spalding & Shepard, 1849.
———. *Poems*. Boston: Ticknor, Reed, and Fields, 1852.
———. *Recollections Personal and Literary*. New York: A. S. Barnes and Company, 1903.
———. *Songs of Summer*. Boston: Ticknor and Fields, 1857.
Story, William Wetmore. *Poems*. Boston: Little & Brown, 1847.
———. *Poems*. Boston: Little, Brown and Company, 1856.
Street, Alfred B. *Drawings and Tintings*. New York: Burgess, Stringer & Co., and M. Y. Beach, 1844.
Talley, Susan Archer. *Poems*. New York: Rudd & Carleton, 1859.
Taylor, Bayard. *At Home and Abroad*. New York: G. P. Putnam's Sons, 1889.
———. *A Book of Romances, Lyrics and Songs*. Boston: Ticknor, Reed, and Fields, 1852.
———. *Poems of the Orient*. Boston: Ticknor and Fields, 1855.
Tennyson, Hallam, Lord. *Alfred, Lord Tennyson, A Memoir by His Son,* two volumes. New York: The Macmillan Co., 1897.
———. (ed.). *Tennyson and His Friends*. London: Macmillan and Co., Limited, 1911.

Thompson, Lawrance. *Young Longfellow.* New York: The Macmillan Company, 1938.

Thompson, Ralph. *American Literary Annuals & Gift Books, 1825–1865.* New York: The H. W. Wilson Company, 1936.

Ticknor, Caroline. *Hawthorne and His Publisher.* Boston and New York: Houghton Mifflin Company, 1913.

Timrod, Henry. *Poems,* ed. Paul H. Hayne. New York: E. J. Hale & Son, Publishers, 1873.

Tinsley, William. *Random Recollections of an Old Publisher,* two volumes. London and Paris: Simpkins, Marshall, Hamilton, Kent & Co., 1905.

Townsend, Henry C. *A Memoir of T. Buchanan Read.* Philadelphia: Printed for Private Circulation, 1889.

Traubel, Horace L. (ed. with others). *In Re Walt Whitman.* Philadelphia: Published by the Editors through D. McKay, 1893.

Trent, William P. *William Gilmore Simms.* Boston and New York: Houghton, Mifflin and Company, 1892.

Tuckerman, Frederick Goddard. *Sonnets,* ed. Witter Bynner. New York and London: Alfred A. Knopf, 1931.

Tuckerman, Henry T. *Thoughts on the Poets.* New York: C. S. Francis & Co., 1846.

Wallace, William Ross. *Meditations in America and Other Poems.* New York: Charles Scribner, 1851.

Weygandt, Cornelius. *The Time of Tennyson. English Victorian Poetry as It Affected America.* New York and London: D. Appleton-Century Company, Inc., 1936.

Whipple, Edwin P. *Essays and Reviews,* two volumes. New York: D. Appleton & Company, 1849.

Wilkins, William Glyde. *First and Early American Editions of the Works of Charles Dickens.* Cedar Rapids, Iowa.: The Torch Press, 1910.

Willmott, Rev. Robert Aris (ed.). *The Poets of the Nineteenth Century.* New York: Harper & Brothers, 1857.

Wilson, James Grant. *Bryant and His Friends.* New York: Fords, Howard & Hulbert, 1886.

Wise, Thomas J. *A Bibliography of the Writings of Alfred, Lord Tennyson,* two volumes. London: Printed for Private Circulation, 1908.

Woolner, Amy. *Thomas Woolner, R. A., Sculptor and Poet: His Life and Letters.* London: Chapman and Hall, Ltd., 1917.

NOTES AND INDEX

NOTES

Chapter I

1. The earliest record that I have of a copy in this country occurs in the accession files of the Boston Athenaeum. The Athenaeum bought the copy which is still in its library from Leonard & Company, Boston booksellers, for fifteen cents on December 24, 1858. Bayard Taylor wrote in May, 1877 (*International Review,* IV, 399), that he knew of but one copy in this country: that in the possession of Dr. Edwin H. Chapin, Universalist minister and rare books collector. In the same year Harper & Brothers made a strenuous search for copies and finally found one, Dr. Chapin's (MS letter, J. W. Harper, Jr. to Evert A. Duyckinck, March 23, 1877, in the Duyckinck Collection, New York Public Library).

2. Most American magazines from 1827 to 1842, of whatever nature, published regularly a list of new books; the eclectic magazines published lengthy lists of new British books. Although I have seen hundreds of such lists, I have not yet found an announcement of *Poems by Two Brothers.*

3. Calling the two quotations "identical," Una Pope-Hennessy (*Edgar Allan Poe,* London, 1934, pp. 54–55) says, "Perhaps this is more than a coincidence"; and Emile Lauvrière (*L'Étrange vie et les étranges amours d'Edgar Poe,* Paris, 1934, p. 68) casually takes for granted that Poe had seen the Tennyson book.

4. In the first place, the Martial quotations were not "identical." The sentence is *Nos haec novimus esse nihil* (*Book XIII, Epigram 2,* line 8). Poe quoted it correctly, but Tennyson had *Haec nos,* etc. Then too, the use of the sentence as a motto was not new in 1827. It had appeared upon the title pages of Dryden's *The Rival Ladies* (1664) and Gay's *The Beggar's Opera* (1728), and it was the motto for an edition of Southey's poems in 1815. Various resemblances between *Poems by Two Brothers* and *Tamerlane and Other Poems* in subject matter and stylistic characteristics can be explained by the fact that they had a common model, Byron, and that both were written by young boys at about the same time. The brief prefaces, strikingly alike, seem obviously to have been influenced by Byron's preface to *Hours of Idleness.* Although its exact date of publication is unknown, *Tamerlane and Other Poems* could not have appeared more than six months later than *Poems by Two Brothers* (see Harold Nicolson, *Tennyson,* London, 1923, p. 49; and Mary E. Phillips, *Edgar Allan Poe, The Man,* Philadelphia, 1926, pp. 305–07). In his recent facsimile edition of *Tamerlane and Other Poems* (New York, 1941, p. xlviii), Thomas Ollive

Mabbott concludes that Poe "could have known nothing" of *Poems by Two Brothers.*

5. See Dorothie Bobbé, *Fanny Kemble* (New York, 1931), p. 27; and a letter, Fanny Kemble to Harriet St. Leger, August 17, 1833, in *Records of a Girlhood* (New York, 1879), p. 581. Miss Kemble's published journal of her voyage to America in 1832 tells in detail of her reading and her literary discussions with the other passengers, but Tennyson is never mentioned. See *Journal of Frances Ann Butler* (London, 1835), pp. 1–48: Her letters and later journals show that she talked frequently of Tennyson during her stay in America, but there is no recorded reference to *Poems by Two Brothers.*

6. See Thomas J. Wise, *A Bibliography of the Writings of Alfred Lord Tennyson* (London, 1908), I, 12–15. An American library now owns the only known copy of the separate print: the William Harris Arnold copy in the Henry E. Huntington Library, San Marino, California.

7. Accession files, item 1396, tenth sale, October 11.

8. No. 91, p. 456 (July 22, 1829). Just founded in 1829, this magazine was read very little, if at all, in America in 1829.

9. I have checked scores of early American booksellers' catalogues and broadsides advertising book auctions, including the excellent collection of the Grolier Club in New York City, which the Club kindly allowed me to use, but I have not yet seen a Tennyson book listed for sale before 1842. It seems true, without exception, that Americans who owned copies before that time either bought them in England or had them sent directly from there.

10. *The Works of Alfred Tennyson,* twelve volumes, ed. William J. Rolfe (Boston, 1895–98), I, 50: hereafter referred to as Tennyson's *Works.* Evert A. Duyckinck's copy of *Poems, Chiefly Lyrical* was in the Duyckinck Collection presented to the Lenox Library of New York City in 1878 (see *Lenox Library Short-Title Lists,* privately printed, 1887). The Lenox Library became a part of the New York Public Library in 1895. The copy, now in the New York Public Library, bears Duyckinck's signature.

11. MS letter, December 29, 1840, Park Benjamin Collection, Columbia University Library.

12. Lowell had a copy for a while both years. He quoted a stanza of "O Darling Room" in the notes of his Harvard Class Poem, published in August, 1838 (see below), and on September 1, 1838, he wrote in a letter to Emerson apologizing for some derogatory lines about Emerson's doctrines in the Class Poem: "I scarcely dare to look at the Tennyson you lent me without expecting some of the devils on the cover to make faces at me" (Horace Elisha Scudder, *James Russell Lowell,* Cambridge, Mass., 1901, I, 59). Since Tennyson's volumes had originally no devils on their covers, Lowell's reference is probably to some of Emerson's drawings. He had a habit of drawing such figures upon his books. Emerson's copy of the *Poems* of 1833 has been lost. Professor William J. Rolfe wrote in 1886 that it had "recently disappeared from Emerson's library and could not be traced" (Preface to his edition of *Select Poems of Alfred Lord Tennyson,* Boston, 1885). Lowell had the book again—or still—in 1839, for five quotations from the 1833 *Poems* written into a commonplace

book which he kept from 1837 to 1839 bear the date May 2, 1839 (MS notebook, James Russell Lowell Collection, Harvard College Library).

13. The manuscript is now in the Pierpont Morgan Library of New York City. The title page is spaced and copied just as it appears in the book, and the poems are carefully copied with pen and ink in double columns on thick paper. All is in Lowell's handwriting.

14. "This P. M. exchanged [pulpits] with Mr. [Nathaniel L.] Frothingham, who tell [*sic*] Charles [Emerson's brother] don't [*sic*] like Tennyson which I lent him as a gem to a virtuoso" (letter to Edward Bliss Emerson, December 25, 1831, in *The Letters of Ralph Waldo Emerson,* six volumes, ed. Ralph L. Rusk, New York, 1939, I, 341: hereafter referred to as Emerson's *Letters*). Emerson's copy of *Poems, Chiefly Lyrical* is now in the vault in Emerson's home at Concord and bears his signature. It was probably the first Tennyson book to reach America.

15. Edward Everett Hale, *Lights of Two Centuries* (New York and Chicago, 1887), p. 497.

16. See *ibid.* Certainly much of the early reading of Tennyson was done from Emerson's books. Sketchy notes and jotted reminders in unpublished portions of Emerson's journals indicate the extent to which his books were circulating. A note, "Tennyson for [F. H.] Hedge," in a list of books to be lent in 1833 shows how early Tennyson was being passed around in the transcendental group (MS "Pocket Note-Book," dated 1833, Papers of the Ralph Waldo Emerson Memorial Association, Cambridge, Mass.).

17. II, 323–25 (December, 1836). The review is unsigned; however, the index to the volume assigns it to the "Editor," and in a letter of April 24, 1861, to Evert A. Duyckinck, Clarke wrote that he was the sole editor of the *Western Messenger* from April, 1836, to May, 1839 (MS letter, Duyckinck Collection, New York Public Library). According to the review, Clarke borrowed *Poems, Chiefly Lyrical* from "a friend," very probably Emerson.

18. XXIII, 305–27 (Jan., 1838). Professor William J. Rolfe says that Dwight told him that he had borrowed both books from Emerson for the preparation of the review (Biographical Sketch in *The Poetic and Dramatic Works of Alfred Lord Tennyson,* one volume, Boston and New York, 1898: hereafter referred to as Tennyson's *Works,* Student's Cambridge Edition).

19. Later Mrs. Nathaniel Hawthorne. For an account of the drawing, see a letter, Elizabeth Peabody to William J. Rolfe, 1884, quoted in Rolfe's Preface to *Select Poems of Alfred Lord Tennyson* (Boston, 1885).

20. *James Russell Lowell and His Friends* (Boston and New York, 1899), p. 21.

21. *Christian Examiner,* XXXIII, 237 (Nov., 1842).

22. *Harbinger,* VI, 158 (March 18, 1848).

23. See Christopher North's review of *Poems, Chiefly Lyrical, Blackwood's Edinburgh Magazine,* XXXI, 721–41 (May, 1832). Tennyson seems never to have realized that many of North's remarks were aimed not at him but at his friends who had praised him too highly.

24. *Journals of Ralph Waldo Emerson,* ten volumes, ed. Edward Waldo Emerson and Waldo Emerson Forbes (New York, 1911), III, 347 (Oct. 27, 1834): hereafter referred to as Emerson's *Journals.* The lines were incorrectly quoted from memory:

Let them rave!
Thou art quiet in the grave.

See Tennyson's *Works,* I, 201. Emerson again quoted the lines as they appear in the *Journals* in "Heroism" of *Essays, First Series* (see *The Complete Works of Ralph Waldo Emerson,* twelve volumes, ed. Edward Waldo Emerson, Cambridge, Mass., 1903, II, 263: hereafter referred to as Emerson's *Works*).

25. *Journals,* IV, 72 (June 22, 1836). Cf. "It would give me new scope to write on topics proper to this age and read discourses on Goethe, Carlyle, Wordsworth, Canova, Thorwaldsen, Tennyson, O'Connell, Baring, Channing, and Webster. To these I must write up" (*ibid.,* V, 17, August 18, 1838). Cf. also "A notice of modern literature ought to include (ought it not?) a notice of Carlyle, of Tennyson, of Landor, of Bettina, of Sampson Reed" (*ibid.,* V, 425, June–July, 1840).

26. *Journals,* V, 57 (Sept. 21, 1838). In a letter to William Henry Furness, September 20, 1838. Emerson wrote "Do you read Tennyson? a beautiful half of a poet" (*Records of a Lifelong Friendship: Ralph Waldo Emerson and Willliam Henry Furness,* New York, 1910, p. 7).

27. *Journals,* V, 6 (July 1, 1838).

28. *Ibid.,* IV, 411–12 (March 18, 1838). The Tennyson quotation is from "The Lotos-Eaters," lines 3–4. It was a favorite quotation with Emerson. He quoted it again in his essay, "Walter Savage Landor" (*Dial,* II, 264, October, 1841). For "The Lotos-Eaters," see Tennyson's *Works,* II, 39.

29. MS letter, undated, in the Craigie House Papers. The letter is quoted in full in Lawrance Thompson, *Young Longfellow* (New York, 1938), pp. 413–14. Longfellow had bought a copy of the 1833 *Poems,* undoubtedly when he was in London in 1835, and in September, 1837, he had the book bound in purple leather, and then presented it to Miss Appleton (MS journals of Longfellow in the Craigie House Papers). The book, bearing the signature, "Fanny C. Appleton," is now in the Craigie House, Cambridge, Massachusetts. The letter probably was written soon after the poems were sent. Of the two quotations in the letter, the first is from "The Lotos-Eaters," and the second is from that portion of "Rosalind" which was omitted in revision (see Tennyson's *Works,* I, 335–36). The misspelling *Tennison* was common with Longfellow for many years. He spelled it thus as late as July 14, 1846 (MS journals, Craigie House Papers).

30. MS letters of Fanny Kemble, 1840, Craigie House Papers.

31. See *Records of a Girlhood,* p. 581; and Margaret Armstrong, *Fanny Kemble, A Passionate Victorian* (New York, 1938), p. 188.

32. *Papers on Literature and Art* (New York, 1846), p. vii.

33. Letter from Margaret Fuller to Emerson, November 24, 1839, in Emerson's *Letters,* II, 239.

34. II, 135 (July, 1841). The review is unsigned, but George Willis Cooke (*An Historical and Biographical Introduction to Accompany The Dial,* Cleveland, 1902, II, 201) assigns it to Margaret Fuller, and internal evidence leaves little doubt of the authorship.

35. Letter, Emerson to Carlyle, July 31, 1846, in *The Correspondence of Thomas Carlyle and Ralph Waldo Emerson, 1834–1872,* ed. Charles Eliot Norton (Boston, 1883), II, 116.

36. Higginson, "A Child of the College," *Atlantic Monthly,* LXXVIII,

767 (Dec., 1896). Maria White, later Mrs. James Russell Lowell and already his close friend, doubtless had got the books through Lowell. In July, 1850, Higginson wrote to Emerson: "During your absence I made a visit to your study . . . [and] saw several things which I coveted, and the first edition of Tennyson was especially tempting; I had pleasant memories of it and had long wished to meet it again. . . . I borrowed it, promising myself to return it in a week. Alas, that the conscience should be so hardened by time, but I have kept it six weeks, and do not feel so guilty as when I first pocketed it" (*Letters and Journals of Thomas Wentworth Higginson, 1846–1906,* ed. Mary Thacher Higginson, Boston and New York, 1921, pp. 33–34).

37. Higginson, "The Equation of Fame," in *Studies in History and Letters* (Cambridge, Mass., 1900), pp. 280–82. Higginson quoted Channing as saying of the passage, "I wish you to say what you think. I regard Tennyson as a great calf, but you are entitled to your own opinion" (*ibid.,* p. 281).

38. "The Poems of Alfred Tennyson," XXI, 152 (Sept., 1842). This unsigned review has been assigned to Poe (*The Complete Works of Edgar Allan Poe,* seventeen volumes, ed. James A. Harrison, New York, 1902, XI, 127: hereafter referred to as Poe's *Works*), but it was obviously by Griswold, editor of *Graham's* from July, 1842, to June, 1843. A Review of Griswold's *Poets and Poetry of America,* published in the Philadelphia *Saturday Museum* for January 28, 1843, assigned the controversial *Graham's* review to Griswold and scornfully analyzed it as a stock example of Griswold's poor judgment and bad writing. This review of Griswold has been widely assigned to Poe (Killis Campbell, *The Mind of Poe and Other Studies,* Cambridge, Mass., 1933, pp. 213–14, 226–27). The anonymous poem, *The Poets and Poetry of America, A Satire by Lavante* (Philadelphia, 1847) quoted from the review in the *Saturday Museum* a passage which it tagged "Poe's critique on Griswold" (see edition by Geoffrey Quarles, New York, 1887, p. 3 of original notes). And Griswold's account of Tennyson in *The Poets and Poetry of England in the Nineteenth Century* (Philadelphia, 1845, p. 445) contained several complete sentences and two factual errors which appeared in the *Graham's* review.

39. Several English anthologies and books of criticism played a small part in acquainting Americans with Tennyson. *The Gem, A Literary Annual* for 1831, a London gift-book to which Tennyson contributed three poems (see Tennyson's *Works,* Student's Cambridge Edition, p. 790), was advertised in Boston in December, 1830, as one of the most attractive of the English annuals (*New England Galaxy,* Dec. 10, 1830). *Specimens of the Table Talk of the Late Samuel Taylor Coleridge,* which contains several references to Tennyson, was published in an American edition in 1835 (New York; Harper & Brothers). Also, an anthology of modern British poetry, *The Book of Gems* (London, 1840), which contained a biographical account and six poems of Tennyson, circulated to some extent in America: the *Orion,* small literary magazine of Penfield, Georgia, quoted from the biographical account in September, 1842 (I, 395).

40. *Blackwood's Edinburgh Magazine,* the *Edinburgh Review,* the *Quarterly Review,* the *Westminster Review,* and the *London Review,* each of which reviewed Tennyson at least once before 1842, were all reprinted in

America in the 1830's (see sets of the American editions listed in the Union Catalogue of the Library of Congress). Notices in newspapers and magazines spoke of the excellence of the reprints and of the financial success of the publishers (Providence, R. I., *Literary Journal,* I, 247, Jan. 4, 1834; *New York Literary Gazette and Journal of Belles Lettres,* No. 8, p. 126, Dec. 5, 1834; New York *Sunday Morning News,* May 8, 1836; etc.).

41. As early as 1828, Edward Willmer, famous Liverpool bookseller, was forwarding English magazines to America "by the very first vessel which sails after they are published" (*Albion,* VII, 127, Sept. 27, 1828), and a little later the firm of Messrs. Wiley and Putnam was delivering at New York, Boston, and Philadelphia "all the magazines . . . by the twentieth of the month on which they are dated, and from a week to fifteen days before they can be reprinted" (*Knickerbocker,* XVIII, 180, Feb., 1841).

42. Phillips, *op. cit.,* pp. 286–90, 590–92.

43. *New World,* V, 238 (Oct. 8, 1842).

44. XLIX, 81–96. This unsigned review is commonly attributed to John Gibson Lockhart, editor of the *Quarterly,* but it was undoubtedly written by Croker. An undated letter, Lockhart to Croker, written apparently just after the completion of the article and recently discovered in the Lockhart Collection of the University of Michigan Library, seems to clear up any uncertainty. The letter is printed in the *Colophon* (New Graphic Series, I, 95, Feb., 1940): "I have read the revised article on Tennyson and think you have more completely effected your purpose, & that as shortly as it cd have been done. It is wonderful that such folly shd pass for poetry with *anybody!* . . . ."

Equally conclusive evidence of Croker's authorship appears in letters between the two concerning John Sterling's favorable review of Tennyson's *Poems* of 1842 in the *Quarterly* (LXX, 385–416, Sept., 1842). Offended by Lockhart's accepting the article, Croker wrote, ". . . it was . . . a public and direct dissent from, and disclaimer of, my opinions," and in a conciliatory tone, Lockhart answered, "By accepting it, I fancied I was taking the easiest way to do Mr. Tennyson justice, and the way most certain to save you from any unpleasant feeling with reference to the article on his early rhymes." These two letters, dated November 20 and 22, 1842, were published in full in the *Quarterly* for April, 1909 (CCX, 775), but until very recently little notice has been taken of them. These letters, together with the one newly discovered, make the assignment of the review to Croker indisputable.

45. To justify his observations, the *Albion's* reviewer quoted the first stanza of "O Darling Room" (N. S., I, 176, June 1, 1833). A popular New York weekly, the *Albion* was composed largely of material selected from British books and journals. It published two songs from Tennyson's "The Miller's Daughter" within six weeks after the appearance of the 1833 volume containing the poem (N. S., I, 33, Feb. 2, 1833).

46. An unsigned review of Grenville Mellen's *The Martyr's Triumph, Buried Valley, and Other Poems,* IV, 325–26.

47. Review of Longfellow's *Ballads and Other Poems, Graham's Magazine,* XX, 189 (March, 1842). The review is unsigned, but it is commonly assigned to Poe. See Poe's *Works,* XI, 64–68; Phillips, *op. cit.,* p. 690; etc. On several occasions before 1842, Poe named Tennyson in the same breath

with the established poets. In January, 1837, he hesitated to assign William Cullen Bryant "a place with the spiritual Shelleys, or Coleridges, or Wordsworths, or with Keats, or even Tennyson, or Wilson, or with some other burning lights of our own day, to be valued in a day to come" (review of Bryant's *Poems, Southern Literary Messenger,* III, 49). See also Poe's "A Notice of William Cullen Bryant," *Burton's Gentleman's Magazine,* VI, 205 (May, 1840).

48. *Graham's Magazine,* XX, 195–99 (April, 1842). The review was signed "C."

49. XXI, 152 (Sept., 1842).

50. Letter to Rufus W. Griswold, July 14, 1842, in *Passages from the Correspondence and Other Papers of Rufus W. Griswold* (Cambridge, Mass., 1898), p. 113.

51. II, 325 (July 16, 1842).

52. Letter from Margaret Fuller to Emerson, December 6, 1840, in Emerson's *Letters,* II, 363. Neither Lowell's letters nor his biographers indicate what sonnets were included in this group. Margaret Fuller was willing to publish the last one in the group if Lowell should consent for it to go alone (*ibid.*). One sonnet of Lowell's appeared in the *Dial* for January, 1841 (I, 366): "Sonnet—To a Voice Heard in Mount Auburn, July, 1839." It possibly owes something to Tennyson: it speaks of "half-sad memories of other years" and draws a comparison between a bird and a girl, as Tennyson liked to do.

53. XXX, 131–34 (March, 1841).

54. LII, 465 (April, 1841). The review is unsigned, but George Willis Cooke (*A Bibliography of James Russell Lowell,* Boston and New York, 1906, p. 77) assigns it to Hillard.

55. "James Russell Lowell," *North American Review,* CLIII, 462 (Oct., 1891).

56. MS notebook, James Russell Lowell Collection, Harvard College Library.

57. *Graham's Magazine,* XIX, 171 (Oct., 1841). The first eight of the sixteen stanzas are quoted.

58. *Poems, Chiefly Lyrical,* pp. 14–18; reprinted in Tennyson's *Works,* I, 159–61.

59. Boston, 1841, pp. 110–11; reprinted with revisions in *The Complete Writings of James Russell Lowell* (sixteen volumes, Cambridge, Mass., 1904), IX, 14: hereafter referred to as Lowell's *Works.*

60. *Poems* (London, 1833), 87–93; reprinted with revisions in Tennyson's *Works,* I, 256–60. The refrain was much revised; see notes.

61. *Graham's Magazine,* XX, 89 (Feb., 1842); reprinted with revisions in *Works,* IX, 53–56.

62. *Graham's Magazine,* XX, 305 (June, 1842); reprinted in *Poems,* ed. Edmund M. Ashe (New York, 1894), pp. 96–97. The second stanza is quoted. The first line, incidentally, suggests Wordsworth's lines to Lucy:

> —Fair as a star, when only one
> Is shining in the sky.

63. *A Year's Life,* p. 104; reprinted in *Works,* IX, 6–10. In a letter to G. B. Loring on May 10, 1839, Lowell quoted two lines from the Choric Song of "The Lotos-Eaters":

Music that gentlier on the spirit lies,
Than tired eyelids upon tired eyes.

Here, he said, Tennyson described gentle, soothing music "more beautifully than any poet I am acquainted with" (*Works,* XIV, 49).

64. Other early poems by Lowell which may be assigned to this Tennysonian group are "The Serenade," "Music," and "Threnodia on an Infant." "The Serenade" and "Music" appeared first in April and May, 1840, in the *Southern Literary Messenger* (VI, 248, 332–33); both were included in *A Year's Life;* and neither is collected in late editions. The "Threnodia" first appeared in the *Knickerbocker* in May, 1839 (XIII, 433), and was reprinted slightly revised in *Works,* IX, 3–6.

65. *Poems, Chiefly Lyrical,* pp. 3–5; reprinted with revisions in Tennyson's *Works,* I, 153–54.

66. *A Year's Life,* pp. 176–78.

67. See *Poems, Chiefly Lyrical,* pp. 21–23; reprinted with revisions in Tennyson's *Works,* I, 164–66.

68. All three are included in *A Year's Life,* and are uncollected in late editions. All first appeared in the *Southern Literary Messenger:* "What reck I of the stars when I," March, 1840 (VI, 213); "Lift up the curtains of thine eyes" and "Isabel," June, 1840 (VI, 416, 468).

69. *Poems, Chiefly Lyrical,* pp. 6–8; reprinted with revisions in Tennyson's *Works,* I, 155.

70. See *ibid.;* and Lowell's *Works,* IX, 10–13. "Irené" first appeared in *A Year's Life* (pp. 112–17). In April, 1842, Lowell in speaking of Jeremy Taylor's "Countess of Carbery" and Tennyson's "Isabel" called them "poems in the truest and highest sense of the word" ("Old English Dramatists," *Boston Miscellany of Literature and Fashion,* I, 151).

71. V, 95 (Aug. 6, 1842). The *New World* was one of the few American magazines which included in their columns some of Tennyson's poems before 1842. That James Aldrich, one of its editors from 1841 to 1845, knew of Tennyson, we have already seen.

72. First published as "The Fifth Psalm" in the *Knickerbocker,* October, 1839 (XIV, 330–31); reprinted in *The Complete Writings of Henry Wadsworth Longfellow* (eleven volumes, Boston and New York, 1904), I, 31–33: hereafter referred to as Longfellow's *Works.*

73. Review of *Voices of the Night, Burton's Gentlemen's Magazine,* VI, 103 (Feb., 1840). The rather long and violent accusation was repeated almost word for word in the *Broadway Journal* for March 29, 1845 (I, 195–96). The two poems were quoted in full in each case.

74. Undated letter to Samuel Ward quoted in Henry M. Hall, "Longfellow's Letters to Samuel Ward," *Putnam's Monthly,* III, 42 (Oct., 1907). Lawrance Thompson (*op. cit.,* p. 416) dates the letter between February 10 and 27, 1840.

75. See Phillips, *op. cit.,* pp. 405, 533–34, 876–77, 1047.

76. XXXII, 321–22 (Jan., 1844). Poe was angered by the article, which he thought was by Dickens, but which was almost certainly by John Forster. See Phillips, *op. cit.,* pp. 900–02; a letter, Lowell to Poe, June 27, 1844, in *Passages from the Correspondence and Other Papers of Rufus W. Griswold,* p. 151; and Killis Campbell's edition of Poe's *Poems* (Boston, 1917), p. 238. Campbell assigned the review to Forster without argument.

77. See Poe's "James Aldrich," *Godey's Magazine and Lady's Book,* XXIV, 16–17 (July, 1846); reprinted in *Works,* XV, 62–64. Also, *The Poets and Poetry of America,* ed. Rufus W. Griswold (Philadelphia, 1850), pp. 399–400.

78. *New York Mirror,* XVII, 283 (Feb. 29, 1840); reprinted in *The Poets and Poetry of America,* p. 400. The second and fourth of five stanzas are quoted. Cf. especially Tennyson's "The Sleeping Beauty," *Poems, Chiefly Lyrical,* p. 143; reprinted in *Works,* II, 222.

79. Poe's "James Aldrich," *Works,* XV, 63–64. The poem was written probably around 1842. For others of Aldrich's Tennysonian poems, see "Lines" (*New World,* I, 433, Dec. 12, 1840); "Beatrice" (*ibid.,* III, 321, Nov. 20, 1841); "Viola" (*ibid.,* V, 16, July 2, 1842); etc.

80. "To Susannah," anonymous, *New York Atlas Magazine,* I, 45 (Feb. 1, 1834).

81. "Kate," anonymous, *Lady's World of Fashion,* I, 104 (April, 1842). Just above the title is a heading "Sonnets on Names," which suggests Lowell, as does the whole poem, and Lowell's "Serenade" appears in the same issue (p. 126); however, "Kate" has never been assigned to Lowell. For other apparent imitations, see "Midnight Mass," *Philadelphia Visitor and Parlour Companion,* V, 232 (August, 1839); "Charming Roselle," *New York Mirror,* XVII, 57 (Aug. 13, 1839); "Why Comes He Not," *Godey's Lady's Book,* XXV, 33 (July, 1842); etc. A remarkable resemblance of a different sort exists between Tennyson's "The Palace of Art" and a poem which George H. Colton, later author of the long poem, "Tecumseh," wrote while a student at Yale. Colton's poem "A Fragment" (*Yale Literary Magazine,* V, 300–07, April, 1840) is entirely different from "The Palace of Art" in form, but the two poems express almost exactly the same philosophy. The *New Englander* in noting the parallel (VII, 237–38, May, 1849) rejected the idea of imitation on grounds of date, but Colton may well have seen Tennyson's poem.

82. *Class Poem* (Cambridge, 1838), p. 48. The quotation is in a note to the lines concerning Wordsworth's "Peter Bells and half-starved asses."

83. Letter to Harriet St. Leger, August 17, 1833, in *Records of a Girlhood,* p. 581.

84. An account of Holmes's lecture on Tennyson and Browning in the series of "Lowell Institute Lectures on English Poetry," *Boston Daily Evening Transcript,* April 20, 1853. The condemned song is undoubtedly the "English War-Song," *Poems, Chiefly Lyrical,* pp. 138–40; reprinted in *Works* (Student's Cambridge Edition), pp. 785–86.

85. Holmes left New York upon his first trip to Europe on April 3, 1833 (John T. Morse, Jr., *Life and Letters of Oliver Wendell Holmes,* Cambridge, Mass., 1896, I, 83), four months after the publication of "The Lady of Shalott." Therefore if the quoted statement is true, Holmes saw the manuscript in America. This is possible but quite unlikely. Possibly Holmes meant that he heard the revised version read before its publication in 1842, or possibly the reporter copied his statement incorrectly. Neither the Boston *Daily Evening Traveller* nor the Boston *Daily Courier* reported the lecture.

86. See Thomas R. Lounsbury, *The Life and Times of Tennyson* (New Haven, Conn., 1915), pp. 446–64.

87. See Clarence Gohdes, *The Periodicals of American Transcendental-*

ism (Durham, N. C., 1931), pp. 17–29; and Frank Luther Mott, *A History of American Magazines* (Cambridge, Mass., 1938), I, 658–63.

88. Only one other of Tennyson's poems appeared in the *Messenger:* "The Mystic" in June, 1838 (V, 160–61).

89. The *Album* contains one other poem by Tennyson: "Lost Hope" in June, 1837 (II, 373).

90. *Arcturus,* II, 161.

91. MS letter to James Russell Lowell, December 17, 1841, Lowell Collection, Harvard College Library. In 1831 Leigh Hunt wrote for his London daily journal, the *Tatler,* four articles upon the poems of Alfred and Charles Tennyson (Feb. 24, 26, and March 1, 3). The first two articles were devoted largely to Alfred, and the last two to Charles. Hunt hailed both of them as great poets.

92. For selections elsewhere, see those already referred to in footnotes; also "Isabel" (*New England Galaxy,* Dec. 8, 1832); "The Death of the Old Year" (Boston *Daily Evening Transcript,* Dec. 31, 1841; the poem had the title "Farewell to the Old Year"); "New Year's Eve" (Lowell, Mass., *Literary Souvenir,* V, 17, Jan. 15, 1842); "Lilian," "The Merman," and "Mariana" (*Lady's World of Fashion,* I, 52, 55, Feb., 1842; and I, 136, May, 1842).

93. "Mariana," I, 9–10 (Feb. 9); "Kate," I, 39 (March 2); "Adeline," I, 67 (March 30); "To J. S." [James Spedding], I, 136 (May 25); "The Ballad of Oriana," I, 137 (June 1); "Margaret," I, 157 (June 15); "To——" ["All good things have not kept aloof"], I, 170 (June 29). "To J. S." and "To——" were entitled merely "Stanzas," with no acknowledgement to Tennyson. Since its first reprinting in 1872, "To——" has as its title its new first line: "My Life is full of weary days." "The Ballad of Oriana" was prefaced by a few original sentences of praise and a paragraph concerning it quoted from John Sullivan Dwight's review in the *Christian Examiner.*

94. "To——" ["All good things have not kept aloof"], III, 140 (Aug. 28, 1841); "Margaret," III, 330 (Nov. 20, 1841); "The Sleeping Beauty," IV, 141 (Feb. 26, 1842); "Adeline," IV, 206 (March 26, 1842); "The May Queen," IV, 411 (June 25, 1842); "The Ballad of Oriana," V, 47 (July 16, 1842). "To——" was entitled "Stanzas," with no acknowledgement to Tennyson. "The Sleeping Beauty" was entitled "The Charmed Sleeper." "The Ballad of Oriana" was prefaced by the same sentences of praise and the same quoted paragraph which had appeared with it in the *Literary Gazette.*

95. Quarto Edition, I, 373 (Sept. 3, 1836), and X, 243 (Jan. 2, 1841). "The Death of the Old Year" had the title "Farewell to the Old Year."

96. XVI, 363 (May 11, 1839); and XVII, 267 (Feb. 15, 1840).

97. MS letter, Craigie House Papers. Probably Longfellow had borrowed *Poems, Chiefly Lyrical* from Emerson, who had told C. C. Little that Longfellow owned a copy of the *Poems.* Emerson owned both books, but probably the *Poems* had been borrowed by someone harder to reach than was Longfellow.

98. The opening sentence of Tennyson's letter of February 22, 1841, to Wheeler, quoted in part below, states that it is an answer to a communication of December 25.

99. See Emerson's letter to Carlyle, July 1, 1842, in *The Correspondence of Thomas Carlyle and Ralph Waldo Emerson,* II, 3. For accounts of Wheeler, see William Augustus Davis, *Biographical Notice of Charles*

Stearns Wheeler (Boston, 1843); and Cooke, *An Historical and Biographical Introduction to Accompany The Dial,* I, 161–65.

100. See Lowell's letter of December 5, 1841, to Evert A. Duyckinck, quoted below.

101. *Alfred, Lord Tennyson, A Memoir by His Son* (New York, 1897), I, 178: hereafter referred to as the *Memoir.*

102. MS letter, Duke University Library.

103. MS letter, December 5, 1841, Duyckinck Collection, New York Public Library. The letter is printed in Lowell's *Works,* XIV, 78. Duyckinck's *News-Gong, A Literary Intelligencer* was issued in three numbers in 1841 and 1842 as a supplement to the *Arcturus.* No copy of any number can be located now. Lowell's letter refers to Duyckinck's comments upon Tennyson in the *News-Gong.*

104. MS letter, Duyckinck to Lowell, December 17, 1841, James Russell Lowell Collection, Harvard College Library.

105. III, 235 (Feb., 1842). The *Lady's World of Fashion* exulted in like manner. Having heard rumors of America's demand for a new edition, the *Lady's World* thought that the Boston edition was to precede the London, and even announced as early as February, 1842, that it had already appeared (I, 45).

Chapter II

1. For a concise discussion of the contents of the two volumes and the revisions of the poems, see Lounsbury, *op. cit.,* pp. 391–415.

2. MS letter, Papers of the Ralph Waldo Emerson Memorial Association.

3. MS letter, November ?, 1842. Widener Collection, Harvard College Library.

4. J. C. Derby, *Fifty Years among Authors, Books and Publishers* (New York, 1884), p. 617.

5. William D. Ticknor & Co., 1833–1845; Ticknor, Reed & Fields, 1845–1854; Ticknor and Fields, 1854–1868; Fields, Osgood & Co., 1868–1871; James R. Osgood & Co., 1871–1878; Houghton, Osgood & Co., 1878–1880; James R. Osgood & Co., 1880–1885; Ticknor & Co., 1885–1889; Houghton Mifflin & Co., 1889–.

6. Caroline Ticknor, *Hawthorne and His Publisher* (Boston and New York, 1913), p. 3.

7. Letter to B. H. Ticknor, September 4, 1889, in Ticknor, *op. cit.,* p. 5.

8. It is often referred to as the earliest (see Derby, *loc. cit.;* and Ticknor, *op. cit.,* p. 3). Several American publishers had paid English authors small portions of the proceeds from American editions as early as 1838 (see William Glyde Wilkins, *First and Early American Editions of the Works of Charles Dickens,* Cedar Rapids, Iowa, 1910, pp. 8–9; and Augustus Ralli, *Guide to Carlyle,* London, 1920, I, 270), but a distinction must be drawn between a payment from the profits of sale and the purchase of the right to reprint. Ticknor's seems to have been a copyright purchase.

9. The Boston *Daily Evening Transcript* of that date announced the "beautiful edition" as "published this morning."

10. The steamship *Britannia* landed at Boston on June 18, and on June 20 Elizabeth Peabody advertised for sale at her book store "a small lot"

of the *Poems* "just received . . . by the Britannia" (Boston *Daily Advertiser,* June 18 and 20, 1842).

11. An anonymous reviewer in the *Southern Literary Messenger* (VIII, 612, Sept., 1842) thought that they compared more favorably with books issued by the London press than any other American books he had ever seen.

12. *New World,* V, 63 (July 23, 1842).

13. MS letter, Wheeler to Emerson, June 11, 1842, Papers of the Ralph Waldo Emerson Memorial Association.

14. William J. Rolfe (Tennyson's *Works,* I, 50) gives 1,500 as the size of the first American edition; Derby (*loc. cit.*) gives 2,000. Figures on the English editions are from Wise, *op. cit.,* I, 80–81, 87.

15. Dated 1846, the edition was noticed as early as Nov. 22, 1845 (*Broadway Journal,* II, 307). For information concerning the American editions of Tennyson, see Appendix A.

16. In May and June, 1843, Elizabeth Peabody advertised for sale at her Boston book store a lot as just received by the steamship *Hibernia* (Boston *Daily Advertiser,* May 6 ff.).

17. July 7 and August 15, 1842.

18. In its review on July 12, the New York *Evening Post for the Country* announced the volumes for sale by Wiley and Putnam of New York. The *Post* had reviewed the *Poems* as early as July 8, but since the reviewer spoke of the "extracts which we have seen," apparently he had not seen the volumes.

19. V, 48 (July 16, 1842).

20. V. 63 (July 23, 1842). The *New World* had already reviewed the English edition with high praise before the American reached its office (V, 48, July 16, 1842).

21. By far the most popular selection was "Godiva." On June 18, before the *Poems* of 1842 had reached New York in any edition, *Brother Jonathan* was enabled "through the politeness of a friend" to present "Godiva" to its readers (II, 213), and with that early start it spread through the news sheets: *Evening Post for the Country,* July 8; *Daily Tribune,* July 12; *Weekly Tribune,* July 16. For the newspaper popularity of "Godiva" outside of New York, see Boston *Morning Post,* July 8; Washington *Daily National Intelligencer,* Oct. 6; and *Boston Daily Advertiser,* Oct. 10.

22. See Lounsbury, *op. cit.,* pp. 424–36. So stereotyped became the expression that Professor Lounsbury spoke of the reviewers as "echoing the cuckoo cry."

23. Letter, Elizabeth Peabody to William J. Rolfe, 1884, quoted in Rolfe's preface to *Select Poems of Alfred Lord Tennyson* (Boston, 1885), pp. v–vi.

24. XIV, 62–77 (Jan., 1844). George William Curtis, who liked the review, made an interesting comment upon it: "Perhaps she [Fanny Kemble] is too masculine a woman to judge correctly his [Tennyson's] delicacy; but she does the whole thing well" (letter to Dwight, March 27, 1844, in *Early Letters of George William Curtis to John S. Dwight,* ed. George Willis Cooke, New York and London, 1898, p. 162).

25. Rufus W. Griswold in *Graham's Magazine* (XXL, 152–53, Sept., 1842) and anonymous reviewers in the *Boston Miscellany of Literature and Fashion* (II, 140, Sept., 1842) and the *Lady's World of Fashion* (II, 114–17, Oct., 1842) also expressed regret over the alterations of the early poems.

The *Lady's World of Fashion* thought that Tennyson had not "improved with years": that "the best of his later poems display more finish, as well as more compactness than the earlier ones cannot be doubted; but much of the airy and seductive grace which charmed us in 'Madeline,' 'Mariana,' 'Adeline,' 'The Lotos-Eaters' and other poems is wanting in the productions of his maturer years."

26. George William Curtis, "Editor's Easy Chair," *Harper's New Monthly Magazine,* XXXVIII, 270 (Jan., 1869). Curtis, who lived for a while at Brook Farm, was pleased to find in the 1842 volume that Nature had confirmed his early judgment of Tennyson. Tennyson's songs, such as "Break, Break, Break," had a charm like unto Shakespeare's. Letter to Dwight, Sept. 1, 1843, in *Early Letters of George William Curtis to John S. Dwight,* p. 109.

27. III, 273–76 (Oct., 1842). The review is unsigned, and George Willis Cooke in his list of contributors (*Historical and Biographical Introduction to The Dial,* II, 205) assigns it to Emerson. The review, however, is undoubtedly by Margaret Fuller. Elsewhere in his *Introduction* (II, 162), Cooke himself refers to the review as Margaret Fuller's, and on October 16, 1842, she wrote to Emerson concerning two typographical errors which occur in the review, "I *am a little vexed,* having hoped my notice might meet the eye of the poet" (Emerson's *Letters,* III, 91).

28. When she first saw these new poems she read herself into many of them. "In Dora, Locksley Hall, The Two Voices, Morte D'Arthur, I find my own life, much of it, written truly out," she wrote Emerson in August, 1842 (*Memoirs of Margaret Fuller Ossoli,* ed. William H. Channing with others, Boston, 1852, II, 66). Such an experience, however, was not unusual with her: as she read Shelley's journals for the first time she found him "affected very much" as she was (MS letter, Margaret Fuller to Emerson, April 26, 1840. Papers of the Ralph Waldo Emerson Memorial Association).

29. Emerson's *Journals,* VI, 218–19 (July, 1842). About the same time Emerson jotted into his journals opposite the name of Tennyson such phrases as "a cosmetic poet" and "tea tray style" (Sept. 26–Nov. 5, 1843, and July 31–Nov. 23, 1846, MS journals O and U, Harvard College Library).

30. *Journals,* VI, 286–88 (Oct., 1842). Cf. Emerson's letter to Margaret Fuller, July 19, 1842 (Emerson's *Letters,* III, 74).

31. *Journals,* VI, 219 (July, 1842), 244 (Sept., 1842).

32. III, 517–18 (April, 1843). The article was headed "Europe and European Books." It appeared also in the New York *Daily Tribune* (April 17, 1843), with the title "Wordsworth and Tennyson."

33. The omitted passage is a comparison of Tennyson's dainty fineness to Ben Jonson's rude manliness. Emerson had drawn the comparison in slightly different words as early as February, 1842. He seems to have thought often of Tennyson and Jonson as opposite extremes (see *Journals,* VI, 158, Jan.–Feb., 1842).

34. Undoubtedly, Poe gained his first knowledge of Tennyson from the British periodicals, which he was reading continually and even contributing to in the thirties (Phillips, *op. cit.,* pp. 286–90, 590–92), but although Poe's attitude toward Tennyson was directly opposed to their low estimate, he seems never to have defended his favorite against them.

35. "William Ellery Channing," *Graham's Magazine,* XXIII, 113 (Aug., 1843). See Poe's *Works,* XI, 174–90.

36. *Broadway Journal,* II, 26 (July 19, 1845). For the assignment of this unsigned article entitled "Alfred Tennyson" to Poe, see Pope-Hennessy, *op. cit.,* p. 241.

37. "Marginalia," *Democratic Review,* XV, 580. Poe is speaking here on a favorite topic. It is Tennyson's purity, "etherisity," and lack of passion, said Poe, which "constitutes him one of the greatest geniuses that ever lived" (Thomas Holley Chivers' account of a conversation with Poe in the summer of 1845, quoted in George E. Woodberry, "The Poe-Chivers Papers," *Century Magazine,* LXV, 447, Jan., 1903). Poe referred to Tennyson's poems again and again as tests of the reader's poetic sensibilities. "Oenone," he said, "exalts the soul not into passion, but into a conception of pure *beauty,* which in its elevation—its calm and intense rapture—has in it a foreshadowing of the future and spiritual life, and as far transcends earthly passion as the holy radiance of the sun does the glimmering and feeble phosphorescence of the glow-worm . . . [and] 'Morte D'Arthur' is in the same majestic vein." If these poems stirred fewer readers than the passionate poems of Byron, the fact proved nothing "more than that the majority of mankind are more susceptible of the impulses of passion than of the impressions of beauty" (a review of R. H. Horne's *Orion, Graham's Magazine,* XXIV, 137, March, 1844. Exactly the same discussion appeared also in an unsigned article, "Increase of Poetical Heresy," probably by Poe, in the *New York Weekly Mirror,* N. S., I, 281, Feb. 8, 1845).

38. *Broadway Journal,* II, 322 (Nov. 29, 1845). Though unsigned, the notice is confidently assigned by biographers to Poe, the "sole editor and proprietor" of the *Journal.* Longfellow clipped the notice from the *Journal,* pasted it inside the cover of his copy of the *Poems* of 1842, and wrote beneath it "Edgar A. Poe." The book is now in the Craigie House.

39. The phrase floats about in Poe and Tennyson criticism, always with quotation marks but without reference. Possibly it has its origin in Bayard Taylor's well known essay on Tennyson (*International Review,* IV, 404, May, 1877). Mary E. Phillips in her biography of Poe (p. 714) varies the phrase but still uses the quotation marks: "the first to hail Alfred Tennyson from across the sea." Miss Phillips has written to me in a letter of November 23, 1939, that she does not remember where she saw the expression.

40. *International Review,* IV, 404–05 (May, 1877).

41. *Century Magazine,* LXV, 447 (Jan., 1903).

42. Letter, Chivers to Poe, Sept. 9, 1845, in Poe's *Works,* XVII, 213. In the last lines, Chivers is touching on his basic disagreement with Poe. Chivers thought that sheer beauty was not enough, that it had to be combined with Truth. Poe thought otherwise. It was natural that Tennyson's early poems should divide them.

43. Letter, Chivers to Poe, Oct. 30, 1845, in Poe's *Works,* XVII, 220.

44. Felton had just read John Sterling's favorable review of the *Poems* of 1842 in the London *Quarterly* (LXX, 385–416, Sept., 1842), was displeased that the *Quarterly* should have shifted its position as established in the earlier Croker review, and was determined not to follow suit (see *Christian Examiner,* XXXIII, 237–38, Nov., 1842). Felton's reference to Sterling's article as a "highly laudatory critique" is puzzling now to anyone who

reads the review. It was often spoken of as highly commendatory, but it was largely noncommittal—at best, mildly favorable.

45. In 1837 Felton, Longfellow, Charles Sumner, George S. Hillard, and Henry R. Cleveland formed a strong friendship and called themselves the "Five of Clubs." They "took a constant interest in each other's studies," and each "sought the criticism of the rest upon his own book, essay, or poem before it was given to the public" (Edward L. Pierce, *Memoir and Letters of Charles Sumner,* Boston, 1877, I, 161–62). Cleveland died in 1843, but the other four continued their close association for several years thereafter (*ibid.,* III, 49). That Longfellow was an early admirer of Tennyson, we have already seen; Sumner warmly welcomed the *Poems* of 1842 (letter to Milnes, Aug. 1, 1842, in T. Wemyss Reid, *The Life, Letters, and Friendships of Richard Monckton Milnes,* New York, 1891, I, 279–80); and a few years later Hillard wrote a poem upon his reading of Tennyson which Ticknor and Fields printed in the front of their "Blue and Gold" editions.

46. X, 240–46 (April, 1844). Edward Sculley Bradley (*Henry Charles Lea,* Philadelphia, 1931, p. 70) assigns the review to Lea.

47. VIII, 612 (Sept., 1842).

48. In August, 1842 (XX, 208), it "read them with admiration, not unmixed with tears" and thought they had "a pathos sweet and winning," and "melody of versification almost faultless." It would give the volumes "more elaborate justice" later. But by December (XX, 582) it had read Felton's review in the *Examiner* and quoted the most abusive passages as expressing its "own opinion" exactly. Then in June, 1845 (XXV, 534–40) it published a laudatory review which Charles A. Bristed, an American student at Cambridge University, had contributed.

49. An anonymous reviewer of Horne's *A New Spirit of the Age* in *Graham's Magazine* (XXV, 47, July, 1844) recommended Horne's laudatory chapter on Tennyson "particularly to our pleasant friend who 'does' the damning for the Southern Literary Messenger."

50. Philadelphia, 1845, p. 445. Griswold's biographical account evaluated Tennyson very much as his review in *Graham's* (XXI, 152–53, Sept., 1842) had done. Tennyson excelled most in his female portraitures, but they were too intangible. Tennyson showed at times a talent for graphic description, but he lacked creative power. In view of this estimate, it is interesting to note that Tennyson ranked fifth in the amount of space devoted to him in the anthology. Only Elizabeth Barrett, Wordsworth, Shelley, and Byron were given more space.

51. See *Ladies' National Magazine* (VII, 71, Feb., 1845), and belated reviews of the 1853 edition in *Presbyterian Quarterly Review* (VI, 656, March, 1858) and *Russell's Magazine* (V, 542, Sept., 1859). That Griswold had changed his mind in the meantime is shown by a quotation from him which Ticknor, Reed, and Fields used in their advertising in 1850: "Of the living poets of England—we include not the few choice spirits of Scotland—Tennyson at this time occupies the highest rank, and he is destined to a wide and high regard" (advertisement of Tennyson's *Complete Poetical Works* enclosed in the back of most issues of *In Memoriam* for 1850).

52. II, 45–48 (July, 1845). The Tennyson criticism is contained in a twenty-nine page review of *The Poets and Poetry of England in the Nine-*

teenth Century. Poe several times took occasion to praise this critique as one of the most appreciative reviews accorded Tennyson by an American (*Broadway Journal,* II, 26, July 19, 1845; and *Graham's Magazine,* XXXVI, 49, Jan., 1850). The review was republished in Whipple's *Essays and Reviews* (New York, 1849), I, 338–46.

53. III, 57–66 (Jan., 1845). The General Index gives Luzerne Ray as the author. Ray (1811–1854) was a minor poet of Connecticut.

54. IV, 91–93 (August, 1845). The review was republished in Tuckerman's *Thoughts on the Poets* (New York, 1846, pp. 273–80), and since the book circulated widely—a new edition was called for in 1848—, the essay on Tennyson doubtless played a significant part in making the poems known.

55. XXV, 534–40 (June, 1845).

56. I, 395 (Sept., 1842). Probably the review was written by William C. Richards, the *Orion's* English-born editor.

57. Lea's MS journal quoted in Bradley, *op. cit.,* p. 70.

58. Newspapers frequently reviewed individual numbers of the British magazines and sometimes evaluated the reviews of Tennyson's *Poems.* The Boston *Morning Post* (Oct. 20 and Nov. 7, 1842) thought John Sterling's review in the *Quarterly* (LXX, 385–416, Sept., 1842) poorly written but just, and Richard Monckton Milnes' review in the *Westminster Review* (LXXVIII, 371–90, Oct., 1842) only fair. The New York *Daily Tribune* (Oct. 19, 1842) thought Sterling's article "discriminating, sympathetic, and written with lofty strength." The *New World* (V, 288, Oct. 29, 1842; VI, 668, June 3) called Milnes' article "weak and common place" but liked James Spedding's review in the *Edinburgh Review* (LXXVII, 373–91, April, 1843). For the eclectic magazine's reprints of Tennyson reviews, see Appendix C.

59. *Democratic Review,* XIV, 62 (Jan., 1844).

60. Probably those in the *Examiner* (No. 1791, pp. 340–41, May 28, 1842) and *Tait's Edinburgh Magazine* (N.S., IX, 502–08, August, 1842) gave highest praise. The review in the *Examiner* is attributed to John Forster (Lounsbury, *op. cit.,* p. 419).

61. Many magazine articles deplored the lack of thoughtful American criticism (see Evert A. Duyckinck, "Criticism in America," *Arcturus,* VII, 401–06, May, 1842; and an article with the same title by W. A. Jones, *Democratic Review,* XV, 241–49, Sept., 1844). Daniel K. Whitaker, editor of the *Southern Literary Journal,* wrote in 1836 an article, "The Puffing System," to condemn "the practice of indiscriminate praise which characterizes the periodical press of our country" (*S. L. J.,* II, 312–15, June, 1836), and Horace Greeley's *New Yorker* (VII, 45, April 6, 1839) pled for a "proper mean" in American criticism: "hyperbolical puffing must give way to the calm expressions of judgement."

62. "In a word, we think that he [Tennyson] would find himself able to fly a higher flight than lyric, idyl, or eclogue, and we counsel him to try it" (*Examiner,* No. 1791, p. 340, May 28, 1842). "His command of diction is complete, his sense and execution of the harmonies of verse accurate and admirable; he has only to show that he has substance worthy of these media . . . that, in fine, he comprehends the function of the poet in this day of ours, to teach still more than he delights, and to suggest still more

than he teaches" (*Westminster Review,* XXXVIII, 390, Oct., 1842). "Powers are displayed in these volumes, adequate, if we do not deceive ourselves, to the production of a great work" (*Edinburgh Review,* LXXVII, 390, April, 1843).

63. Letter to John Sullivan Dwight, Feb. 25, 1844, in *Early Letters of Curtis to Dwight,* p. 150.

64. Two separate editions were published in New York in 1844, one by Harper & Brothers and the other by J. C. Riker.

65. *Southern Literary Messenger,* X, 620 (Oct., 1844).

66. XXV, 47 (July, 1844).

67. Published in London in 1847 and republished by Harper & Brothers in New York the same year. The book remained popular for years. In August, 1857, *Russell's Magazine* (I, 474) reviewed a new English edition, quoted from the chapter on Tennyson, and called it "capital criticism."

68. Longfellow, Margaret Fuller, and Charles Stearns Wheeler had hoped to see him on earlier trips abroad, but in each case circumstances had intervened (see Samuel Longfellow, *Life of Henry Wadsworth Longfellow,* Boston, 1886, I, 434–35, and *Memoirs of Margaret Fuller Ossoli,* II, 190). In August, 1842, soon after completion of his editing of Tennyson's *Poems,* Wheeler sailed for Europe, leaving Lowell to care for Tennyson's interests if any matters should arise requiring an agent for the author—in a letter of Nov. 14, 1842, to John Francis Heath, Wheeler referred to Lowell as serving in such a capacity, and when Tennyson wrote Wheeler that Ticknor had not sent him a copy of the American edition, Wheeler wrote Lowell, on Nov. 24, 1842, to have Ticknor send one at once (MS letters, Harvard College Library). Soon after Wheeler reached Europe, Tennyson wrote him a long and friendly letter wishing him pleasant travels and inviting him to England: "I ought not to forget that your bond with England is nearer and dearer than with Greece or Italy. . . . When do you intend to visit England? You must give me a little notice beforehand, or I may be out of the way, & I should be sorry to miss the pleasure of seeing you" (MS letter, November ?, 1842, Widener Collection, Harvard College Library). Wheeler proudly quoted from this letter in his correspondence with friends back home (see MS letters to Emerson, Nov. 11, 1842, and to Lowell, Nov. 24, 1842, Harvard College Library), and to one, he wrote in November, 1842, "I count on a very kind reception from him some eighteen months hence" (unidentified letter quoted in Davis, *op. cit.,* p. 10). This expectation was never realized, for Wheeler died suddenly in Heidelberg, Germany, on June 13, 1843.

69. In a letter of August 5, 1844, Carlyle described Tennyson's physical features and personal habits at length, and on September 30, Emerson replied, "The sketch you drew of Tennyson was right welcome, for he is an old favorite of mine,—I owned his book before I saw your face;—though I love him with allowance. O cherish him with love and praise, and draw from him whole books full of new verses yet" (*Correspondence of Carlyle and Emerson,* II, 66–68, 76). Henry Reed's knowledge of Tennyson came through letters from Wordsworth, with whom Reed corresponded regularly in the early 1840's (see *Wordsworth & Reed,* ed. Leslie Nathan Broughton, Ithaca, N. Y., 1933, pp. 144, 148).

70. See MS letters, Wheeler to Lowell, Nov. 8, 1842 (James Russell Lowell

Collection, Harvard College Library), and Wheeler to Emerson, Nov. 11, 1842 (Papers of the Ralph Waldo Emerson Memorial Association).

71. Published in London in 1846 and republished by Carey & Hart of Philadelphia the same year. The poem was published anonymously, but soon the name of the author was widely known.

72. Philadelphia, Carey & Hart, 1847.

73. "Poetry and Imagination," XLII, 263 (March, 1847). A review of *The New Timon* in the Washington *Daily National Intelligencer* for May 17, 1847, also approved. It spoke of the author's "just aversion" to Tennyson's "namby-pamby" poetry.

74. LXIV, 467 (April, 1847).

75. Anonymous review of *The New Timon,* XIII, 84 (Feb., 1847). For other protests against *The New Timon* and strong approvals of Tennyson's pension, see *Littell's Living Age,* VIII, 16 (Jan., 1846), and the *Democratic Review,* XIX, 317 (Oct., 1846).

76. I, 69 (Jan. 15, 1842). Cf. *George Cruikshank's Omnibus,* VIII, 260 (Dec., 1841). The parody, entitled "The Clerk," was prefaced by a paragraph (from *Cruikshank's Omnibus*) praising "Mariana at the Moated Grange" and assuring readers that no irreverence to the beautiful poem was intended.

77. XXI, 189 (Feb., 1843). The parody was taken from *Tait's Edinburgh Magazine* (N. S., IX, 803, Dec., 1842), but the *Knickerbocker,* at the moment under the spell of Felton (see above), wrote an introduction of its own: "The annexed stanzas . . . introduce us to that nice dandy-poet, Mr. Alfred Tennyson; a little man, who writes with little thought in a little room on a little piece of paper." "To Isaac Tomkins' Child" is not a harsh parody. The Boston *Daily Evening Transcript* for December 11, 1854, quoted it as an example of one having less caricature than most of Bon Gaultier's.

78. When Robert Southey died in 1843, Tennyson was among the poets considered for the laureateship. For *Tait's Edinburgh Magazine* for May (N. S., X, 273–76), Bon Gaultier wrote "Lays of the Would-Be Laureates," supposed petitions for the honor written by the various aspirants. Tennyson's was "The Laureate." It was both clever and genial. Several American newspapers reprinted it at once (Boston *Daily Advertiser,* July 10, 1843, and Washington *Daily National Intelligencer,* July 13, 1843), and it became popular.

79. New York: J. S. Redfield. Neither Roorbach's *Bibliotheca Americana* nor the Union Catalogue of the Library of Congress lists an earlier edition.

80. See *Albion,* 4th Ser., XI, 153 (March 27, 1852); XIII, 244 (May 27, 1854); *Sartain's Magazine,* X, 437–38 (May, 1852); and the Boston *Daily Evening Transcript,* Jan. 9, 1855.

81. X, 438 (May, 1852).

82. XVIII, 429–33 (July, 1852).

83. Some fun is made of Tennyson in advertisements and in what were called "patchworks"—individual lines from many different poems pieced together to form one—, but neither of these are worth considering (see "Claribelle" in advertisement of Smith Brothers, Clothiers, New York *Daily Tribune,* March 15, 1858; see "patchworks" in *Putnam's Monthly Magazine,* IX, 439–43, April, 1857, and in San Francisco *Evening Bulletin,* Oct. 30, 1857). In an article entitled "Puffs and Poetry," Bon Gaultier had

in October, 1843 (*Tait's Edinburgh Magazine,* N.S., X, 649–54), parodied several poems as advertisements of various wares. *Brother Jonathan* (VI, 228–32, Oct. 28, 1843) reprinted the article. In it, parts of "Morte d'Arthur" were made into an advertisement of Mechi's steel razors.

84. *Godey's Lady's Book,* XXV, 275 (Dec., 1842). The poem was signed "J. Tomlin, Esq., Jackson Tennessee."

85. *American Whig Review,* IV, 117–18 (August, 1846). The poem (98 lines in all) was entitled "Emily, Some Memories in the Glass of Tennyson." When it was reprinted in Parker's collected *Poems* (Auburn, N.Y., 1850, pp. 137–40), "Emily" was changed to "Floralie" in the title and throughout the poem.

86. Far the most popular of the few parodies by Americans was "Eagle Ye Second," by "G. Whilikins" (see New York *Independent,* X, 1, June 3, 1858; St. Louis *Daily Missouri Republican,* June 14, 1858; *Harper's Weekly,* II, 462, July 17, 1858; etc.). Incidentally, Anna Cora Mowatt's comedy, *Fashion; or Life in New York,* first acted in New York in 1845, contained a character, "T. Tennyson Twinkle, a Modern Poet"; but in the play neither his acting nor his quoted verses burlesqued Tennyson.

87. See reviews by Margaret Fuller (New York *Daily Tribune,* Jan. 4, 1845), Poe (*Broadway Journal,* I, 17–20, Jan. 11, 1845), Henry Charles Lea (*Southern Literary Messenger,* XI, 236–37, April, 1845), Charles A. Bristed (*Knickerbocker,* XXV, 540–42, June, 1845), etc.

88. *Broadway Journal,* I, 17–20 (Jan. 11, 1845).

89. *Southern Literary Messenger,* XI, 341–42 (June, 1845).

Chapter III

1. The Boston *Daily Evening Transcript* had announced on February 9 that Ticknor & Company would publish *The Princess* "this afternoon."

2. Samuel Longfellow, *op. cit.,* II, 109. Professor Thomas R. Lounsbury (*op. cit.,* pp. 557–58) felt that Longfellow must have been mistaken and that Fields must have told him of the sale of "some new edition of the 'Poems' previously published," and not of *The Princess;* but Professor Lounsbury's belief is based on two errors: first, that "there is no record of the publication of the work [*The Princess*] in this country before the middle of February," and second, that Longfellow's entry in the journal was "under date of January 25." Intervening material between quotations from the journal in Samuel Longfellow's *Life,* to which Professor Lounsbury refers, makes the dating of the entry uncertain, but the entry in the MS journal (Craigie House Papers) closely follows another marked February 15, showing that the month is February and not January. Although the interval is short, there is no reason why Ticknor could not have known by February 25 that he would need more copies of *The Princess,* which he had published on February 9.

3. I have seen or had minute descriptions of six copies of Ticknor's edition dated 1848, and the only differences found were in various sheets of advertisements bound at the beginning and at the end. The size, pagination, and text do not vary. It seems, therefore, that the word in *Graham's* and in Longfellow's journal should be *impressions* and not *editions,* but that

Ticknor printed from his original plate several times in 1848 seems beyond question.

4. The Boston *Daily Evening Transcript* for September 4, 1848, announced the "new and enlarged edition . . . including 'The Princess'" as published "today."

5. See Wise, *op. cit.*, I, 99–104.

6. Although a dozen copies of Ticknor's edition of *Poems* dated 1851, 1852, and 1853, have been checked, none has been found containing a later version of *The Princess* than the first London edition. The *Poems* dated 1854 but reviewed as early as September, 1853 (*Graham's Magazine*, XLIII, 336), contained *The Princess* printed from the fourth London edition of April, 1851.

7. Ticknor and Fields's "Blue and Gold" pocket edition of the *Poems* of that date contained *The Princess* with all the additions and emendations of the fifth London edition. The chief difference between the fourth and the fifth editions was the addition in the fifth of the fourteen-line section in the Prologue beginning "O miracle of women."

8. February 11, 1848. The review was signed "S."

9. February 14, 1848. Since Margaret Fuller was contributing to the *Tribune* from Europe at this time, this review may be hers; however, that is quite unlikely. Such contributions were usually headed "By our foreign correspondent," and this is not so marked.

10. XIII, 155 (April, 1848).

11. XXXII, 300 (May, 1848).

12. I, 79 (Nov., 1848).

13. *Massachusetts Quarterly Review*, I, 257 (March, 1848). The review is unsigned; for its assignment to Lowell, see Scudder, *op. cit.*, II, 429.

14. *Literary World*, III, 61–62 (Feb. 26, 1848). Incidentally, the reviewer was "speaking out" against a statement which his own journal had quoted with strong approval two weeks earlier (III, 28). For the review in the *Examiner*, see No. 2084, pp. 20–21 (Jan. 8, 1848).

15. *Harbinger*, VI, 158 (March 18, 1848). Theodore Winthrop, minor New England poet and novelist, the following year expressed the same opinion concerning Tennyson's change. Upon re-reading Tennyson with pleasure in 1849, Winthrop wrote into his journal: "He has exquisite power over language, and his poems have blood in them, and are really classic" (*The Life and Poems of Theodore Winthrop Edited by His Sister* [Laura Winthrop Johnson], New York, 1884, p. 26).

16. See Leonora Cranch Scott, *The Life and Letters of Christopher Pearse Cranch* (Boston and New York, 1917), pp. 156–61. For the poem, see Cranch's *The Bird and the Bell with Other Poems* (Boston, 1875), pp. 1–22. Cranch was one of the early transcendentalist admirers of Tennyson. In 1844 he painted a scene from "The Lady of Shalott" (see letter, Curtis to Dwight, March 27, 1844, in *Early Letters of George William Curtis to John S. Dwight*, p. 162).

17. *The Bird and the Bell with Other Poems*, pp. 283–84.

18. "The Poetic Principle." This famous lecture of Poe's, which he delivered at least twice in 1848 (see Phillips, *op. cit.*, p. 1313), was first published in the *Home Journal*, August 31, 1850. It is republished in *Works*, XIV, 266–92. Incidentally, biographers and editors of Poe give *Sartain's*

Union Magazine, VII, 231–39 (Oct., 1850), as the earliest publication of "The Poetic Principle," but the *Home Journal* published it in full more than a month earlier "from advance sheets of the new vol. by Mr. Poe, in the press of Mr. [J. S.] Redfield."

19. "The Late Edgar A. Poe," *Southern Literary Messenger,* XV, 696 (Nov., 1849).

20. See J. F. A. Pyre, *The Formation of Tennyson's Style* (Madison, Wis., 1921), pp. 174–79.

21. Journal, Feb. 7, 1848, quoted in Samuel Longfellow, *op. cit.,* II, 106. James T. Fields had lent Longfellow a copy of the English edition. Thus Longfellow was privileged to read the poem before its publication in America (see *ibid.*).

22. Letter to Mary Agnew, February 13, 1848, quoted in Marie Hansen-Taylor and Horace E. Scudder, *Life and Letters of Bayard Taylor* (Boston, 1884), I, 119.

23. *The Living Authors of England* (New York, 1849), pp. 55–59. Some idea of the appeal of Powell's book may be gained from an enthusiastic letter written him by James Mathewes Legaré, a total stranger, soon after its publication. Legaré added the "fresh masterly" volume to the limited number of his "pet-books," and had not words with which to express his esteem for this "pleasant, brilliant, and critically accurate" work (MS letter, Nov. 26, 1849, Boston Public Library).

24. II, 275 (May, 1848).

25. XIV, 264 (April, 1848).

26. F. M. Finch, "A Frolic with Tennyson," *Yale Literary Magazine,* XIV, 112–22 (Jan., 1849).

27. *Literary World,* III, 61 (Feb. 26, 1848).

28. *American Literary Magazine,* II, 275–81 (May, 1848).

29. "The Sphere of Woman," *Sartain's Union Magazine,* II, 270–73 (June, 1848).

30. The most quoted seems to have been the lines from Part VII beginning

> For woman is not undeveloped man,
> But diverse.

See *Godey's Lady's Book,* XL, 75 (Jan., 1850); Henry Reed, *Lectures on English Literature, from Chaucer to Tennyson* (Philadelphia, 1855), pp. 46–47; *Peterson's Magazine,* XXVII, 23–24 (Jan., 1855); *Graham's Magazine,* L, 269 (March, 1857); etc.

31. August 20, 1853. Religious periodicals offered some of the best examples of Americans' reading into Tennyson's poems whatever they wished to find. The *Methodist Quarterly Review* (XXXIV, 359, July, 1852) had an unusually good one: *The Princess* was "designed to convey the prophetic anticipation of a better age, already knocking at our door, when the supremacy of intellect, which has caused our present confusion, shall in consequence of its own restoration to health, give place to the nobler dominion of religious sentiment and moral duty."

32. XIII, 155 (April, 1848).

33. *Yale Literary Magazine,* XIV, 122 (Jan., 1849). An interesting reaction of a different sort came from another college student. The anonymous author of an article "Musings by Lamplight" in the *Nassau Literary Maga-*

zine (VIII, 116, Dec., 1848), Princeton College student publication, had also had a reverie with *The Princess* but thought it too "metaphysical" and had rather read "Evangeline" instead.

34. I, 78–79 (Nov., 1848).

35. Professor Lounsbury, who made a careful study of the British criticism of the poem, summarized the British reaction: "Never was greater reluctance to accept a work as the author designed it more pronounced and more violently proclaimed than in the sort of welcome with which 'The Princess' was greeted at its first appearance. Stupid as well as malignant criticism fell to Tennyson's lot. . . . In general, it ranged all the way from semi-approval to positive condemnation" (*op. cit.,* pp. 540–41).

36. ". . . until we took up the little book before us, we had no idea of meeting with anything so *bizarre,* indeed grotesque, as this correctly enough named 'medley' " (*Eclectic Review,* 4th Ser., XXIII, 415–16, March, 1848). "Mr. Tennyson has here engrafted the weaknesses and affectations of the Cockney school upon the worst peculiarities of his own style; he has chosen a subject which is narrow, uninteresting, unnatural, and absurd, not to say offensive in itself . . . namby-pamby is the true characteristic of the execution. There is a forced simplicity which is flat and literal; an affectation of nature, which produces nothing natural" (*Spectator,* XXI, 41–42, Jan. 8, 1848; this excerpt was quoted in the Boston *Daily Evening Transcript,* Feb. 11, 1848).

37. "Lecture Rooms and chivalric lists, modern pedantry and ancient romance, are antagonisms which no art can reconcile. With the power which Mr. Tennyson has here evinced for the familiar and the ideal regarded separately, it is much to be deplored that by their unskilful combination he has produced simply—the grotesque" (*Athenaeum,* No. 1053, p. 8, Jan. 1, 1848). "Why does he not assume his mission? Why does he discredit it with trifling and with puerilities unworthy of him? . . . . In the *Princess* we have more decisive evidence of his powers for a sustained and solid exercise of poetry than has heretofore been given. But it is yet only an omen for the future. Its glorious promise has yet to be fulfilled" (*Examiner,* No. 2084, p. 21, Jan. 8, 1848).

38. "The second title of this lively performance points out its principal defect; it is a *medley,* and, we must think, a somewhat incongruous one" (*Quarterly Review,* LXXXII, 445, March, 1848). "His very title-page declares 'The Princess' to be a 'Medley.' In the Prologue we have this avowal in detail. . . . But this consciousness of an eccentric plan can scarcely excuse it. We fancy that the Prologue is in reality an apologetic supplement. If so, there is hope that an error spontaneously discerned and confessed will in future be avoided" (*Athenaeum,* No. 1053, p. 7, Jan. 1, 1848).

39. ". . . may we yet expect from him some more prolonged strain, some work fully commensurate to the undoubted powers he possesses? It were in vain to prophesy. This last performance, *The Princess,* took, we believe, his admirers by surprise. It was not exactly what they had expected from him—not of so high an order. Judging by some intimations he himself has given us, we should not be disposed to anticipate any such effort from Mr. Tennyson. Should he, however, contradict this anticipation, no one will welcome the future epic, or drama, or story, or whatever it may be, more cordially than ourselves" (*Blackwood's Edin-*

burgh Magazine, LXV, 467, April, 1849). "We only regret that so much wealth has been lavished upon a subject which we cannot but think was hardly worthy of it. . . . We hope some day to welcome from his pen a work which shall combine them all [Tennyson's talents], with yet higher reach than he has attempted" (*Sharpe's London Magazine,* VI, 141, April, 1848).

40. Reviews in *Howitt's Journal* (III, 28–29, Jan. 8, 1848) and the *Gentleman's Magazine* (N. S., XXIX, 115–31, Feb., 1848) were favorable.

41. "A Talk about the Princess," *American Review: A Whig Journal,* VIII, 28–39 (July, 1848).

42. *Massachusetts Quarterly Review,* I, 256–59 (March, 1848).

43. *New Englander,* VII, 193–215 (May, 1849). This unsigned review was included in Hadley's *Essays Philological and Critical* (New York, 1873), pp. 276–324. Three lengthy passages are quoted verbatim from the review of *The Princess* in the *North British Review,* IX, 43–72 (May, 1848), and numbers of paraphrased criticisms could come from any one of several of the unfavorable British reviews already referred to, especially that in the London *Quarterly Review,* LXXXII, 427–53 (March, 1848).

44. See Aubrey de Vere's review in the *Edinburgh Review* (XC, 388–404, Oct., 1849); Charles Kingsley's in *Fraser's Magazine* (XLII, 245–55, Sept., 1850); etc.

45. See the *Knickerbocker,* XXV, 183–84 (Feb., 1845) and XXVIII, 174–75 (Aug., 1846). The *Knickerbocker* never tired of felicitating itself upon having given Dempster the suggestion (see the "Editor's Table," XXIX, 380 (April, 1847); XLIX, 532 (May, 1857); and LIV, 553 (Nov., 1859).

46. The work was sold in four different forms: the three parts bound together, and each part bound separately as an individual piece. It was entered for copyright in April 9, 1845, and Ditson reissued the work several times in 1845 and 1846. For a description of this and other American editions of Tennyson sheet music, see Appendix A.

47. XXVI, 590 (Dec., 1845), and XXVIII, 175 (Aug., 1846).

48. Reporters of the concerts almost invariably described "The May Queen" as the most memorable number on the program. In Charleston, South Carolina, it was "the treat of the evening" ("a Charleston journal" quoted in the "Editor's Table," *Knickerbocker,* XXXVIII, 77, July, 1851); in a New York asylum for the blind, it was by far the "most touching of all" Dempster's songs (*Knickerbocker,* XXX, 548, Dec., 1847); and after a concert in Brooklyn, "its thrilling lines" lingered in the ear and the heart of a reporter and "would not away" (New York *Independent,* IX, 1, March 12, 1857). See also *Albion,* 3rd Ser., IV, 239 (May 17, 1845); *Anglo-American,* X, 20 (Oct. 23, 1847); etc.

49. The *Knickerbocker* warned its readers: "It's great popularity has induced other vocalists to take it up; but reader, do you hear Mr. Dempster sing it, if you would have justice done to it" (XXV, 470, May, 1845). On a tour of England and Scotland in 1845 and 1846, Abby Hutchinson sang "The May Queen" on every program, often being forced to repeat it because of the applause with which it was greeted (John Wallace Hutchinson, *Story of the Hutchinsons,* Boston, 1896, I, 174, 186, 208–09). It was her singing at Grasmere which caused Hartley Coleridge to write his sonnet, "To Alfred Tennyson," expressing the wish that the author could

have heard his lines embalmed in such perfect music (*ibid.*, 208–09). Tennyson regretted that he did not hear the Hutchinsons when they were in England (*Memoir*, I, 239).

50. Clark devoted three pages of his "Editor's Table" to the poem in March, 1844, and frequently reprimanded reviewers and anthologists, including Rufus W. Griswold, for not giving the poem more attention (*Knickerbocker*, XXIII, 291–93, March, 1844; and XXIV, 594, Dec., 1844). Three-fourths of the review of the 1842 *Poems* in the *Christian Parlor Magazine* for December, 1844 (I, 231–35) was devoted to "The May Queen."

51. "Music in Boston," *Harbinger*, II, 77 (Jan. 10, 1846).

52. Dempster sang his cantata before Tennyson himself, and Tennyson is said to have remarked with tears in his eyes that not until that moment had he felt the full effect of his own lines (*Knickerbocker*, XXIX, 380, April, 1847). John Sullivan Dwight's own *Journal of Music* confessed in 1858 that "Dempster's genius" had "contributed largely to the popularity of Tennyson's beautiful ballad, the 'May Queen'" (unsigned notice of Dempster's *Songs and Ballads*, XIV, 296, Dec. 11, 1858). For an interesting though unconvincing suggestion that Washington Irving's "Pride of the Village" in *The Sketch Book* may have suggested to Tennyson the plot of "The May Queen," see D. Barron Brightwell, "Tennyson and Washington Irving," *Notes and Queries*, 5th Ser., XII, 65 (July 26, 1879).

53. See *Harbinger*, VI, 115 (Feb. 12, 1848); *Saturday Evening Post*, Sept. 14, 1850; *Knickerbocker*, XXXVIII, 410 (Oct., 1851); *Dwight's Journal of Music*, I, 74 (June 12, 1852); etc.

54. Review of *In Memoriam*, *Southern Literary Messenger*, XVI, 688 (Nov., 1850). The review was signed "E. C."; for its doubtful assignment to Cooke, see David K. Jackson, *The Contributors and Contributions to The Southern Literary Messenger* (Charlottesville, Va., 1936), p. 101. Incidentally, Colonel J. T. L. Preston, husband of Margaret Junkin Preston, published an entire article on the song in October, 1867 (*Land We Love*, Charlotte, N. C., monthly, III, 470–75).

55. Tennyson's name on the title page was spelled *Tenneyson*. The line forming the title, which is not contained in Tennyson's poem, was written by Woodbury and inserted as a refrain at the close of each of Tennyson's four stanzas. Woodbury also made two minor changes of wording within the stanzas.

56. "Death-Verses: A Stroll through the Valley of the Shadow of Death with Tennyson . . . ," *American Whig Review*, XIII, 536 (June, 1851). This review of *In Memoriam* was signed "J. S."

57. In all probability, more than a hundred different American publications printed the songs before their inclusion in an American edition. From 1850 to 1852 they are found galore. Sometimes in groups and sometimes singly, they bore such headings as "New Songs by Tennyson," "Overlooked Novelties," "Poems by Tennyson Which Have Not Yet Appeared in this Country," etc. See New York *Daily Tribune*, Dec. 14, 1850; *Literary World*, VII, 482 (Dec. 14, 1850); Boston *Daily Evening Transcript*, Dec. 16, 1850; *Holden's Dollar Magazine*, VII, 173 (April, 1851); *Dwight's Journal of Music*, I, 18 (April 24, 1852); etc.

58. "The Poetry of California," *Pioneer,* I, 26 (Jan. 1854). Ewer called his magazine the first "periodical of a purely literary type" in the far West (*Pioneer,* I, 1, Jan., 1854).

59. See *New York Musical Review and Gazette,* VII, 116 (April 19, 1856).

60. According to Mr. J. Francis Driscoll of Brookline, Massachusetts, copies are still easy to find. In his enormous collection of American sheet music, he has two copies. The Library of Congress, The Harvard College Library, and The Boston Public Library own copies. Published by Oliver Ditson of Boston, the copies, apparently all exactly alike, listed five agents throughout the country.

61. *Albion,* 4th Ser., X, 579 (Dec. 6, 1851).

62. Review of *Poems* by Alexander Smith, *Graham's Magazine,* XLIII, 111 (July, 1853). The review is unsigned, but the *Literary World* (XII, 547–48, July 9, 1853) in reprinting parts of it tagged the excerpts, "From a subtle review from the pen of E. P. Whipple, in *Graham's Magazine* for July." Whipple was writing reviews for *Graham's* at the time (Mott, *op. cit.,* I, 553), and internal evidence would give the review to him. The review contained several derogatory digressions concerning Philip James Bailey's *Festus,* Whipple's pet aversion.

63. XLIII, 336 (Sept., 1853).

64. MS journal, Aug. 22, 1851, Craigie House Papers.

65. Quoted below.

Chapter IV

1. Letter to his mother, 1850, quoted in *Letters and Journals of Thomas Wentworth Higginson,* pp. 32–33. Higginson had got his information from his Harvard friend, William Henry Hurlbut, just returned from a visit to England (see *ibid.,* pp. 29–32).

2. MS letter in the Craigie House Papers. For calling my attention to this item, I am indebted to Mr. J. Lee Harlan, Jr., Columbia University graduate student.

3. The London *Times* for June 3 announced it to be ready by June 8.

4. MS letter, Duyckinck Collection, New York Public Library.

5. Copies of two separate impressions have been seen. Alike in size and pagination, one was marked as printed by Metcalf & Co. of Cambridge and the other by Hobart & Robbins of Boston. For information concerning the American editions, see Appendix A.

6. Moxon's first edition numbered five thousand copies, and by January, 1851, a fourth edition had been issued (Wise, *op. cit.,* I, 108–13). In a letter to me dated Sept. 21, 1940, the Houghton Mifflin Company lists eight issues of Ticknor, Reed, and Fields's first edition of *In Memoriam* through 1855. No information is available concerning the first four, but the others are listed as numbering five hundred copies each.

7. See *Literary World,* VII, 12–13 (July 6, 1850); Boston *Daily Evening Transcript,* July 9 and 13, 1850; New York *Daily Tribune,* July 9, 1850; *Saturday Evening Post,* July 27, 1850; etc.

8. I, 34 (July 8, 1850); cf. *Spectator,* XXIII, 546 (June 8, 1850). *Littell's Living Age* (XXVI, 167–71) reprinted the same review and also one from the London *Examiner* (No. 2188, pp. 356–57, June 8, 1850) in its issue

dated July 27 but advertised as ready for sale much earlier (see Washington *Daily National Intelligencer,* July 17, 1850, and New York *Independent,* July 18, 1850).

9. July 22, 1850.

10. Letter to George H. Boker, Dec. 17, 1850, in Hansen-Taylor and Scudder, *op. cit.,* I, 197.

11. Letter to Lord Morpeth, April 8, 1851, quoted in Pierce, *op. cit.,* III, 76.

12. See Letter to Charles Eliot Norton, Aug. 11, 1855, in Lowell's *Works,* XIV, 311. Lowell contrasted *In Memoriam* and one of his favorites, "Maud." See also *Tennyson and His Friends,* ed. Hallam, Lord Tennyson (London, 1911), p. 358.

13. *Journals,* VIII, 163 (Jan. 1–14, 1851). Cf. Moncure Daniel Conway, *Emerson at Home and Abroad* (Boston, 1882), p. 359: "The Work of Tennyson he [Emerson] liked least was 'In Memoriam.'"

14. Reed, *op. cit.,* p. 324.

15. XVI, 48 (Jan., 1851). *Poole's Index to Periodical Literature* assigns this unsigned review of *In Memoriam* to George P. Fisher, Yale theologian.

16. *Monthly Religious Magazine,* X, 152 (April, 1853). The review was signed "F."

17. XVI, 690 (Nov., 1850).

18. VII, 539–40 (Oct., 1850). The *International Weekly Miscellany,* which did not like Tennyson (see I, 34, July, 1850), reprinted the harshest parts of the review on November 1, 1850 (I, 477).

19. The twenty-volume *Works of Orestes A. Brownson,* edited by his son, Henry F. Brownson (Detroit, 1882–87), does not assign the review to him, but the *International Weekly Miscellany* (I, 34, July 8, 1850) referred to the review as by "Dr. Brownson," and internal evidence would indicate that it was his. Earlier a member of the Transcendental Club but always unstable in his beliefs, Brownson had become by 1850 one of the strongest opponents of the transcendentalists. For his diatribes against them and their philosophy, see *Works,* VI, 1–243.

20. XVIII, 134 (Sept., 1850).

21. 4th Ser., IX, 381 (August 10, 1850).

22. XVIII, 535–36 (Nov., 1850). Coming in a series of "Critical Notices" at the end of the number, this unsigned review may have been by the editor, William Gilmore Simms. The list of Simms's "Chief Contributions to Magazines" in William P. Trent's *William Gilmore Simms* (Boston and New York, 1892, pp. 339–41) does not contain the review, but the brief list names only major articles.

23. "Death-Verses," XIII, 538–39 (June, 1851). The article was signed "J. S."

24. "Recollections of Poets Laureate—Tennyson," *American Whig Review,* XV, 522 (June, 1852).

25. *Home Journal,* Feb. 14, 1853.

26. XXVII, 205 (Sept., 1850). The review was signed "S. E. B."

27. VIII, 598–615 (Nov., 1850). The General Index gives Increase N. Tarbox, Boston minister and Biblical scholar, as the author of the review.

28. XXXVII, 198–99 (Sept., 1850).

29. I, 570 (Sept., 1850).

30. May 29, MS, Craigie House Papers. The first part of the dialogue is copied into Felton's unpublished journals of travel, 1853 (Felton Collection, Harvard College Library). There the conversation reaches Tennyson but breaks off just before the passages on *In Memoriam.* The dialogue does not appear in any of Felton's published journals of travel.

31. *Literary World,* VII, 30 (July 13, 1850).

32. *Southern Literary Messenger,* XVI, 688 (Nov., 1850).

33. *Literary World,* VII, 30 (July 13, 1850). One young reviewer, a student at Princeton, felt that the anonymity did not excuse Tennyson for "thus making a parade" of his sorrow: what more right had Tennyson than anyone else "to obtrude his private griefs upon the public notice?" (*Nassau Literary Magazine,* X, 62–65, Oct., 1850.)

34. XLIX, 290 (Sept., 1850). William Cushing's *Index to the Christian Examiner* (Boston, 1879, p. 111) assigns this unsigned review of *In Memoriam* to C. C. Smith.

35. VIII, 612 (Nov., 1850).

36. X, 153–58 (April, 1853). The review was signed "F."

37. XVI, 48–50 (Jan., 1851).

38. See *New Englander,* VIII, 602 (Nov., 1850).

39. Mott, *op. cit.,* I, 369.

40. XXIX, 122 (August 3, 1850).

41. "Infidelity in England," VI, 181 (Feb. 12, 1851). The article was signed "C. B. W." The Boston *Daily Evening Transcript* (March 11, 1851) reprinted the "able" article as a matter of information "without endorsing either the facts or the conclusions of the writer." Lines of *In Memoriam* are quoted from Sections LVI, stanza 5; LIII, stanza 9; and XCVI, stanza 3. The last stanza is misquoted: *There is more faith* should be *There lives more faith.* Sections CXVIII–CXX, which in outlining the evolution of man from a lower state approximate the later notorious Darwinian theory of evolution, seem to have aroused no opposition. The great furor over the theory came, of course, with the publication of Darwin's *The Origin of the Species* in 1859.

42. Letter, Dec. 19, 1850 or 1851, quoted in Morse, *op. cit.,* II, 277. Lord Herbert of Cherbury, Ben Jonson, and Sir Philip Sidney had used the same rime scheme, but according to J. F. A. Pyre (*op. cit.,* p. 105), "Tennyson neither stumbled upon this arrangement nor did he adopt it from any of his predecessors. It was a natural product of his experiments." Tennyson himself wrote, "I had no notion till 1880 that Lord Herbert of Cherbury had written his occasional verses in the same metre. I believed myself the originator of the metre, until after 'In Memoriam' came out, when some one told me that Ben Jonson and Sir Philip Sidney had used it" (*Memoir,* I, 305–06).

43. Letter, Oct. 6, 1850, quoted in Richard Henry Stoddard: *Recollections Personal and Literary* (New York, 1903), pp. 189–90. For praise by Stoddard, see his article, "Alfred Tennyson," in the *National Magazine,* IX, 408–15 (Nov., 1856).

44. *National Magazine,* IV, 15–17 (Jan., 1854).

45. XXXVII, 198–99 (Sept., 1850).

46. It was given various titles: "The Ending and Beginning Year," New York *Daily Tribune,* Dec. 31, 1850; "Carol for the New Year," *Harper's*

Monthly, II, 396 (Feb., 1851); "The Dying Year," Boston *Daily Evening Transcript,* Dec. 31, 1851; etc.

47. "The Poetry of Sorrow," London *Times,* Nov. 28, 1851.

48. Feb. 14, 1852. When the *Boston Weekly Museum* (IV, 303, Feb. 28, 1852) reprinted the article from the London *Times,* it quoted the *Home Journal's* approval.

49. 4th Ser., XI, 51 (Jan. 31, 1852).

50. Feb. 28, 1852. The contributor signed his article "New Hampshire." The article was reprinted in the *Boston Weekly Museum,* IV, 315 (March 13, 1852).

51. VII, 256 (Oct., 1850).

52. *North American Review,* LXXXIII, 115 (July, 1856). This review of *In Memoriam* together with reviews of two other works formed an article entitled "The Literature of Friendship."

53. "Death Verses," *American Whig Review,* XIII, 535–36 (June, 1851). The review was signed "J. S."

54. Increase N. Tarbox, *New Englander,* VIII, 615 (Nov., 1850). The quotation was from Charles Kingsley's review in *Fraser's Magazine* (XLII, 252, Sept., 1850): ". . .—in our eyes, [*In Memoriam* is] the noblest English Christian poem which several centuries have seen." Tarbox quoted the passage incorrectly: "In our eyes it is the noblest Christian poem, which England has produced for two centuries."

55. Kingsley's statement quoted above was not at all extraordinary. Cf.: "This is a glorious work, and worthy of the chief efforts of the chief minds" (*North British Review,* XIII, 553, August, 1850). "Not thus [comparison with Milton and Petrarch], however—nor by comparison even with the extraordinary friendship, love, and grief, commemorated in the sonnets of Shakespeare—should we commemorate the highest and most distinctive claims of this *In Memoriam"* (*Examiner,* No. 2188, p. 256, June 8, 1850). ". . . it is the finest poem the world has seen for very many years" (*Tait's Edinburgh Magazine,* N. S., XVII, 505, August, 1850). Nowhere in American criticism have such superlative statements been found before 1855.

56. Hallam Tennyson wrote in the *Memoir* (I, 298), "At first the reviews of the volume were not on the whole sympathetic," and Professor Harold Nicolson (*op. cit.,* p. 163), doubtless expanding upon that statement wrote that "at first the reviewers were generally unfavorable." But these statements are somewhat inexplicable. Of a score of reviews which I have seen in leading British periodicals, only one—that in the *Times*—was definitely unfavorable. Cf. Professor Lounsbury's statement (*op. cit.,* p. 620): "'In Memoriam' had one distinction which none other of Tennyson's works had ever enjoyed. From the very moment of its publication it was greeted with an almost unanimous chorus of approval by the critical press." All of the Tennyson biographers were basing their statements upon the British reviews. Except for Professor Lounsbury, who had seen one, they had obviously not seen any of the unfavorable American reviews.

57. "The Poetry of Sorrow," Nov. 28, 1851.

58. See especially "The 'Times' and the Poets," *Tait's Edinburgh Magazine,* N. S., XIX, 18–21 (Jan., 1852). Several eclectic magazines reprinted the article in America.

59. Cf.: "Our laborious analysis of 'The Princess' sufficiently showed that

we had faith in Mr. Tennyson for something more than the exquisite polished expression of ordinary thought and sentiment, upon which his mere popularity rests and his reviewers for the most part dwell; we felt that careful study had given us a right to express ourselves freely concerning what seemed to us to be the errors of that poem; and the fact that we did so express ourselves is a proof of our impartiality that ought, perhaps, to be mentioned at the commencement of the notice of a poem [*In Memoriam*] . . . concerning which we have nothing but praise to utter (*North British Review,* XIII, 532, August, 1850). "It has been often asked why Mr. Tennyson's great and varied powers had never been concentrated on one immortal work. The epic, the lyric, the idyllic faculties, perhaps the dramatic also, seemed to be all there, and yet all sundered, scattered about in small fragmentary poems. 'In Memoriam,' as we think, explains the paradox. Mr. Tennyson had been employed on higher, more truly divine, and yet more truly human work than either epos or drama" (*Fraser's Magazine,* XLII, 254–55, Sept., 1850).

60. Few Englishmen preferred Tennyson's early poems to his later. Edward Fitzgerald, who "gave up all hopes of him [Tennyson] after 'The Princess,'" was an exception, and because of the belief was, as he put it, "considered a great heretic" (*Memoir,* I, 253).

61. Letter, August 1, 1842, quoted in Reid, *op. cit.,* p. 280.

62. Cf.: ". . . the dainty trick of Tennyson cloys when caught by a whole generation of versifiers, as the style of a great poet never can be" ("Swinburne's Tragedies," 1866, in *Works,* II, 158). In his review of *Enoch Arden* (*North American Review,* XCIX, 626, Oct., 1864) Lowell accused Tennyson of vainly trying to imitate his "former self" and ranked Tennyson in the "highest order of minor poets." Lowell's change of attitude toward Tennyson was due partly to a change within himself. In his earlier days he liked the purely aesthetic more than he did later, but that he always preferred the earlier poetry of Tennyson to the later is beyond question.

63. *International Weekly Miscellany,* I, 34 (July 8, 1850).

Chapter V

1. *International Weekly Miscellany,* I, 105 (July 1, 1850).

2. *Ibid.;* and *Home Journal,* June 8, 1850. The *Home Journal* had heard that Mary Howitt, Elizabeth Barrett Browning, and Caroline Norton were all being considered.

3. *Boston Weekly Museum,* III, 69 (August 10, 1850).

4. "Valley of Diamonds," August 2, 1850.

5. Hansen-Taylor and Scudder, *op. cit.,* I, 197. See *Literary World,* VII, 481 (Dec. 14, 1850); and *Boston Weekly Museum,* III, 220 (Dec. 21, 1850). The only expression of disappointment which has been found appeared in the *International Monthly Magazine* (II, 180, Jan., 1851), which had already shown its dislike for Tennyson. It merely paraphrased—without giving credit—Henry F. Chorley's tirade in the London *Athenaeum,* No. 1204, p. 1218 (Nov. 23, 1850). Chorley had championed the cause of Elizabeth Barrett Browning and was indignant when she did not receive the appointment.

6. "On Some of the Characteristics of Modern Poetry and on the Lyrical

Poems of Alfred Tennyson," *Englishman's Magazine,* I, 616–28 (August, 1831). For a concise discussion of the English attitude in the eighteen-forties that Tennyson was the "true prophet of the new times," see Leslie A. Marchand, *The Athenaeum, A Mirror of Victorian Culture* (Chapel Hill, N. C., 1941), pp. 275–77.

7. *New World,* V, 63 (July 23, 1842).

8. Review of *Poems* (1842), *Knickerbocker,* XXV, 534–35 (June, 1845).

9. H. H. Clements, "Tennyson," *New York Illustrated Magazine of Literature and Art,* II, 241–44 (Sept., 1846).

10. The best discussion of this which I have seen is in an unpublished doctoral thesis (1936) in the University of North Carolina Library: Guy Adams Cardwell, Jr., *Charleston Periodicals, 1795–1860.* See chapters entitled "The Heritage from Eighteenth Century England," "Changing standards," and "Byron and Byronism in Charleston" (pp. 56–159).

11. *The Autobiography of William J. Grayson,* ed. Robert Duncan Bass (unpublished Ph. D. thesis, University of South Carolina, 1933), pp. 247–48. Grayson's *Autobiography,* written in 1862, has never been published.

12. Simms was editor of the *Magnolia,* 1842–43, the *Southern and Western Magazine,* 1845, and the *Southern Quarterly Review,* 1849–55. Curiously, in spite of his general coolness to modern poets, Simms espoused the cause of one at a time when that poet had few followers: Simms was among the earliest to like Browning. See Trent, *op. cit.,* p. 197.

13. "Literature in the South," *Russell's Magazine,* V, 386–87 (August, 1859). John Russell's personal set of *Russell's* now in the New York Public Library has this unsigned article marked Timrod's. Guy A. Cardwell, Jr. (*op. cit.,* p. 385), who had seen other sources for ascription of authorship in *Russell's,* also assigns the article to Timrod.

14. Evert A. Duyckinck wrote into his diary on December 1, 1859, that he had asked Irving a short time before whether he was an admirer of Tennyson and had received the confession quoted (MS, Duyckinck Collection, New York Public Library).

15. Bryant was widely quoted as having praised Tennyson's brief poem, "The Eagle." Of its fourth line, "The wrinkled sea beneath him crawls," he thought "perhaps no single line in our language conveys so forcible an idea of height" (see Boston *Daily Evening Transcript,* Jan. 25, 1854; and *Harper's Magazine,* XII, 860, May, 1856). One magazine quoted him as having praised the "compact expressiveness" of a passage in "Locksley Hall" (*Crayon,* V, 90, March, 1858).

16. Parke Godwin, *A Biography of William Cullen Bryant* (New York, 1883), II, 21–23.

17. A letter, Halleck to Samuel Ward, August 25, 1862, quoted in James Grant Wilson, *Bryant and His Friends* (New York, 1886), pp. 265–66.

18. Joel Benton, "Some Reminiscences of Fitz-Greene Halleck," *Frank Leslie's Illustrated Newspaper,* XXV, 243, (Jan. 4, 1868), and Evert A. Duyckinck, "Fitz-Greene Halleck," *Putnam's Monthly Magazine,* N.S., I, 246 (Feb., 1868). In recording Halleck's estimate of Tennyson, Duyckinck turned aside long enough to assure his readers that Halleck was doing Tennyson an injustice.

19. Benton, *loc. cit.* Like Bryant, Halleck liked a few scattered passages from Tennyson. Bayard Taylor described his vain efforts to convince Hal-

leck of Tennyson's genius. After reading poem after poem without effect, Taylor read "The Eagle," and a sudden light flashed into Halleck's eye, " 'Ringed with the azure world,' " Halleck repeated; "yes, that's poetry!" (Taylor, "Fitz-Greene Halleck," *North American Review,* CXXV, 65, July, 1877). For favorable comment by Halleck on a few other lines from Tennyson, see Frederick S. Cozzens, *Fitz-Greene Halleck. A Memorial* (New York, 1868), p. 18.

20. Merwin & Hitchcock, San Francisco booksellers, advertised the poems in the early eighteen-fifties, and later J. J. Lecount, proud of his "most extensive assortment [of books] on the Pacific Coast," also advertised them. See San Francisco *Daily Herald,* Dec. 4–31, 1852; San Francisco *Weekly Pacific,* Dec. 10, 1852—Feb. 11, 1853; San Francisco *Evening Bulletin,* Dec. 18–31, 1858; etc.

21. San Francisco *Weekly Pacific,* July 23, 1852. For an early California review of Tennyson's poems, see the *Pioneer; or, California Monthly Magazine* (III, 28–34, Jan., 1855). Written by Charles E. Havens, minor California poet, the review mixed praise and blame fairly equally. Havens thought Tennyson's versification faultless and his "musical simplicity of style" unexcelled, but felt that Tennyson lacked the inventive faculty; and without explaining himself Havens objected to the "profanity" of *In Memoriam* and the general "Transcendentalism" of Tennyson's philosophy. That Havens liked Tennyson better in practice than in theory is indicated by his imitations quoted below.

22. The "Editor's Table" of *Russell's* directly answered the article on ancient and modern poetry in the *Home Journal.* ". . . if search had been made among the vast body of English Poets from Chaucer downward, this caviller could not have selected an author whose writings are more distinguished for consistent, unvarying, wonderful clearness—clearness of design, diction, imagination, metaphor, and allusion—than Alfred Tennyson" (I, 182, May, 1857).

23. Letter to his mother, Nov. 3, 1857, quoted in Laura Stedman and George M. Gould, *Life and Letters of Edmund Clarence Stedman* (New York, 1910), I, 142–43.

24. Letter to Henry C. Townsend, Nov. 21, 1856, quoted in Henry C. Townsend, *A Memoir of T. Buchanan Read* (Philadelphia, 1889), p. 103.

25. "Alfred Tennyson," *National Magazine,* IX, 415 (Nov., 1856).

26. Examples are to be found throughout American magazines from the late eighteen-forties on. See reviews of the poems of Thomas Buchanan Read (*Ladies' National Magazine,* XI, 125, March, 1847), of Philip Pendleton Cooke (*Illustrated Monthly Courier* [Philadelphia], I, 57–58, Oct. 2, 1848), of Browning, (*Graham's Magazine,* XXXV, 378, Dec., 1849), etc.

27. "Tennyson," *Presbyterian Quarterly Review,* VI, 657 (March, 1858). The Boston *Daily Evening Transcript* (March 18, 1858) reprinted parts of the article and gave its strong approval.

28. When Tennyson finally republished "The Deserted House" and "The Sea-Fairies" from *Poems, Chiefly Lyrical* in 1851 and 1853 respectively, they went their rounds in American newspapers and magazines. They had been favorites with Americans in the eighteen-thirties, and their reception now was just as warm. Of "The Deserted House," the Boston *Daily Evening Transcript* (May 16, 1853) wrote, "For simplicity of conception and

language, in appropriateness of imagery and the solemn tone it breathes, this little poem has been rarely surpassed." F. C. Ewer clipped "The Sea-Fairies" from some newspaper for inclusion in his *Pioneer: or, California Monthly Magazine* ("Editor's Table," IV, 68, July, 1855) as one of the most "exquisite" and "exceedingly delicate" poems he had ever read. Ticknor & Fields included the poems in an American edition in 1854. The *Literary World* found *Timbuctoo* somewhere and reprinted it as a "rarity" in 1852 (X, 93, Jan. 31), and the *Southern Literary Messenger* (XVII, 252, April, 1851) found the sonnet, "But Were I Loved As I Desire to Be," of the 1833 *Poems.* Not knowing where the poem came from, John R. Thompson described it in his "Editor's Table" as a new sonnet of Tennyson's "just from the mint." Incidentally, in the eighteen-sixties and seventies Ticknor & Fields and Harper's waged a spirited contest to see who could find more "new" poems by Tennyson. Digging into the early suppressed poems, they published everything they could find.

29. Charles E. Havens, "The Poems of Alfred Tennyson," *Pioneer; or, California Monthly Magazine,* III, 33–34 (Jan., 1855); "Tennyson," *Presbyterian Quarterly Review,* VI, 657–58 (March, 1858); and a review of Ticknor's "Blue and Gold" pocket edition of Tennyson's *Poetical Works, Arthur's Home Magazine,* VIII, 181 (Sept., 1856).

30. Delivered at the Lowell Institute in Boston in April and at Hope Chapel in New York in December, the lecture on Tennyson was reported in the Boston *Daily Evening Transcript* (April 20) and in the New York *Daily Times* (Dec. 5). The lectures were obviously the same. The *Times* gave much the longer and more detailed of the two reports.

31. New York *Times's* report (Dec. 5, 1853) of Holmes's lecture.

32. Review of Tennyson's poems, *Southern Literary Messenger,* XIX, 657 (Nov., 1853).

33. "Family Portraits," *Putnam's Monthly Magazine,* I, 334 (March, 1853). Another called the poem a telling blow struck at "haughty pride" (*Southern Literary Messenger,* XVI, 691, Nov., 1850).

34. *Southern Literary Messenger,* XIX, 658 (Nov., 1853).

35. Review of Coventry Patmore's *The Angel in the House, Putnam's Monthly Magazine,* VIII, 23 (July, 1856).

36. "Wordsworth and Tennyson," *Yale Literary Magazine,* XIX, 299 (July, 1854). The article was signed "W. W."

37. *Southern Literary Messenger,* XIX, 658 (Nov., 1853).

38. Clements, *op. cit.,* pp. 241-42.

39. Review of *Poetical Works of Henry Alford, Graham's Magazine,* XLII, 503 (April, 1853).

40. The *International Weekly Miscellany* (I, 34, July 1, 1850) wrote that people flocked to the bookstores for every new poem of Tennyson's; the New York *Independent* (IX, 8, April 16, 1857) described the sale of Tennyson's poems as "unexampled"; etc.

41. For the high prices demanded by Tennyson from his English publishers, see William Tinsley, *Random Recollections of an Old Publisher* (London and Paris, 1905), I, 236 ff.; and Frank A. Mumby, *The House of Routledge, 1834–1934* (London, 1934), pp. 80–81 and 185 ff. Upon his becoming Poet Laureate, Tennyson received from his English publishers hundreds of pounds for every new work, but no record has been found

of Ticknor's ever paying over one hundred and fifty dollars. Ticknor paid that amount for the 1842 *Poems*. According to the New York *Literary American* (II, 380, April 21, 1849) he paid that amount in 1849 for "reprinting an edition" of Tennyson's poems. And on October 26, 1855, concerning the publication of *Maud, and Other Poems,* Tennyson wrote to Ticknor, "I have this morning received your draft for £30 for which I request yourself & Mr. Fields to accept my thanks" (MS in James T. Fields's autograph album, Harvard College Library). Just how often Ticknor sent such drafts to Tennyson cannot be determined, but one can be certain that their total never rivaled that of the English royalties.

42. The English figures below are from Wise, *op. cit.,* I, 80 ff. The American figures are listed in Roorbach's *Bibliotheca Americana,* Ticknor's sales catalogues, and throughout Boston and New York newspapers. These prices for the plain paper board editions (both American and English publishers, of course, sold more expensive editions) in America showed no variation from year to year, and the prices in New York were the same as those in Boston. The English editions were sometimes advertised in this country (Wiley and Putnam of New York listed the Boston and London editions of *Poems* side by side in their sales catalogue for 1844 with prices: Boston, $1.50; London, $3.50), but after the mid-eighteen-forties advertisements of the English editions were extremely rare. That Ticknor's editions were practically duplicates of the London edition has been noted many times.

43. "Diffusion of Books," N. S., VI, 198–200 (Sept. 19, 1846). Incidentally, the absence of international copyright worked both ways. Longfellow's poems, for instance, sold in London at much cheaper prices than did the works of English poets, and, partly in consequence, Longfellow was one of the most widely read poets in the British Isles during the middle of the nineteenth century. Charles Eliot Norton wrote to Mrs. George Ticknor from London on June 21, 1850, "Everybody here says there is no poet in England to be compared with Mr. Longfellow" (*Letters of Charles Eliot Norton,* ed. Sara Norton and M. A. De Wolfe Howe, Boston and New York, 1913, I, 69). See Clarence Gohdes, "Longfellow and His Authorized British Publishers," *PMLA,* LV, 1165–79 (Dec., 1940).

44. John R. Thompson in 1858 replied to a censorious English criticism with a detailed comparison of Longfellow and Tennyson: "Mr. Longfellow has often been compared with Tennyson, and a recent English critic, in a paragraph of flippant depreciation of America, has arraigned him as only a feeble imitator of the Tennysonian model. But a more unjust accusation could not have been made. In some respects indeed, the two laureates are alike. A quiet, thoughtful melancholy pervades the poems of both. Each of them has enwreathed legendary lore with poetic garlands, each sings of love and ambition and sorrow and longings for the world beyond the grave. But in their modes of expression and in their manner of treatment no two writers could be more different. . . . It is the strongest possible proof of the essential difference between Tennyson and Longfellow, that while many have challenged the genius of the former because of his indistinctness, as many have denied to the latter great powers because of the clearness and simplicity which belong to the enunciation of his thoughts. . . . Upon the principle of *omne ignotum pro magnifico,*

Mr. Longfellow is, indeed, but a mere versifier; upon the principle that what proves nothing is worth nothing, Mr. Tennyson is but a cloudy rhapsodist. Yet is each undeniably a true child of genius" (review of *The Courtship of Miles Standish and Other Poems, Southern Literary Messenger,* XXVII, 389–90, Nov., 1858). The *Nassau Literary Magazine* noted that Longfellow was called "the American Tennyson" and set out to prove that he was "no lunar copy" (IX, 337, June, 1850). The *Southern Quarterly Review* wrote, "We are not afraid to compare Longfellow and Bryant with Tennyson and Cunningham. . . . Longfellow's *Midnight Mass for the Dying Year* is as far superior to Tennyson's *Death of the Old Year,* as one piece of poetry can surpass another of the same class" ("Fugitive Poetry of America," signed "A. S. P.," XIV, 114, July, 1848); and the *Southern Literary Messenger* quoted the New York *Express* as having declared concerning Poe's "The Raven" that no one could "pretend to enter into competition with it, except, perhaps, Alfred Tennyson, and he only to be excelled out of measure" (XI, 187, March, 1845). See also *Knickerbocker,* XLIV, 435–36 (Oct., 1854); and *Peterson's Magazine,* XXXIV, 448–49 (Dec., 1858).

45. Letter to Ferdinand J. Dreer, Dec. 15, 1860, quoted in Townsend, *op. cit.,* p. 118.

46. Ticknor and Fields printed the letter in the front of their two-volume edition of *Poems,* 1856, and in many editions thereafter.

47. The earliest edition that I have found by another American publisher appeared in 1862, when G. Routledge and Sons issued through their New York office an elaborately illustrated edition of *Works.* Very possibly other non-Ticknor editions appeared earlier, but they were not widely advertised, no copies now exist in the largest American libraries, and no record of them is listed in the several large union catalogues in the country.

48. "Editor's Table," L, 94 (July, 1857).

49. New York *Daily Tribune,* June 20, 1856.

50. *Putnam's Monthly Magazine,* VIII, 98 (July, 1856). The pocket edition sold for seventy-five cents.

51. "The Little-Book Epidemic," June 20, 1857.

52. Ticknor and Fields printed the poem in the front of later issues of the pocket editions and used it extensively in their advertising. That the poem was especially addressed to Fields and that it was written by Hillard are facts shown by a letter, Fields to Evert A. Duyckinck, June 7, 1856. Copying the poem in full, Fields prefaced it with the sentence, "A few days ago I sent you a little pocket Tennyson, which I hope you will like as much as Hillard who addressed to me these lines" (MS, Duyckinck Collection, New York Public Library).

53. New York *Daily Tribune,* Dec. 6, 1856.

54. New York, 1857, pp. 432–55. Willmott's original English edition contained only "The May Queen" and "Break, Break, Break"; Duyckinck added the other three (see p. xi of Table of Contents).

55. Philadelphia, 1859, pp. 313–24. The volume was reviewed as early as December 2, 1858 (Boston *Daily Evening Transcript*).

56. For a general description of the literary annuals and their contents, see Ralph Thompson, *American Literary Annuals & Gift Books* (New York, 1936), pp. 1–36. Professor Bradford A. Booth of the University of California at Los Angeles, who is preparing an index of American annuals,

1825–1865, has written to me in a letter of February 15, 1941, that he has found 75 poems of Mrs. Hemans, 21 of Byron's, 20 of Tom Moore's and 19 of Wordsworth's, as compared with 17 of Tennyson's. It should be remembered with reference to the comparison that Tennyson came into prominence later in the period than any other of the group. For a list of Tennyson items in American annuals, see Appendix B.

57. This rare gift-book, not listed in Ralph Thompson's catalogue (*op. cit.,* pp. 102–63), has been found only in the library of the Boston Athenaeum.

58. Boston, 1854, pp. 116–21. The Prologue, the first four stanzas of Section XXXIII, Section LIV, and Section CVI ("Ring Out, Wild Bells") were quoted. The book was reprinted in entirety the same year as *An Excursion among the Poets* (Richmond, Va.) with H. C. Foster named on the title page as editor.

59. Curiously, all four poems were taken from Tennyson's early volumes, and not from the *Poems* of 1842. "The Grasshopper" and "The Deserted House" of *Poems, Chiefly Lyrical* were not reprinted in 1842, and textual variations in the other two items, "The May Queen" and "New Year's Eve" show that they were printed from the *Poems* of 1833; none of the corrections which Tennyson made in the 1842 version appear. When a second volume, called "Part Second," of *Poetry for Home and School* appeared in 1846, three other poems of Tennyson—all from the 1842 volume—were added, to bring his total to seven and give him a representation within the first five in a collection of poets, American and English, from Chaucer to contemporary times.

60. Cincinnati, 1857, pp. 206–09, 328–29. I have carefully checked the several hundred McGuffey texts in the almost complete collection of the Library of Congress and have found no other Tennyson item in a reader as early as 1858.

61. William and Anna U. Russell, *Introduction to the Young Ladies' Elocutionary Reader,* (Boston, 1845) pp. 162–64. As in the *Poetry for Home and School,* the text is that of the 1833 *Poems.*

62. Francis T. Russell (New York, 1847), pp. 93–94.

63. "Bayard Taylor's Poems," *American Whig Review,* XV, 33 (Jan., 1852).

64. Review of *Poems* by Owen Meredith, *Southern Literary Messenger,* XXVIII, 473 (June, 1859). This review has been doubtfully assigned to John R. Thompson (Jackson, *op. cit.,* p. 142).

65. Cf. S. Foster Damon, *Thomas Holley Chivers, Friend of Poe* (New York and London, 1930, pp. 185–86): "After Tennyson's volume of 1842, melodious feminine names had become common."

66. Professor Damon (*op. cit.,* p. 210) gives 1841 as the date of "Isadore," but his only reference is to an article by W. C. Richardson in the Boston *Daily Evening Transcript* for April 24, 1897, which states that the poem was "written and published" in 1841. Neither biographer tells *where* it was published, and apparently no one knows.

67. *Eonchs of Ruby* (New York, 1851), p. 97. The first stanza is quoted.

68. Professor J. F. A. Pyre wrote in 1921 (*op. cit.,* p. 248) concerning "Locksley Hall" and its English followers, "These poems immediately crossed the Atlantic and created there the rhythms of Poe's *The Raven*

(1845) and its congeners." The influence of "Locksley Hall" seems clear, but if "Isadore," apparently the earliest of the Poe-Chivers group using the rhythm, appeared earlier than "Locksley Hall," Professor Pyre's statement must be revised.

Several verbal echoes strengthen the connection between Tennyson and "The Raven." Tennyson's "No More," a contribution to *The Gem: A Literary Annual* for 1831, repeated its title as a refrain, and "Anacreontics," another contribution to the same annual, used the name "Lenora" (see "Literary Gossip," *Athenaeum,* No. 2473, p. 395, March 20, 1875). The line from "No More," "Surely all pleasant things had gone before," instantly suggests Poe's

> Other friends have flown before—
> On the morrow *he* will leave me, as my hopes have
> flown before.

Also, Tennyson's line from "Adeline" of *Poems, Chiefly Lyrical,* "Take the heart from out my breast," suggests Poe's "Take thy beak from out my heart." Tennyson's "The Sea-Fairies," "All Things Will Die," "Madeline," and "Eleanore," all contain elements which may have contributed to the refrain of "The Raven," but since such refrains were being used frequently at the time, one cannot speak with definiteness of the Tennyson influence there. See Robert S. Forsythe, "Poe's 'Nevermore': A Note," *American Literature,* VII, 439–52 (Jan., 1936).

69. Professor Pyre (*op. cit.,* pp. 244–49) concluded that the meter was Tennyson's invention.

70. *Graham's Magazine,* XXII, 35 (Jan., 1843); see Longfellow's *Works,* I, 211–14. The first two stanzas are quoted.

71. *Works,* I, 219–23. A note (p. 219) dates the poem in the spring of 1844.

72. *The Dream of a Day and Other Poems* (New Haven, Conn., 1843), pp. 193–94.

73. *Poems* (Boston, 1847), pp. 138–39. Story dated the poem 1843. The fifth and sixth stanzas are quoted. For a later copying of the rhythm by Story, see his "Prologue—Spoken at the Inauguration of Crawford's Bronze Statue of Beethoven, at the Boston Music Hall, March 1, 1856" (*Poems,* Boston, 1856, pp. 296–305).

74. First published as "Verses Suggested by the Present Crisis" in the Boston *Daily Courier,* December 11, 1845. See Lowell's *Works,* IX, 185–91. The first stanza is quoted.

75. *Poems* (Boston, 1847), p. 1. For "Inez," see pp. 42–45. "Inez" first appeared in a gift-book for 1847 which was published in late 1846: *Leaflets of Memory* (Philadelphia), pp. 25–27.

76. *Poems of the Orient* (Boston, 1855), pp. 105–10. Stanzas VI and VIII are quoted. For a use of the rhythm in *A Book of Romances, Lyrics and Songs* (Boston, 1852), see "Manuela," pp. 75–80.

77. See, for instance, Story's, "The Mistake" (*Poems,* Boston, 1847, pp. 96–115) and Read's "The Fairer Land" (*Lays and Ballads,* Philadelphia, 1849, pp. 115–17). "The Fairer Land" had been published a year earlier as the proem to an anthology, *The Female Poets of America* (Philadelphia, 1848), of which Read was editor.

78. *Songs of Summer* (Boston, 1857), p. 198. The first four lines of Sec-

tion III are quoted. The poem is dated 1853. Stoddard varied his four-line stanzas, mixing in some *aabb* rimes toward the last.

79. *Virginalia; or Songs of My Summer Nights* (Philadelphia, 1853), pp. 28–29. The poem is written in eight-line stanzas. The first four lines of the third stanza are quoted. For other examples of Chivers' use of the rhythm, see "Bessie Bell," "Rosalie Lee," and "Lily Adair," all in the same volume.

80. "Song" ["That I loved thee—aye, adored thee"], *The Boudoir Annual* for 1846 (Boston), p. 30.

81. *The Brilliant,* a gift-book for 1850 (New York), pp. 110–11.

82. See Mulchinock's *Ballads and Songs* (New York, 1851), pp. 110–18. The connection with both "Locksley Hall" and "The May Queen" is obvious. The poem is divided into Parts as is "The May Queen." Mulchinock's girl directs her doleful but brave complaint to her mother, and Tennyson's refrain "mother dear" is repeated many times.

83. *Pioneer; or, California Monthly Magazine,* II, 149–50 (Sept., 1854). Stanzas eleven, twelve, and thirteen are quoted. Several months earlier, a poem, "Sea-Side Musings," signed "C. E. H." and very probably by Havens, in the same magazine (I, 311–13, May, 1854) explained Tennyson's "argosies of magic sails" and "pilots of the purple twilight":

> Yonder cloud, so slowly sailing through the blue dome of the world,
> Like an argosy, full freighted, with its canvas all unfurled,
>
> Shall be anchored ere the twilight in some distant horizon
> Crimson with the setting splendor of the slowly sinking sun.

Cf. Susan Archer Talley's "A Soul's Creed":

> Pilots of the coming twilight floating on the Southern gale
> Laden with costly treasure—amethyst and topaz pale

(*Southern Literary Messenger,* XV, 222–23, April, 1849; reprinted in Susan Archer Talley's *Poems,* New York, 1859, p. 22).

84. Henry Latham in his poem, "The Age" (*The Forget-Me-Not* for 1856, New York, pp. 60–64) used the stanza and paraphrased the same passage, and Mulchinock's long series of poems, "Chants for Toilers" (*op. cit.,* pp. 40–74), freely lifted both expressions and ideas from "Locksley Hall." Compare, for instance,

> Many a morning by the waters of the far resounding sea
> Have I walked in meditation all my spirit fancy free—(p. 65)

to Tennyson's

> Many a morning on the moorland did we hear the copses ring.
> And her whisper throng'd my pulses with the fulness of the spring
> (ll. 35–36).

Also compare

> From the chord of self-evoking music, wild but sweet to hear,
> Fraught with mystic strange revealings to the earnest thinker's ear
> (p. 160).

to Tennyson's

> Love took up the harp of Life, and smote on all the chords with might;
> Smote the chord of Self, that, trembling, past in music out of sight (ll. 33–34).

Verbal borrowing from "Locksley Hall," especially among the major poets was infrequent, but copies of the rhythm are to be found everywhere. By including verses written anonymously and by unknowns in American periodicals and gift-books, one could continue the list indefinitely.

85. "American Authorship—Hawthorne," XXIII, 498 (April, 1853). The article was signed "R. H. N., Macon, Geo."

86. *Poems,* Philadelphia, 1844, p. 15. The stanzas were dated June, 1836. For another such example, see Alfred B. Street's "To the Brown Thrush," *American Literary Magazine,* Hartford, Conn., III, 145–46 (Sept., 1848).

87. *Southern Literary Messenger,* XVII, 104 (Feb., 1851). The first two stanzas are quoted.

88. D. Parish Barhydt, "On the Death of James Fenimore Cooper," *Literary World,* IX, 252–53 (Sept. 27, 1851). The ninth, tenth, and eleventh stanzas are quoted. Barhydt enjoyed using the stanza, ill-treating it just as badly in other contributions to the *Literary World:* "The Hill," IX, 369 (Nov. 8, 1851), and "The River," X, 106 (Feb. 7, 1852). A New York sociologist, Barhydt wrote one long poem: *Life* (New York, 1851).

89. Pp. 140–41. For other examples, see "The Moon on the Spire" (pp. 103–04) and "I Lay His Picture on My Knee" (pp. 224–29). "Great and Small" first appeared in *Graham's Magazine,* XLIII, 332 (Sept., 1853).

90. "H. W. L.," *The Bells: A Collection of Chimes* (New York, 1851), p. 24. The first two stanzas are quoted.

91. *A Vision of Faery Land and Other Poems* (Boston, 1853), 201–03. Incidentally, Henry Timrod's later Confederate War poem, "Christmas," suggests "Ring Out, Wild Bells" and in its closing invocation to peace is very close to Section XI in *In Memoriam.* See *The Poems of Henry Timrod,* ed. Paul H. Hayne (New York, 1873), pp. 104–07.

92. *Graham's Magazine,* XXXVIII, 184 (March, 1851); reprinted in *Poems* (Boston, 1860), pp. 169–71. "Grace Greenwood" was the pseudonym of Mrs. Sara Jane Lippincott—traveler, poet, and voluminous writer. In her *Poems* (Boston, 1851) she twice used the "Locksley Hall" stanza: "Arnold de Winkelried" (pp. 179–86) and "The Gold-Seekers" (pp. 170–74). For Julia Ward Howe's use of the *In Memoriam* stanza, see her *Words for the Hour* (Boston, 1857), pp. 32–34, 49–51, etc.

93. William Roderick Lawrence, "Isadore," *Peterson's Magazine,* XXV, 202 (March, 1854). A frequent contributor to *Peterson's,* Lawrence consistently used the *In Memoriam* stanza. See "La Violette," XXVI, 383 (Dec., 1854); "Rosa Sine Spina," XXVII, 200 (March, 1855); etc.

94. "Death of the Old Year," *The St. Lawrence and the Saguenay and Other Poems* (New York, 1856), pp. 92–94. For the review of the volume, see the *Albion,* 4th Ser., XV, 393 (Aug. 16, 1856). In this volume, which reminds one of some poem of Tennyson's on almost every page, Sangster used the *In Memoriam* stanza again in "Fanny" (pp. 220–21).

95. *International Monthly Magazine,* IV, 169 (Sept., 1851). In 1849, John

Esten Cooke copied into his commonplace-book a rimed tetrameter version of "Tears, Idle Tears" (John O. Beaty, *John Esten Cooke, Virginian,* New York, 1922, p. 20).

96. "Lancelot of the Lake," *Sartain's Union Magazine,* X, 6–7 (Jan., 1852).

97. For a full description of Tennyson's blank verse, see Pyre, *op. cit.,* pp. 68–93, 113–59.

98. *Democratic Review,* XIII, 147–53 (Aug., 1843); reprinted in *Works,* IX, 112–23. Lines 95–103 and 360–64 are quoted.

99. *Poems* (Boston, 1849), II, 3–16; reprinted in *Works,* IX, 154–63. Lines 104–13 are quoted.

100. *Russell's Magazine,* I, 46 (Apr., 1857); reprinted in *The Poems of Henry Timrod,* pp. 172–73. Lines 16–27 are quoted.

101. "He . . . will soon rank as one of the very noblest of American poets. In fact, he *is* so *now,*" "Marginalia," *Southern Literary Messenger,* XV, 600 (Sept., 1849); see Poe's *Works,* XVI, 175–77.

102. *Meditations in America and Other Poems* (New York, 1851), pp. 89–92. Lines 20–28 and 37–45 are quoted. For "Last Words of Washington" and "Wordsworth," see pp. 69–75, 81–88.

103. "Ulysses," lines 6–11. The poem first appeared in the 1842 *Poems.* See *Works,* II, 185–88. For a blank verse monologue by Bayard Taylor written in the "Ulysses" manner, see "In Articulo Mortis" (*Poems of the Orient,* pp. 186–92); and for an unusually clear verbal echo of "Ulysses," see William Gilmore Simms's Sonnet LV of "Grouped Thoughts and Scattered Fancies" (*Southern Literary Messenger,* XI, 442, July, 1845):

> "We are a part of all we hear and see,—
> We share in their existence—we are taught
> By what they suffer—with their feelings fraught."

Cf. "Ulysses": "I am a part of all that I have met. . . ." (l. 18).

104. Aldrich, *op. cit.,* pp. 87–88.

105. *Passion-Flowers* (Boston, 1854), pp. 8–25, 46–58.

106. For the first two, see *Poems* (Boston, 1843), pp. 1–9, 115–18; for the last, see *Poems* (Boston, 1847), pp. 27–34.

107. New York, 1844. See especially "The Mill" (pp. 29–30) and "The Garden" (pp. 31–32).

108. *Poems* (Boston, 1852), pp. 70–73.

109. *Russell's Magazine,* II, 438 (Feb., 1858); see *The Poems of Henry Timrod,* p. 191. For Stoddard's imitation, see "Rattle the Window, Winds!" *Songs of Summer,* p. 45.

110. *Lays and Ballads* (Philadelphia, 1849), pp. 12–18. The fifth and fifteenth stanzas are quoted. For Read's other imitation of "The Lady of Shalott," see "Olivia," *Poems* (Boston, 1847), pp. 38–41.

111. See Henry B. Hirst's "Florence" (*The Penance of Roland and Other Poems,* Boston, 1849, pp. 108–28) and James Barron Hope's "The Lover to the Maiden" (*Leoni Di Monota and Other Poems,* Philadelphia, 1857, pp. 207–09). A poem, "Reading Tennyson" by Mary W. S. Gibson (*Knickerbocker,* XLVIII, 276, Sept., 1856) imitated and highly praised "The Lady of Shalott."

112. *The Coming of the Mammoth and Other Poems* (Boston, 1845), pp. 85–87. The sixth stanza is quoted.

113. *Ballads and Songs,* pp. 181–83. The sixth stanza is quoted. See also "A Lament for Thomas Davis" (*ibid.,* pp. 238–40), William Gibson's "Oralie" (*op. cit.,* pp. 204–10), and Thomas Bailey Aldrich's "Berthabell" (*op. cit.,* pp. 89–90). Such poems are, of course, suggestive of numbers of poems containing oft-repeated refrains. They are akin to Poe's and Chivers' poems with lyrical refrains, and the Irish poet, James Clarence Mangan, is sometimes credited with popularizing such refrains (see Henry Edward Cain, *James Clarence Mangan and the Poe-Mangan Question,* Washington, D. C., 1929, pp. 45–66). Mangan's "The Karamanian Exile," first published in 1844 (*Dublin University Magazine,* XXIII, 536, May) is typical of several of his poems of the "Oriana" type, all of which may have been influenced by the earlier "Oriana" (1830).

114. "The Funeral of Time" and "The Burial of Eros" (*The Coming of the Mammoth and Other Poems,* pp. 31–36, 60–63), and "The Death of the Year," *Graham's Magazine,* XXXVII, 333 (Dec., 1850). See also Mary E. Hewitt's "A Lament for the Old Year" (*Songs of Our Land and Other Poems,* Boston, 1846, pp. 107–08), and W. H. C. Hosmer's "Winter Sprites" (*Knickerbocker,* XXVII, 228–30, March, 1846).

115. See Lowell's *Works,* IX, 301–24; and Scudder, *op. cit.,* I, 266–69. "The Sleeping Palace" is Section I of "The Day-Dream" (Tennyson's *Works,* II, 219–21). There is an interesting parallel between the famous line in "The Vision of Sir Launfal," "What is so rare as a day in June?" and a line in the "Huntsman's Song" of *Poems by Two Brothers* (see 2nd ed., London and New York, 1893, pp. 61–62): "Oh! what is so sweet as a morning in spring." The "Huntsman's Song" is doubtfully assigned to Charles Tennyson (*ibid.,* p. 62). It is very unlikely that Lowell saw *Poems by Two Brothers* as early as 1848, but the lines are remarkably alike. One other close parallel between well known passages in Lowell and Tennyson is worthy of notice. The following lines from Lowell's "A Glance behind the Curtain" remind one of the oft-quoted line in "Locksley Hall," "Better fifty years of Europe than a cycle of Cathay" (l. 184):

> We learn our souls more, tossing for an hour
> Upon this huge and ever vexed sea
> Of human thought where kingdoms go to wreck
> Like fragile bubbles yonder in the stream,
> Than in a cycle of New England sloth

(*Democratic Review,* XIII, 236–40, Sept., 1843; see *Works,* IX, 144).

As has been noted already, many of the most Tennysonian of Lowell's early poems were uncollected in later editions of Lowell's poems, and Tennyson echoes are much rarer in his later poems than in his earlier. When Lowell revised his early poems, he invariably made them less Tennysonian. This point is discussed at some length in an unpublished Master's Essay (Columbia University, 1923): Allegra Stewart, *A Comparison of Lowell and Tennyson.*

116. *Poems* (Boston, 1847), pp. 96–115. In both Tennyson's and Story's poems, a lover reminisced over meetings with his sweetheart upon the meadow under a great tree, and both the tree and the flower shared their secrets. For another imitation of "The Talking Oak," see Hirst's "To an Old Oak" (*The Coming of The Mammoth and Other Poems,* pp. 92–94).

117. See Mulchinock's "The Dying Girl" (*op. cit.*, pp. 110–18) and I. B. Woodbury's "Mother Dear, O Pray for Me" (*American Monthly Musical Review*, I, 1–9, Nov. 1, 1850).

118. John R. Thompson printed the improvement, which was written, he said, by "an adventurous writer in the interior of our state," in his "Editor's Table" of the *Southern Literary Messenger* (XXIII, 470–71, Dec., 1856). With the improvement Thompson printed Tennyson's poem, together with harsh reprimands to the "improver." See also William W. Story's "No More" (*Poems*, 1847, pp. 89–90):

> Flow on, sad stream, unto the sea!
> Thou flowest on as ever,
> But the heart most dear no more is here,
> Forever and forever.

Tennyson's "A Farewell" begins in the same manner:

> Flow down, cold rivulet, to the sea,
> Thy tribute wave deliver:
> No more by thee my steps shall be
> Forever and forever

(first published in 1842 *Poems;* see *Works,* II, 282).

119. See Hirst's "The Owl" (*The Coming of the Mammoth and Other Poems*, pp. 118–19) and Thomas B. Read's "The Windy Night" (*Poems*, Boston, 1847, pp. 62–64).

120. Besides those already noted, see Chivers' "Cradle-Song" (*Virginalia*, p. 128), which is most like Tennyson's "Sweet and Low" (Part II, ll. 456–72); and anonymous "Lines" ["Ask Me not, with simple grace"] (*The Garland: or, Token of Friendship*, New York, 1855, pp. 30–31), which plagiarize "Ask Me No More" (Part VI, ll. 364–79).

121. *Words for the Hour* (Boston, 1857), pp. 35–37. The first three stanzas are quoted. For Hope's "The Charge at Balaklava," see *op. cit.*, pp. 79–86. For Meek's "Balaklava," see his *Songs and Poems of the South* (New York, 1857), pp. 89–93. Of the three imitations, Meek's is least like Tennyson, but Meek's poem was directly inspired by Tennyson's. Challenged by a friend to write a poem on a subject treated by an English poet and to sign the name of an English poet to it in order to see how popular it would become, Meek wrote "Balaklava" for the New Orleans *Sunday Delta* in 1855 over the name of Alexander Smith (Herman Clarence Nixon, *Alexander Beaufort Meek*, Auburn, Ala., 1910, pp. 20–21). As Smith's, "Balaklava" attracted wide attention both in England and America (*ibid.*). When it was included in *Songs and Poems of the South,* Meek stated in the preface (p. vi) that "by some error of the press" the poem had been attributed to Alexander Smith, but for many years it was still referred to as Smith's. For comparisons of "Balaklava" and "The Charge of the Light Brigade," see "Smith and the Poet Laureate," Boston *Daily Evening Transcript,* March 15, 1855, and "Editor's Table," *Pioneer; or, California Monthly Magazine,* III, 279–80 (June, 1855).

122. "Kane," *Southern Literary Messenger,* XXIV, 257–60 (Apr., 1857). For the assignment of this anonymous poem to Cooke, and for a discussion of its relation to Tennyson's "Ode," see Beaty, *op. cit.*, p. 67.

123. *Songs of Summer,* pp. 166–67. Tennyson's song is from "Maud," I,

850–923. Points of resemblance between the two poems are discussed in William Purviance Fenn, "Richard Henry Stoddard's Chinese Poems," *American Literature,* XI, 421 (Jan., 1940).

124. *Lyra and Other Poems* (New York, 1852), pp. 30–32. Lines 34–48 are quoted. Several other poems in this volume are close to "Mariana." See especially "Madela" (pp. 91–92). See also Alice Cary's "Rosalie" (*Poems,* Boston, 1855, pp. 171–73).

125. *Poems* (Boston, 1847), pp. 80–81. The first stanza is quoted. Cf. Bayard Taylor's "Moan, Ye Wild Winds" and "The Mid-Watch" of *Poems of the Orient* (pp. 92, 197–98), and William Ellery Channing's "Mariana" (*Poems,* Boston, 1847, pp. 142–43). Annuals and magazines contain numbers of poems which sound like parodies of "Mariana." See "Marianne" by W. H. Carpenter (*Godey's Lady's Book,* XXVI, 127, March, 1843), "Eleanore" (*Ladies' National Magazine,* IV, 132, Oct., 1843), and "The Maiden's Wail" by Oscar G. Hughan (*The Book of the Boudoir,* Boston, 1853, pp. 194–97). "Eleanore," signed "C," sounds like Chivers, who in 1843 was contributing to the *Ladies' National Magazine,* but the poem has not been assigned to him.

126. Aldrich, *op. cit.,* pp. 35–36. The first stanza is quoted.

127. Boker, *The Podesta's Daughter and Other Poems* (Philadelphia, 1852), pp. 138–39. The poem first appeared in an annual for 1849: *The Book of Pearls* (New York), pp. 223–24. The first stanza is quoted. The last line was repeated as a refrain in all four stanzas. Cf. "Oenone" by Howard H. Caldwell (*Poems,* Boston, 1858, pp. 109–18).

128. *Poems* (Boston, 1847), pp. 13–25. The second stanza is quoted.

129. *Poems* (Boston, 1855), pp. 75–78. The first stanza is quoted. Cf. Aldrich's "The Golden Island" (*op. cit.,* pp. 121–23), Stoddard's "The Castle in the Air" (*Poems,* Boston, 1852, pp. 3–20), and Hirst's "On a Summer Night" (*The Penance of Roland and Other Poems,* p. 81). Several reviewers of George William Curtis's *Nile Notes of a Howadji* noted parallels between passages of Curtis's prose and Tennyson's "The Lotos-Eaters" (see John Esten Cooke, "A Handful of Autumn Leaves: from the Lowlands of Virginia," *Southern Literary Messenger,* XVIII, 714, Dec., 1852—for assignment to Cooke, see Beaty, *op. cit.,* p. 166; and see also an anonymous article, "George W. Curtis," *National Magazine,* IV, 28, Jan., 1854).

130. "The Sea-Fairies" first appeared in the 1833 *Poems,* and "The Merman" and "The Mermaid" in *Poems, Chiefly Lyrical.* See *Works,* I, 192–94, 210–15.

131. *Poems* (Boston, 1847), pp. 125–26. The first stanza is quoted.

132. *Romances, Lyrics and Songs,* pp. 142–44. The first stanza is quoted. Cf. Christopher P. Cranch's "The Sweet-Flower" and "The Ocean" (*Poems,* Philadelphia, 1844, pp. 21–23, 67–69) and Stoddard's "The Song of the Syrens" (*Songs of Summer,* p. 8).

133. New York, 1849, pp. 8–12.

134. For the four poems specifically referred to, see the *Saturday Evening Post,* Sept. 21, 1850; Aldrich, *op. cit.,* pp. 129–30; Alice Cary, *Lyra and Other Poems,* pp. 23–24; and Clarence May, *The Book of the Boudoir* (Boston, 1853), pp. 302–03.

135. "William Ellery Channing," *Graham's Magazine,* XXIII, 113–17 (Aug., 1843); see Poe's *Works,* XI, 174–90.

136. Review of Lowell's *Poems* (1849), VI, 35 (Jan. 12, 1850).

137. Review of Lowell's *Poems* (1844), *North American Review,* LVIII, 286 (April, 1844). The review is unsigned; for its assignment to Felton, see William Cushing, *Index to the North American Review* (Cambridge, Mass., 1878), p. 66.

138. Letter to Ferdinand J. Dreer, Dec. 15, 1860, in Townsend, *op. cit.,* p. 118.

139. See Townsend, *op. cit.,* pp. 75, 113, 118; John R. Tait, "Reminiscences of a Poet-Painter," *Lippincott's Magazine,* XIX, 320 (March, 1877); and I. C. Keller, "Thomas Buchanan Read," *University of Pittsburgh Bulletin,* XXIX, 1–4 (Jan., 1933).

140. Letter to Ferdinand J. Dreer, Feb. 5, 1858, in Townsend, *op. cit.,* p. 113.

141. Tennyson wrote to Charles Stearns Wheeler just after Wheeler's arrival in Europe in 1842, "I do not fear that you will bring among us the spirit of Fenimore Cooper" (MS letter, Nov., 1842, Widener Collection, Harvard College Library).

142. Arthur Hugh Clough praised the bust to Emerson in a letter of March 23, 1857, and suggested "you ought to buy it in America" (*Emerson-Clough Letters,* ed. Howard F. Lowry and Ralph L. Rusk, Cleveland, 1934, letter No. 30). Liking Clough's suggestion, Emerson forwarded the letter to James Elliot Cabot with the recommendation that the matter be brought to the notice of the Library Committee of the Boston Athenaeum (letter, May 8, 1857, in Emerson's *Letters,* V, 75). On February 22, 1858, Woolner wrote to Mrs. Alfred Tennyson that a Dr. Bellows of Boston [doubtless Henry W. Bellows, Unitarian minister and scholar] wished to buy the bust and even felt "inclined to buy it unseen, having heard so much about [it] from Emerson" (Amy Woolner, *Thomas Woolner, R. A.,* London, 1917, p. 143). It was in reply to this letter that Mrs. Tennyson wrote Woolner on February 25, 1858, expressing her own disapproval of the bust's leaving England and quoting Alfred as saying "tell him not to part with that to America[;] he is sure to find a purchaser in England" (*ibid.,* p. 145).

143. Phillips, *op. cit.,* p. 1606.

144. First published in the *Examiner,* No. 2297, p. 86 (Feb. 7, 1852), it was not included in any editions of Tennyson's *Works* till thirty years later, when the two stanzas in praise of America were deleted. It seems that American newspapers and magazines would have reprinted the poem from the *Examiner,* and doubtless some did, but no instances have been found.

145. Even Read spoke of Tennyson's cordiality to him personally (letter to Ferdinand J. Dreer, Feb. 5, 1858, in Townsend, *op. cit.,* p. 113).

146. *Journals,* VII, 444–47 (May 6?, 1848).

147. See letter, Tennyson to Tuckerman, July, 1855, quoted in Witter Bynner's introduction to *The Sonnets of Frederick Goddard Tuckerman* (New York and London, 1931), pp. 28–29.

148. Letter to his brother Edward, quoted in Bynner, *op. cit.,* pp. 26–27. The manuscript is now in the possession of Tuckerman's grand-daughter, Mrs. Orton Loring Clarke, of Amherst, Massachusetts.

149. See Bynner, *op. cit.,* pp. 26–30.

150. Letter to a Mrs. Eckley, June 10, 1873, quoted in *ibid.,* p. 30.

151. See Taylor, *At Home and Abroad* (New York, 1889), pp. 445–46;

and Hansen-Taylor and Scudder, *op. cit.,* I, 333–34. Taylor's letter to Boker, undated, is quoted in Hansen-Taylor and Scudder, I, 334.

152. Thomas Wentworth Higginson's account of the experience of his Harvard friend, William Henry Hurlbut (*Letters and Journals of Thomas Wentworth Higginson,* p. 33). Hurlbut visited England in 1850 (see *ibid.,* pp. 29–33).

153. Entry of July 19, 1853, in Madame LeVert's journal, *Souvenirs of Travel* (Mobile, 1857), I, 79.

154. For the entire account of Hawthorne's experience, see entry of July 30, 1857, in his journal (*The Heart of Hawthorne's Journals,* ed. Newton Arvin, Boston and New York, 1929, pp. 241–45).

155. Fields, *Yesterdays with Authors* (Boston, 1872), p. 81.

156. The letter, dated by Taylor "June, 1857," is reproduced in James Grant Wilson, "Thackeray in the United States," *Century Magazine,* LXIII, 337 (Jan., 1902).

Chapter VI

1. "Alfred Tennyson," VI, 390 (Oct., 1855).

2. "Tennyson's Maud as a Work of Art," *Yale Literary Magazine,* XXIV, 89 (Dec., 1858).

3. The Boston *Daily Evening Transcript* for July 31, 1855, stated, "The laureate has sent the proof sheets of 'Maud, and other Poems' to his American publishers, Messrs. Ticknor & Fields."

4. *Norton's Literary Gazette,* N. S., II, 259 (June 15, 1855).

5. From August 15 to 18 in the Boston *Daily Evening Transcript,* Ticknor and Fields advertised the edition to be published "on Saturday, August 18." A list of Ticknor and Fields editions sent to me by the Houghton Mifflin Company in a communication of September 21, 1940, gives August 18 as the date of publication.

6. Thomas Gold Appleton recorded in his journal on August 9, 1855, that he, Longfellow, George William Curtis, and Julia Ward Howe were enjoying reading "Maud" from proof sheets which Fields had sent them (Susan Hale, *Life and Letters of Thomas Gold Appleton,* New York, 1885, p. 294).

7. Taylor wrote to Fields in a letter of August 6, 1855, "Many thanks for 'Maud,' which came safely, and will be reviewed at once, probably in tomorrow's paper" (Hansen–Taylor and Scudder, *op. cit.,* I, 305). *Maud, and Other Poems* was reviewed in the *Tribune* on August 7. At the head of the review, the edition was listed as that of Ticknor and Fields, but, curiously, the heading listed the number of pages of the book being reviewed as 154, the number of pages in the first English edition. Ticknor and Fields's edition had 160 pages. Fields evidently had sent Taylor some proof sheets of the English edition.

8. See *Albion,* 4th Ser., XIV, 346 (July 21, 1855); *Home Journal,* July 21, 1855; Boston *Daily Evening Transcript,* August 2, 1855; etc.

9. Letter, Taylor to Fields, quoted in Hansen-Taylor and Scudder, *op. cit.,* I, 305.

10. Houghton Mifflin Company possesses complete, and presumably accurate, records of the editions of *Maud, and Other Poems.* According to

their communication to me (Sept. 21, 1940), the first printing, issued on August 18, 1855, numbered 3000 copies, the second (later in August) numbered 2000, the third (September, 1855) numbered 2400, and the fourth (March, 1856) numbered 1000.

11. The "Ode" was first published in pamphlet form on November 18, 1852, the day of the funeral of the Duke of Wellington; a second edition in pamphlet form with greatly revised text was published in 1853 (Wise, *op. cit.,* I, 122–24). The *Literary World* announced on April 9, 1853 (XII, 290), that Ticknor, Reed, and Fields had "in press" an American edition of the "Ode," but no other trace of any kind can be found of such an edition now. Probably it was projected but never published. "The Charge of the Light Brigade" was first published in the London *Examiner,* No. 2445, p. 780 (Dec. 9, 1854).

12. For the "Ode," see Boston *Daily Evening Transcript,* Dec. 6, 1852; *Southern Literary Gazette,* II, 284–85 (Dec. 18, 1852); *Literary World,* XII, 290–91 (April 9, 1853); etc. For "The Charge of the Light Brigade," see New York *Daily Tribune,* Jan. 4, 1855; *Albion,* 4th Ser., XIV, 1 (Jan. 6, 1855); San Francisco *Weekly Pacific,* Feb. 2, 1855; etc.

13. See *Memoir,* I, 160–61; and Lounsbury, *The Life and Times of Tennyson,* pp. 269–78. A MS copy of the "Stanzas" dated 1833 is still extant (Wise, *op. cit.,* I, 305). Professor Lounsbury gives a detailed discussion of the relationship between the "Stanzas" and "Maud." Both poetically portrayed insanity in the form of mental hallucination, and in both the demented lover was haunted by visions of his lost sweetheart and memories of their former bliss together.

14. XXV, 487–88 (June, 1845). Sixty-six of the original 110 lines were printed in the *Knickerbocker* and there bore the title, "My Early Love." The poem also bore a note by the editor of the *Knickerbocker* stating that the unpublished verses had been contributed by Bristed, who "had been permitted to read them in the manuscript of the author." Professor Lounsbury (*The Life and Times of Tennyson,* p. 277) used the fact that Bristed at Cambridge thought the poems unpublished to prove that *The Tribute* had been utterly forgotten, but Bristed knew that the poem had been published, and he had not read them from manuscript. It was the editor, Lewis Gaylord Clark, who was in error. As soon as Bristed received his copy of the *Knickerbocker* for June, he wrote to Clark correcting the error: "I did not read the poem in the author's manuscript; I have not the honor of his acquaintance; and I am unable to recall to mind a syllable of my communication, from which such an inference could have been legitimately drawn. I expressly stated that the lines in question had been printed, but subjoined as a reason for your reprinting them, that they were not generally known to the American public" ("Editor's Table," *Knickerbocker,* XXVI, 288, Sept., 1845).

15. See *Broadway Journal,* I, 348 (May 31, 1845); New York *Daily Tribune,* May 30, 1845; and *Harbinger,* VI, 74 (Jan. 8, 1848). Although of earlier date, the *Journal* and the *Tribune* acknowledged the *Knickerbocker* for June as their source for the poem.

16. XLVI, 525–26 (Nov., 1855).

17. Letter, Lowell to Charles Eliot Norton, Aug. 11, 1855, in Lowell's *Works,* XIV, 311.

18. Letter to Mabel Lowell, July 1, 1869, in Lowell's *Works,* XV, 214–15.

19. *Journals,* VIII, 526 (1855).

20. LXXXI, 544 (Oct., 1855). For assignment of the unsigned review to Hale, see Cushing, *Index to the North American Review,* p. 66.

21. Susan Hale, *op. cit.,* p. 294.

22. Entry of August 5, 1855, quoted in Samuel Longfellow, *Life of Henry Wadsworth Longfellow* (Boston and New York, 1891), II, 290. Note that this is not the edition previously referred to. Because of variations in the two, it has been necessary to use both the 1886 and the 1891 editions.

23. The journals of Julia Ward Howe quoted in Hildegarde Hawthorne, *The Poet of Craigie House* (New York and London, 1936), p. 193.

24. Review of *Maud, and Other Poems,* VI, 318 (Sept., 1855). Compare a later statement in the same periodical ("Alfred Tennyson," VI, 386, Oct., 1855): "'Maud' has the felicitous mannerism of Tennyson's earlier verse, with the stern and vigorous thought of the later."

25. XLVI, 525 (Nov., 1855).

26. VIII, 87 (Dec. 15, 1855); for another review in the same periodical, see X, 62 (Nov. 22, 1856).

27. See reviews in *Southern Literary Messenger,* XXI, 639 (Oct., 1855); and the Boston *Daily Evening Transcript,* Dec. 19, 1855.

28. XXI, 639 (Oct., 1855).

29. Nov. 13, 1855. See also *Putnam's Magazine,* VI, 388–89 (Oct., 1855).

30. MS letter, Tuckerman to Tennyson, October 22, 1855, Harvard College Library. "Maud" is extremely unorthodox in its versification. It has no set stanza form. The lines vary in length from three to five stresses, and iambic, trochaic, dactylic, and anapaestic meters are all represented. See J. F. A. Pyre, *op. cit.,* pp. 189–95.

31. "Editor's Easy Chair," *Harper's Monthly Magazine,* XI, 705 (Oct., 1855). From 1853 to 1859 the "Editor's Easy Chair" was handled by Curtis and Donald G. Mitchell (Mott, *op. cit.,* II, 389). William Dean Howells several times referred to this item as Curtis's. See Howells's essay on Tennyson in *My Literary Passions* (New York, 1895), pp. 150–64.

32. *My Literary Passions,* p. 153.

33. *Ibid.,* pp. 155–57. Cf.: "Like every other great poet he [Tennyson] somehow expressed the feeling of his day, and I suppose that at the time he wrote "Maud" he said more fully what the whole English-speaking race were then dimly longing to utter than any English poet who has lived." Tennyson was always Howells's favorite: "But when I think over all the other poets I have read, he is supreme above them in his response to some need in me that he has satisfied so perfectly" (*ibid.*).

34. "New Poetry, English and American," Dec. 19, 1855. This review of *Hiawatha, Maud,* and Browning's *Men and Women* was signed "W."

35. *Harper's Monthly Magazine,* XII, 262 (Jan., 1856). This item was doubtless by Curtis.

36. New York *Daily Times,* Nov. 13, 1855. See also *Graham's Magazine,* XLVII, 371 (Oct., 1855).

37. *Albion,* 4th Ser., XIV, 417 (Sept. 1, 1855). See also "Tennyson's Maud," an amusing dialogue between the fictitious character, Jeremy Short, and the editor in *Peterson's Magazine* XXVIII, 307–09, Nov., 1855). Jeremy Short vigorously attacked the poem, and the editor defended it.

Jeremy Short complained especially of "Maud's" irregular versification: if Tennyson "had stuck to legitimate metres," he "might have made the poem better."

38. New York *Daily Times,* Nov. 13, 1855; "The British Periodicals," *Theological and Literary Journal,* VIII, 528 (Jan., 1856); and "The Assembly of Extremes," *Crayon,* III, 31 (Jan., 1856).

39. *Graham's Magazine,* XLVII, 371 (Oct., 1855).

40. *Home Journal,* Sept. 15, 1855, and Oct. 27, 1855. William J. Grayson wrote in July, 1857, of the "poem, which to some readers, is Tennyson's 'Maud,' but to others is Tennyson's 'Maudlin'" ("What Is Poetry," *Russell's Magazine,* I, 331. Guy A. Cardwell, *op. cit.,* p. 378, assigns this unsigned article to Grayson).

41. *Albion,* 4th Ser., XIV, 417 (Sept. 1, 1855).

42. "The Assembly of Extremes," *Crayon,* III, 31 (Jan., 1856).

43. LX, 135 (Jan., 1856). In its eight-page review of six books of poetry, including *Maud, and Other Poems,* this was the only sentence which the *Examiner* devoted to Tennyson's book.

44. "The British Periodicals," IX, 352 (Oct., 1856); see also same title, VIII, 528 (Jan., 1856).

45. O. J. Victor, review of *Maud, and Other Poems,* XVIII, 422 (July, 1858). See also *Bibliotheca Sacra,* XII, 851 (Oct., 1855).

46. 4th Ser., XIV, 417 (Sept. 1, 1855).

47. XXI, 638–39 (Oct., 1855). Jackson (*op. cit.,* p. 125) doubtfully assigns the review to Thompson.

48. "An English and an American Poet," *American Phrenological Journal,* XXII, 90–91 (Oct., 1855). The review was included as Whitman's in *In Re Walt Whitman,* ed. Horace L. Traubel, Richard Maurice Bucke, and Thomas B. Harned (Philadelphia, 1893), pp. 27–32. In later years Whitman and Tennyson became great admirers of one another. Whitman sent Tennyson an autographed copy of the *Leaves;* Tennyson invited Whitman to visit him on the Isle of Wight; and the two praised one another's poetry. See *Memoir,* II, 343–45, 424; *Tennyson and His Friends,* p. 203; and Harold Blodgett, *Walt Whitman in England* (Ithaca, N.Y., 1934), pp. 122–35.

49. *Crayon,* III, 30–32 (Jan., 1856).

50. *Tennyson and His Friends,* p. 359.

51. *English and Scottish Sketches. By an American* (London, 1857), p. 157.

52. Letter to Arthur Hugh Clough, August 20, 1855, in *Letters of Charles Eliot Norton,* I, 130–31. Norton was privileged to read *Hiawatha* several months before its publication in December, 1855. Another of Longfellow's friends, also reading the poem in manuscript, wrote that it was "the very antipodes of Tennyson's Maud, which is a poem of the present day, very poetical, very morbid, irreligious and painful" (unidentified "private letter" quoted in the *Crayon,* II, 121, Aug. 22, 1855). George William Curtis wrote Longfellow on December 17, 1855, concerning his favorite poems which he used in his attacks upon stupid and severe critics of poetry: "My battle-cry has been changed from 'Maud' to "Hiawatha'—and I have battered the enemy with knotted clubs" (MS letter, Craigie House Papers).

53. "Editor's Table," XLVII, 360–61 (Oct., 1855).

54. August 6, 1855, quoted in Hansen-Taylor and Scudder, *op. cit.,* I, 305.

55. "Alfred Tennyson," *National Magazine,* IX, 415 (Nov., 1856).

56. Letter to his mother, Nov. 3, 1857, quoted in Stedman and Gould, *op. cit.*, p. 143.

57. Review of *Maud, and Other Poems, North American Review,* LXXXI, 545 (Oct., 1855). A particularly ingenious justification of the peculiar variations of versification in "Maud" appeared in the "Editor's Table" of *Graham's Magazine* (XLVIII, 71, Jan., 1856): Tennyson had created that "rough-and-tumble kind of hand-gallop" in order to throw the horde of imitators off his track.

58. *Harper's Monthly Magazine,* XII, 262 (Jan., 1856).

59. "Editor's Easy Chair," *Harper's Monthly Magazine,* XI, 705 (Oct., 1855).

60. *North American Review,* LXXXI, 544–45 (Oct., 1855).

61. Like the American, the British criticism of "Maud" was rather sharply divided. Some reviews approved, but others gave the harshest condemnation. Cf.: "And even seen in the light of the most reverential criticism, the effect of 'Maud' cannot be favorable to Tennyson's fame. Here and there only it contains a few lines in which he does not fall below himself. With these slight exceptions, he is everywhere saying, if not something that would be better left unsaid, something that he had already said better; and the finest sentiments that animate his other poems are entirely absent" (*Westminster Review,* N. S., VIII, 597, Oct., 1855). "Besides, as we have already observed, the rhythm is sometimes rough, if it is not actually imperfect, and the sentiment is unpoetic and commonplace, if it be not something worse than that—actually vulgar" (*Dublin University Magazine,* XLVI, 339, Sept., 1855). ". . . it ["Maud"] must always stand as a heavy item on the debtor side of his [Tennyson's] reputation account" (*National Review,* I, 404, Oct., 1855).

62. Probably the stricture most oft-repeated in the British journals was the objection to Tennyson's approval of war (see *Athenaeum,* No. 1449, p. 893, Aug. 4, 1855; *Bentley's Miscellany,* XXXVIII, 264, Sept., 1855; *Blackwood's Edinburgh Magazine,* LXXVIII, 319, Sept., 1855; etc.), and, curiously, this objection appeared rarely in America. The few instances of it were greatly outweighed by defenses of Tennyson's attitude, such as that in the *Graham's* review (quoted above). Those who were not willing to go so far as a blanket approval of war, set about showing that Tennyson was advocating a peculiar kind of war and only certain attributes of it (see *Putnam's Magazine,* VI, 390, Oct., 1855; *Harper's Monthly Magazine,* XI, 701, Oct., 1855; New York *Independent,* VII, 48, Feb. 7, 1856; *Yale Literary Magazine,* XXIV, 90–92, Dec., 1858; etc.).

63. See *Memoir,* I, 393–412. Although biographers have not emphasized the misunderstanding of *The Princess* as they have that of "Maud," it seems that on the basis of the British reviews, *The Princess* better deserves the title of the most persecuted. Several little-noticed British reviews of "Maud" were highly laudatory. Note the estimate in the *Spectator,* "As a whole, *Maud* is perfectly intelligible in its action, the character of the autobiographic hero is well marked, and the changes of passion are indicated with a dramatic force and singleness of aim which Mr. Tennyson has never before reached" (XXVII, pp. 813–14, Aug. 4, 1855). See also the encomium in the *Examiner,* "Containing hardly a weak line, full of deep feeling and purpose, exquisitely musical, and instinct with the subtlest perceptions of

the poet, *Maud* impresses us as one of the most perfect works of the Laureate" (No. 2479, p. 484, Aug. 4, 1855). No such statements as these have been found in British reviews of *The Princess* during the first two years after its publication.

64. In reply to a letter from Fields, Tennyson wrote, Oct. 26, 1855, "The English Press has (as you remark being [*sic*] 'stupid' enough: but I have as far as I know, always been attacked in a similar fashion whenever I have put forth a fresh publication. This time the assault has been a little harder than usual" (MS letter, James T. Fields Autograph Album, Harvard College Library).

65. MS letter, Tuckerman to Tennyson, October 22, 1855, Harvard College Library. The review of *Maud, and Other Poems* in *Blackwood's* (LXXVIII, 311–21, Sept., 1855) was one of the most severe of the British criticisms.

66. See reviews in London *Times,* Nov. 15, 1852; *Athenaeum,* No. 1308, p. 1263 (Nov. 20, 1852); *Literary Gazette,* No. 1870, pp. 852–53 (Nov. 20, 1852); etc.

67. II, 284–85 (Dec. 18, 1852).

68. II, 365 (Nov. 27, 1852).

69. I, 108 (Jan., 1853).

70. Nov. 22, 1854; Jan. 4, 1855. Upon reading the note objecting to his statement, the correspondent recanted (*Tribune,* Feb. 20, 1855).

71. *Autobiography,* p. 261.

72. "Editor's Table," XLVI, 276–77 (March, 1855).

73. MS letter, Tennyson to Tuckerman, July, 1855 (Harvard College Library): "You will find in my little volume 'The Charge of the Light Brigade' with the 'blunder'd' that offended you & others, omitted." In the introduction to his edition of Tuckerman's *Sonnets,* Witter Bynner printed the letter and read the word *blunder'd* incorrectly as *blunders* (p. 29). The *Knickerbocker* noted that "many" objected to the line (review of *Poems* by Erastus W. Ellsworth, XLVI, 291, Sept., 1855).

74. "Editor's Table," XXVII, 252 (March, 1855).

75. "Tennyson's Battle Ode," Jan. 16, 1855. The article was signed "Philo-Tennyson." Ferdinand C. Ewer wrote, in the "Editor's Table" of his *Pioneer; or, California Monthly Magazine* (III, 279–80, June, 1855), one of the strongest encomiums that "The Charge of the Light Brigade" received. Ewer contrasted at length Tennyson's "immortal poem" and A. B. Meek's imitation, "Balaklava," cited above, which he thought to be by Alexander Smith. For attempting to write in competition with Tennyson, said Ewer, Smith deserved "to be put into the penitentiary."

76. For the many textual variations, see Wise, *op. cit.,* I, 143–48. A few days after the appearance of *Maud, and Other Poems,* Tennyson became dissatisfied with the second version and published a third, in pamphlet form (*ibid.*).

77. "Editor's Table," XXXII, 219 (Sept., 1857); and review of *Maud, and Other Poems,* Nov. 13, 1855. *Putnam's Magazine* (VI, 391, Oct., 1855) compared the revisions to the unforgivable "pranks he [Tennyson] played with the 'Lady of Shalott,'" but concluded that none of his revisions had ever been "more unfortunate" than those of "The Charge of the Light Brigade."

78. *North American Review,* LXXXI, 546 (Oct., 1855).

79. *Putnam's Magazine,* VI, 390 (Oct., 1855).

80. Letter to his mother, Nov. 3, 1857, quoted in Stedman and Gould, *op. cit.,* I, 143.

Conclusion

1. "Tennyson," *International Review,* IV, 418 (May, 1877).

2. Letter to James T. Fields, Aug. 12, 1859, quoted in Samuel Longfellow, *op. cit.* (1886 ed.), II, 341.

3. See Ticknor and Fields's advertisement of the *Idylls of the King* in the Boston *Daily Evening Transcript,* Aug. 12, 1859. Both Ticknor and Fields and another Boston publisher, J. E. Tilton, published editions of *Enoch Arden* in 1864. Houghton Mifflin Company's letter of September 21, 1940, to me lists 40,000 copies of the Ticknor and Fields edition as printed during the first year. Tilton's edition of *Enoch Arden* was one of the earliest American editions of Tennyson issued by a publisher other than Ticknor and Fields. The *North American Review* (C, 306–07, Jan., 1865) severely reprimanded Tilton for publishing his edition. He had "committed this dishonorable action knowingly," for Tennyson had publicly declared that Ticknor and Fields were his authorized American publishers. Since there was no law by which Tilton could be punished, the *Review* hoped that booksellers and bookbuyers would refuse to handle Tilton's edition.

4. Hamilton W. Mabie, "The Influence of Tennyson in America," *Review of Reviews,* American Edition, VI, 556 (Dec., 1892). The tremendous popularity of Tennyson among the uneducated in America at the time of his death is discussed at length in Cornelius Weygandt, *The Time of Tennyson* (New York and London, 1936), pp. 99–104.

5. G. E. Woodberry, *Atlantic Monthly,* LVII, 425–26 (March, 1886).

6. *Victorian Poets* (Boston, 1875), p. 160.

7. See Lowell's review of *Enoch Arden, North American Review,* XCIX, 626 (Oct., 1864), and J. C. Heywood, *How They Strike Me, These Authors* (Philadelphia, 1877), pp. 126–47.

8. "Tennyson," *International Review,* IV, 418 (May, 1877).

9. "The Influence of Tennyson in America," *Review of Reviews,* VI, 556 (Dec., 1892).

INDEX